American Writers in Istanbul

Contemporary Issues in the Middle East

OTHER TITLES IN CONTEMPORARY ISSUES IN THE MIDDLE EAST

The Arabic Novel: An Historical and Critical Introduction, Second Edition
ROGER ALLEN

The Druze and Their Faith in Tawhid
ANIS OBEID

Islam, Arabs, and the Intelligent World of the Jinn
AMIRA EL-ZEIN

The Kurdish National Movement: Its Origins and Development
WADIE JWAIDEH

Middle Eastern Lives: The Practice of Biography and Self-Narrative
MARTIN KRAMER, ed.

One Family's Response to Terrorism: A Daughter's Memoir
SUSAN KERR VAN DE VEN

Painting the Middle East
ANN ZWICKER KERR

Turkish Islam and the Secular State: The Gülen Movement
M. HAKAN YAVUZ and JOHN L. ESPOSITO, eds.

Veils and Words: The Emerging Voices of Iranian Women Writers
FARZANEH MILANI

Writing Off the Beaten Track: Reflections on the Meaning of Travel and Culture in the Middle East
JUDITH CAESAR

American Writers in *Istanbul*

Melville, Twain, Hemingway, Dos Passos, Bowles, Algren, Baldwin, and Settle

Kim Fortuny

With a Foreword by Roger Allen

SYRACUSE UNIVERSITY PRESS

First Edition 2009

09 10 11 12 13 14 6 5 4 3 2 1

∞ The paper used in this publication meets the minimum requirements of the American National Standard for Information Sciences—Permanence of Paper for Printed Library Materials, ANSI Z39.48-1992.

For a listing of books published and distributed by Syracuse University Press, visit our Web site at SyracuseUniversityPress.syr.edu.

ISBN: 978-0-8156-3236-8

Library of Congress Cataloging-in-Publication Data

Fortuny, Kim.

American writers in Istanbul : Melville, Twain, Hemingway, Dos Passos, Bowles, Algren, Baldwin, and Settle / Kim Fortuny. — 1st ed.

p. cm.

Includes bibliographical references and index.

ISBN 978-0-8156-3236-8 (cloth : alk. paper)

1. Authors, American—Homes and haunts—Istanbul (Turkey) 2. Americans—Istanbul (Turkey)—Intellectual life. 3. Literature and society—Istanbul (Turkey) 4. American literature—Turkic influences. 5. Istanbul (Turkey)—In literature. 6. Melville, Herman, 1819–1891—Criticism and interpretation. 7. Twain, Mark, 1835–1910—Criticism and interpretation. 8. Hemingway, Ernest , 1899–1961—Criticism and interpretation. 9. Dos Passos, John R. (John Randolph), 1844–1917—Criticism and interpretation. 10. Bowles, Paul, 1910–1999—Criticism and interpretation. 11. Algren, Nelson, 1909–1981—Criticism and interpretation. 12. Baldwin, James, 1924–1987—Criticism and interpretation. 13. Settle, Mary Lee—Criticism and interpretation. I. Title.

PS144.I88F67 2009

818'.309—dc22 2009041239

Manufactured in the United States of America

For Jill and Isabelle

For people like me, *Istanbullus* with one foot in each culture, the "western traveler" is often not a real person; he can be my own creation, my fantasy, even my own reflection.

—ORHAN PAMUK,
Istanbul: Memories and the City

KIM FORTUNY is a Fulbright recipient and an assistant professor of English at Boğaziçi University in Istanbul, Turkey. Her first book, *Elizabeth Bishop: The Art of Travel,* was published by University Press of Colorado in 2003.

Contents

Illustrations

Foreword

ROGER ALLEN

ISTANBUL HAS ALWAYS BEEN, it almost goes without saying, one of the world's most fabled cities, whether the word or phrase that triggers relevant ideas and images is Constantinople (Constantine's city), Istanbul (the Greek "into the city"—*eis ten polin*), the Bosphorus, the Hellespont, the Dardanelles, Gallipoli, etc. I myself have visited the city twice, with a considerable interval between the two: once as a student in 1963 on my return from Lebanon to England; and a second time exactly one week ago (I write this in March 2009) when I encountered a vastly transformed and expanded city of many millions of people, with increasingly large housing projects straddling both the European and Asian sides of the world-famous waterway, the Bosphorus, that links the Black Sea with the Aegean. The city now has two airports, one on each continent. At the conclusion of my recent bus- and boat-tour of the city (once we had crossed the permanently traffic-jammed suspension bridge joining the two sides), we were invited to step out of the bus and into Asia. I have also recently "revisited" Istanbul in textual form, producing a translation and study (*Spies, Scandals, and Sultans,* 2008) of the city as seen through Egyptian eyes during the highly tense period that was the reign of one of the last Ottoman Sultans, Abdulhamit II, who come to the throne in 1876 and proceeded, among other things, to establish one of the most elaborate surveillance systems of the era, and in both Ottoman dominions and elsewhere. Kim Fortuny's book is a further illustration of the fact that in my own fascination with this magical city, I am far from alone; indeed I am preceded by some of the most illustrious names in American (and, through Nelson Algren's relationship with Simone de Beauvoir, European) writing.

It is important to underline at the outset that this book is not intended to be a tourist guide about Istanbul, nor a history of the city and its own littérateurs. Rather it is presented as a survey—a chronological one at that—of American writing: writing in prose—sometimes fictional, sometimes in the form of a very particular kind of nonfictional narrative, the travel account. It treats the lives and travels of a number of famous writers—all of them prominent contributors to the history of American letters writ large—and examines both the ways in which each author reacts to the great city and the placement of their writings about Istanbul (and sometimes Turkey as a whole) within their total oeuvre. It almost goes without saying that the ways in which the author of this study incorporates commentary on various aspects—critical, cultural, and historical—of these authors' writings allows for some interesting contributions to such contemporary intellectual debates as those surrounding "Orientalism" and postcolonial theory. As such, they may serve as an apposite reflection of both American letters in their more outward-looking mode and the realities of the confrontation between cultures—hardly irrelevant themes as we approach the end of the first decade in the twenty-first century.

This then is a glimpse across time into the city of Istanbul as seen through the lenses of several American writers. It thus reflects the changing modes of American fiction and the equally shifting cultural attitudes that are to be found in the progression of their writings. And therein lies its value.

Rabat
March 2009

Acknowledgments

SPECIAL THANKS TO Dr. Cevza Sevgen for her support and guidance over the years. To Dr. John Freely who helped me begin thinking about this book and who is an inspiration to so many of us here. To Feza Kurkcuoğlu for his generous contribution of photographs and time and Sedat Pakay for the donation of his superb Baldwin photographs. To Mini Garwood and Engin Cezzar for their insights. Thank you to Boğaziçi University for its support and to Vice President Professor Gülay Barbarosoğlu for her kind efforts. Thanks to all the Boğaziçi University Western Languages and Literatures Teaching Assistants, with special acknowledgment of Cihan Yurdaun and student assistant Tuba Kaya. Thanks to Padraic Rohan and Julie DuSablon for their help with the text. To Mary Selden Evans at Syracuse University Press for her perseverance. To my friends Tonguç Rador, Gülen Güler, Sibylle and Demet Çizenel, Muhittin Mungan, Meg Russett, Haluk Oral, and "cuz" Recep Molu for help, direct and indirect. Special appreciation to Ahmet Dinç and Zilli. To my dear mother, Darlene Fortuny. To our wonderful students at Boğaziçi University for their enthusiasm and trust. And finally, special thanks to Istanbul, past and present.

Introduction

THIS BOOK, *American Writers in Istanbul,* has been conceived of in a spirit similar to that of Lady Mary Montagu's *Turkish Embassy Letters.*

> Since my last [letter] I have stayed quietly at Constantinople, a city that I ought in conscience to give your ladyship a right notion of, since I know you can have none but what is partial and mistaken from the writings of travelers. 'Tis certain there are many people that pass years here in Pera without having ever seen it, and yet they all pretend to describe it. (Lady Mary Wortley Montagu, letter 46, Constantinople, April 10, 1718; Montague 1994)

Lady Mary Wortley Montagu was a rare tourist. She came to the capital of the Ottoman Empire in the early eighteenth century blessed with an admirable cache of personal curiosity and national self-doubt. Understanding the precarious challenge of creating the "right notion" of a place, she nevertheless attempted in her letters home to correct, in her slant way, Occidental prejudices about the Ottomans passed down through chronicle and letter since the fifteenth century.

Working under the like assumption that most foreign accounts of Istanbul or Turkey are necessarily partial, the aim in this book is to approach the American writers and the Turkish subjects they engage, with an equal eye for the readily knowable and the partially understood. The book explores what these American writers have written about Istanbul, what terms they have employed to translate to others the complexities of a culture that has always existed within yet just beyond the reaches of the Christian world. It addresses what Istanbul had to say to these writers and how the city itself disrupts common conjectures about the gateway to the Muslim East.

The American writers examined in this text either lived in Istanbul for various lengths of time or passed through during different periods of history. Some of their discussions of Asia Minor have received attention from Western scholars, but overall the attention has been minimal. Thus, it is in keeping with a contemporary inclination for reevaluating the fine print of American letters that this book partially derives its present purpose. Academic multiculturalism encourages us to reassess our literary heritage. And because the writers in this book are for the most part canonical writers, the book joins others of its kind in questioning the assumptions readers make, or have been asked to make, concerning the writers' contributions to the promotion of North American culture abroad. More often than not, we now tend to locate a hegemonic agenda—sometimes subtle, sometimes not—at the controls of American literary culture. This book, however, has a somewhat different purpose: it asks what would be the case, for example, if the "outside" has been alive, and for years, well inside North America's literary and cultural conscience? What if, for example, Istanbul—and everything the place-name conjures up for an Occidental audience—had since at least the nineteenth century been active, though perhaps ignored, at the aesthetic and cultural center of American letters; active not only in the form of the intertextual adaptations we see in the poetry of Emerson and Whitman, but as a real place, directly experienced? This is not only a question of influence but also a question of the integration of constructs traditionally at opposition in the heart of the Occidental body.

The "Levant" and the "Levantine" are confusing terms. The first technically indicates those countries on the Eastern edges of the Mediterranean—Lebanon, Syria, Israel—but not necessarily Asia Minor (or modern-day Turkey). The latter, "Levantine," refers historically to people of Italian (Venetian, Genoese) or French descent who lived in Asia Minor during the Ottoman Empire (fifteenth to twentieth centuries) and who were the descendants of crusaders or traders. Byron, however, like many other nineteenth-century European writers, tends to refer to the west coast of Asia Minor as the Levant and its Greek inhabitants as Levantines. Thus, one's application of these terms depends on how one imagines borders as well as the natural rotation of the earth. "Levant" means "to rise." The Levant is the place where the sun rises in the East. It is a place associated in the Western literary imaginary with ascension, hope, rebirth, the promise of innocence and beauty beyond the disappointments and decadence of the West. W. B. Yeats, in one of his most famous poems, "Sailing to Byzantium," imagines the Levant and its capital as an ahistorical realm, a place of transcendence beyond the "paltry" lives of mortal men. The atmosphere of Byzantium, part the material effect of artifice—the gold mosaics of St. Sophia—part the immaterial imaging inspired by myth and rumor, promises spiritual and intellectual sustenance to a subject weighed down by mortal passions and the needs of "dying generations—at their song" in the material West.

> And therefore I have sailed the seas and come
> To the holy city of Byzantium.
> . . .
> Oh sages standing in God's holy fire
> As in the gold mosaic of a wall,
> Come from the holy fire, perne in a gyre,
> And be the singing-masters of my soul
> Consume my heart away; sick with desire
> And fastened to a dying animal
> It knows not what it is
>
> YEATS 1979, 1976–77

Byzantium promises salvation through aesthetics: the plastic arts, music, dance. Eastern modes of representation promise alternatives to death in the West.

Byron, toward the end of his long poem *The Giaour,* similarly associates the Levant with a purifying fire that promises to liberate the soul from the mortal body through the destruction of desire.

> 'Yes, Love indeed is light from heaven—
> A spark of that immortal fire
> With angels shar'd—by Allah given,
> To lift from earth our low desire.
>
> BYRON 1986, 1131–34

The Muslim Prophet is given the benefit of Byron's profound Christian doubt, at least in the context of the poem. And, the form that love takes in these lines, much as the form knowledge would take in Yeats's Byzantium, is located in the possibility of beauty and chance for renewal, which the Levant offers. Though the majority of the poem reiterates the fanatical nineteenth-century European preoccupation with Turkish "turbans" that "now pollute Sophia's shrine," there are many moments, particularly toward the conclusion, where political or religious abstractions give way to the exploration of individual human hearts: Muslim or Christian—Hassan or Giaour—the narrator's allegiances in the poem are relatively flexible. Furthermore, Byron's notes to the poem tell a parallel story of the writer's esteem for the Ottomans (as well as his disdain for European Christians), which further complicates an Orientalist reading of the Eastern frontier: "The Ottomans, with all their defects, are not a people to be despised . . . If it be difficult to pronounce what they are, we can at least say what they are *not:* They are *not* treacherous, they are *not* cowardly, they do *not* burn heretics, they are *not* assassins, nor has the enemy advanced to *their* capital (Byron 1986, 103). Like Lady Mary Montagu, George Byron takes a case of national self-doubt, or self-loathing, abroad with him. As a popular writer he is perhaps less inclined to create the "right notion" of a place if it means low sales, yet his letters contradict or "correct" the Occidental prejudices he markets.

BUT THIS IS POETRY. Most European travel prose about the Levant tell other stories about the Ottomans, stories of a people slavish, ignorant, covetous, proud, cruel, despotic. These terms are most often found in intertextual or armchair accounts of the empire, writing based on other writing rather than direct experience. Stereotypes abound: they confirm and reconfirm each other like nervous, small town gossip. Largely preoccupied with the Turkish slave markets, Europeans chronicles are often drawn to the figure of the Christian female slave for sale to the highest Muslim bidder. Fascinated, if not aroused, by the veil worn by Ottoman women, writers eroticize the concealed, enigmatic female body in their narratives as often as they sexualize the body on public display, and ethics are adjusted to gratify a voyeuristic interest in the exotic coupling of Muslims and Christians. That Turks are lascivious is the foregone conclusion. And it is not without a small dose of poignant, self-directed social irony that Lady Mary Wortley Montagu offers the following reassessment of this popular slave market narrative:

> I know you'll expect I should say something particular of that of the slaves, and you will imagine me half a Turk when I don't speak with the same horror other Christians have done before me, but I cannot forbear applauding the humanity of the Turks to those creatures. They are never ill used and their slavery is in

> my opinion no worse than servitude all over the world. 'Tis true they have no wages, but they give them yearly clothes to a higher value than our salaries to an ordinary servant. But you'll object men buy women with an eye to evil. In my opinion they are bought and sold as publicly and more infamously in all our Christian great cities. (Montagu 1994, 130)

Taking into account Lady Montagu's patrician disregard for the servant classes in both the English and the Ottoman Empires, the favorable comparison of the condition of "those creatures" to the English women for sale on the marriage market in her own socioeconomic circles makes for deft, early feminist irony. Montagu would later go on to publish tracts protesting the eighteenth-century's system of dowry. What she makes clear in this rewriting of male travel narratives, however, is that tales of the female slave trade have been passed on without the conscientious critical distance necessary to speak objectively of another culture.

But, as is true of most fixed assessments of foreign cultures, the prejudices say more about the fears and weaknesses of the speaking subject, or subject nation, than the objectified enemy. According to the majority of Western texts written during and since the Crusades, Muslim Turks have been out to destroy Christian Europeans. According to one political writer of the Italian Renaissance, Giovanni Botero: "There is no public enemy against whom he [the defender of the Christian faith] may prove his valor: an enemy whose constant object is the oppression of Christianity, and whose might is such that to resist it, let alone overcome it, is to win far greater glory than can ever be achieved by bearing arms against Christians" (Cirakman 2002, 74). The Turk offered a common enemy to an early modern society weakened by domestic discord. In language familiar to that at the turn of the century in the United States, the rhetoric of homeland security becomes indistinguishable from the platitudes of faith. Bearing arms under the banner of a vengeful god inspires a people to exchange the dull enemies they know, have always known, for an exotic one about whom they know next to nothing.

In the following century, the Ottoman Turks proved as dangerous to the English as they had earlier to the Italians. In fact, the Ottomans posed an equal and opposing problem to any Christian colonial power with Eastern-directed political or economic aspirations. In his conclusion to *The History,* Sir Walter Ralegh echoes Botero's call for unification in the face of a shared threat to the physical/spiritual security of Europe. His appeal, however, suggests steps toward the pacification rather than the destruction of a common European enemy, which had proved as aggressive in its imperial ambitions as had the English.

> But as the Turk is now counterpoised by the Persian, so instead of so many millions as have been spent by the English, French and Netherlands in a defensive war, and in diversions against them, it is easy to demonstrate that with the charge of two hundred thousand pound continued but for two years or three at the most, they may not only be persuaded to live in peace, but all their swelling and overflowing streams may be brought back into their natural channels and old banks. These two nations, I say, are at this day the most eminent and to be regarded—the one seeking to root out the Christian religion altogether, the other, the truth and sincere profession thereof; the one, to join all Europe to Asia, the other, the rest of all Europe to Spain. (Ralegh 1956, 516–17)

For Ralegh, the most outspoken as well as most heeded of Renaissance colonial explorers, the Ottoman threat existed in direct contradistinction to England's own hopes for Asia Minor, hopes that would not come to fruition for the English for another four hundred years. In the meantime, the Turks served at least one positive purpose for the English: a prevailing sixteenth-century Protestant idea was that God was using Turks to punish Christians. An opinion made popular by Martin Luther, Luther initially argued that it was better to obey the Ottomans than the Pope, but then modified his view in the face of increased Ottoman strength and supported war against them.

IN WESTERN LITERARY TEXTS, Istanbul, due in part to its geographical location, has always symbolized the longing and resentment that comes with unfulfilled desire. This is an old trope in the travel literature. The Bosphorus Straits separate not only the Asian continent from the European continent but the city from itself. And such a topology and typology has been the source of tension and voyeuristic pleasure since pre-Hellenic times. The Byzantine Empire thrived from the fourth century to the middle of the fifteenth century when internal problems, as well as external pressures, led to its decline and eventually to its fall to the Turks in 1453. Though ultimately the prize and problem of the Ottomans, the empire's capital had always been a spectacular object of admiration and a source of administrative discomfort for the Holy Roman Empire. Despoiling Orthodox shrines in order to displace them to Catholic soil, Western European crusaders through the Middle Ages displayed a paradoxical attitude vis-à-vis their Eastern Christian outpost. In their drive to destroy in order to possess the unruly, markedly more female Orthodox Church, crusaders on their way to liberate the Holy Land from the infidels made frequent stops in Constantinople to sack vulnerable Orthodox shrines. Roman Christians carried away the artifacts the Orthodox iconoclasts had left behind in their various campaigns to reduce the Byzantines' heretic penchant for aesthetic displays of faith. Why on earth this obsession with glamorous surfaces, the iconoclasts would ask as various empresses maneuvered to save art from the destroying hands of the protesting fathers. Much of what they did not destroy the Catholics took back to Europe and installed in town squares: spoils of war, monuments to a beauty not their own. The lions that used to hold sentinel over St. Marks Square in Venice attest to this double function of faith.

This European relationship to Constantinople/Istanbul, characterized by its destabilizing tendency toward both attraction and repulsion, is not without its sequel in modern times. The European debate over the entry of Turkey into the European Union shows signs of this ancient play of magnetism and aversion. Istanbul is like a Western city in many ways—an eighteen-year-old cruising Istiklal Street on a Friday covets the same fashions and ignores the same world crises as any eighteen-year-old on Broadway Avenue. Yet hiding behind its hip, cosmopolitan façade is a vast population that does not quite fit in the big city. The floral headscarves make Christian Democrats in Germany uncomfortable, as they do Nationalists in Ankara. Europeans on vacation take pictures of flushed peasants piled on the back of hay trucks (waving happily?) after a long day's work in the sun, but they do not want to live next door to them in Ealing or Erzurum. Popular consensus in Europe suggests that while the faded but still attractive "Byzantium" may be an asset to the growth of the Union, the lands and people beyond—Asia Minor and the Anatolians who live there—are forces not so much to be embraced as held at bay.

Turkey, as "erratic, eccentric, accidental" in the eyes of the contemporary West as it was to the West's medieval ancestors, thus exists "on the margins of metropolitan desire," according to Homi Bhabha's theory of colonial mimicry and Orientalism (Bhabha 1994, 92). Yet this "ambivalent world of the 'not quite/not white'" that we note in Western discourse is not only the byproduct of representational authority, as Bhabha directs us to see; it is also the site of potential rupture in the shaky seams of colonial tales of the East. The American writers discussed in this volume contribute either willfully or reluctantly to this rupture. James Baldwin, for example, was living in Istanbul at the time he was writing one of the most contentious, and most successful, political essays of his long, controversial career. "The Fire Next Time," an examination of the Nation of Islam in North America, constitutes a paradoxical literary inversion of the return of the oppressed. From the distance/proximity of the Muslim frontier, Baldwin spoke to America of its racial phobias and the subsequent ideological "disorder" of its marginalized African American communities.

A European or an American writing about Istanbul "comes up against the Orient as a European or American first, as an individual second," writes Edward Said (Said 2000, 77). The American writer of this text comes to the subject with a willed double perspective: direct experience of Istanbul and Turkey has lead to a heightened awareness of the gaps that may exist between the historical-cultural position of the "ex-patriot" and personal associations with the country and its people. This heightened awareness puts an increased pressure on the critical eye when turned toward the writing of other Americans abroad.

> To be a European or an American in such a situation is by no means an inert fact. It meant and means being aware, however, dimly, that one belongs to a power with definite interests in the Orient, and more important, that one belongs to a part of the earth with a definite history of involvement in the Orient almost since the time of Homer. (Said 2000, 77)

To write about Istanbul, or write about other Americans writing about Istanbul, is to be conscious of the precarious dangers of speaking for others. It necessarily questions the rights of centralizing authorities even as it insists that a responsible story is possible.

The American writers discussed in this book have only recently entered history's literary engagement with Istanbul. Herman Melville's mid-nineteenth-century journal entries describing his brief visit to the capital of the Ottoman Empire offer the earliest example of American writing on Istanbul in the collection. Melville's impressions coincide with the rapid geopolitical expansion of the United States during this historical period. It could therefore be argued that his writing contributes to the early authorizing of the United States as a nascent imperial power. While entitlement has always tended to accompany, or precede, the fact- and fancy-finding missions of writers abroad, from Herodotus to Marco Polo to Paul Theroux, it is sometimes not so easy to determine, even with the help of much postcolonial theory, whether the writing has helped or hindered the demarche of history. Like many of his European predecessors, Melville is taken aback by the crowds of Istanbul, "these millions of fellow beings, some of whom seem not unwilling to accept our civilization, but with one consent rejecting much of our morality & all of our religion" (Melville 1955, 95). Unlike many of the armchair accounts he would have inherited from European sources, however, Melville looks at the ancient city with an eye for the concrete as well as the fancied detail. At times, he passes sentence, but he allows the reader to observe the contours of the place without passing the predictable kinds of cultural judgment many travel narratives impose:

> Out of every window look faces (Jew, Greek, Armenian) which in England or America would be a cynosure in a ball room.—Wretched looking houses & and filthy streets. *Tokens of pauperism without the paupers.* Out of old shanties peep lovely girls. like lillies *& roses growing* in *cracked flower-pots.* (Melville 1955, 90)

This is not to say that Herman Melville is a more generous observer than are his European counterparts. On the contrary. Like many American writers of the period and after, he seems to have little sense of the political or economic relationship his country might have with the Ottoman Empire, which by the mid-nineteenth century is an empire much less threatening to the West due to power shifts in the world order.

Melville's account of Istanbul verges on the disinterested. From this disinterest, however, emerges a particular kind of grounded beauty. Melville's attention to the concrete textures of Istanbul illustrates Edward Said's now classic appeal to Western writers and readers to avoid the "common human failing to prefer the schematic authority of a text to the disorientations of direct encounter with the human" (Said 2000, 93). Later, Said writes of French lamentations over the "betrayed dream" of Orientalism:

> The modern Orient disputes imagination, sends one back to the imagination as a place preferable for the European sensibility, to the real Orient. For a person

> who has never seen the Orient, Nerval once said to Gautier, a lotus is still a lotus; for me it is only a kind of onion. To write about the modern Orient is either to reveal an upsetting demystification of images culled from texts, or to confine oneself to the Orient of which Hugo spoke in his original preface to *Les Orientales,* the Orient as "image" or "*pensée,*" symbols of "*une sorte de preoccupation générale.*" (Said 2000, 101)

Unlike these French Orientalists, Melville seems generally unconcerned with the *preoccupation générales* that preceded him to Istanbul. He appears as interested in the onion as in the lotus. If nineteenth-century English poets such as Byron demonize the Turks in order to feed a necessary social hunger—a need to project internal cultural insecurities on an available and distant enemy—or early twentieth-century Irish writers such as Yeats romanticize the Levant as an aestheticized alternative to the realities of postwar Europe, Melville assesses the city, its beauty and its desolation, as he would any other city old enough and wise enough to put into question the permanence of human structures.

ALL EMPIRES COME TO AN END, of course. At the height of the empire, the Ottomans controlled approximately two times the territory ever controlled by the Romans, territory that spanned from the eastern borders of Europe in the Balkans to North Africa and the Middle East. The empire, whose "fall" is dated to around the mid-nineteenth century, existed as a global power for three hundred years, one hundred more than is officially recognized for the Romans and almost two hundred years more than is allowed the United States at the time of this writing. But in 1864, the empire was winding down as the United States began to steam ahead with its youthful trust in technology and the limitlessness of the resources its machines would require to do the work of many men in a fraction of the time. Melville, like Mark Twain, was skeptical from the start. Ernest Hemingway and Paul Bowles went abroad in search of stories that dramatized the shifts and revisions of power relations from various cultural points of view. The Ottomans are not so much memento mori in these texts as living examples of the knowledge that comes when the "swelling and overflowing streams" of a global power are "brought back into their natural channels and old banks" by new money and world war. American writers in Istanbul are often shocked by the chaos of the city. And the ease, or at least forbearance, with which Turks negotiate this apparent anarchy seems to provide an answer to some existential question only the experienced can ask. James Baldwin expressed the view that Turkey had a unique role to play in the modern world. With access to knowledge that has come with the rise and the fall of their own empire, Turks have gained a hard-earned familiarity with the painful cycles of domination and loss. Baldwin identifies this familiarity with cultural maturity.

TURKISH INTELLECTUALS, academics, and even students are generally bored now with the word "Oriental." The indiscriminate application of the noun/adjective in reference to vast regions and various peoples—any place or anybody of traditionally Muslim or of non-Christian origin—has reduced the once politically volatile signifier to one more inflated catchword, a term, to borrow George Orwell's phrase from "Politics and the English Language," that gives an appearance of solidity to pure wind. Theories of "the Other" have been domesticated beyond recognition. And this is happening in what appears to be direct and ironic contradistinction to twenty-first-century international crises between Christians and Muslims. Despite more than twenty years of concentrated discussion by cultural critics, academics, and their students, official and popular constructions of Muslim cultures in the West have changed relatively little since the 1970s, or the Middle Ages.

Red and orange alerts posted by American consulates for the edification and safety of American citizens residing in or visiting Muslim countries around the world after September 11, 2001, attest to an increased urge to distance American nationals from what is regarded as universal Muslim fanaticism. Emails circulated by local U.S. embassies advised U.S. citizens to watch their backs, be wary of their neighbors. Americans abroad are told to regularly, but not systematically, change their routes, be prudent about developing habits in their interaction with local populations. Like any institution concerned with public liability, the American government's "outposts" abroad are primarily concerned with the immediate and pragmatic protection of its own citizens. However, the price of prudence is anxiety, fear, and the inevitable move toward isolation that results.

The challenge for Americans who live and write beyond Christian frontiers is to resist such advice. This is not to say that Americans when abroad should wear their colors with pride. Neither does this mean one has a national duty to practice the fearlessness, even recklessness, we still like to associate with our frontier culture. Quite the contrary. Americans, like anyone who hopes to live abroad (or at home) with conviction, must make a sustained effort to listen and observe and learn something about the language people use to talk about themselves. Moreover, this means distrusting one's own language, the language one has inherited to talk about East-West relations, be it "enlightened" academic discourse or popular public speech. Terms like "Oriental" that have become rhetorically naturalized to the point of invisibility come under increased pressure in the face of political realities of the historical moment. Nothing can be taken for granted, because very little goes according to plan. The slippage, the excess that confuses the official language about the Middle East, is proof of this fact. When leaders repeat with conviction that "America will prevail," we must insist that the grammar functions be clarified: if America is the subject of this rallying phrase, who or what is the silent object in the catch phrase? And when the listener is criticized or ridiculed for these "academic," thus extraneous questions (the enemy, apparently, is clear), she must remind the audience that the language we use to cheer ourselves up as a nation may be precisely the language that is causing us, and others, the most international trouble.

Looking at texts by writers who (except for Paul Bowles) do not necessarily define themselves as Orientalists—or, as in the case of Twain, define themselves as "anti-Orientalists" only to fall into the common traps and tropes of the field—serves a multiple function. It allows us to broaden the possible ways of thinking about one complex, idiosyncratic city of the world, even if it does not help us to understand intimately the city and its people from the distance an armchair makes. This book avoids the kinds of Orientalist enthusiasm or wariness that clouds the perception of, in this case, a culture of the Near East. Rather, because the present study attempts to interject something fresh into the historical "disparity between texts and reality" that hampers much Orientalist discourse, as Edward Said had noted back in 1978, it begins with the assumption that it has no business wandering very far from either the written word at hand or the historical reality of the city.

> The contemporary intellectual can learn from Orientalism how, on the one hand, either to limit or enlarge realistically the scope of his discipline's claims, and on the other, to see the human ground (the foul-rag-and-bone shop of the heart, Yeats called it) in which texts, visions, methods, and disciplines begin, grow, thrive and degenerate. (Said 2000, 110)

By paying attention to the "worldly, historical circumstances" that give rise to its own construction, this book hopes to avoid the "overreaching aspirations" of classical Orientalist studies and offer a modest but poignant reading of eight American writers and a city.

Thus, a second function of the book is to study the literary representations of Istanbul and trace how these particular Istanbul passages in each writer's career add to the oeuvre of each as a whole. Hemingway, for example, learns much that he knows about war from observing the War of Independence in Turkey as a young correspondent based in Istanbul in 1922. His dispatches are prosaic finger exercises for the novels and stories of war to come. Nelson Algren's dyspeptic observations not just of Istanbul but of the U.S. presence abroad in the context of Turkish-American relations tell the story of a prose style crippled by political and aesthetic disillusion. Because most travel literature tells us more about the country of origin of the writer than it does about the foreign landscape at hand, it would be disingenuous to exaggerate Istanbul's place in the text. The city functions almost as a character in the book, but a character whose idiosyncrasies tease out and expose vital information about how each writer filters and translates a "strange" environment. Equal attention is thus paid to form and content in the hope that this conjunction might shed light not only on a great city of the world but also on the work of important American writers who traveled to it usually in search of a scoop for an article or two but came away with much more.

A third goal of the book is to push the claim that in conceiving of canonical American writers as international or transnational writers we are urged to loosen our collective national grip on literature as the product of place. One unfortunate byproduct of the otherwise beneficial practice of contextualizing literature according to culture has been an exaggerated emphasis on national borders. We will conceive of Hemingway as an American in Paris because we are used to that. And because Africa figures directly in his short fiction, there has been work done there. We spend less time, however, on Hemingway's sojourns in other, less well-known parts of the world. In the context of postwar Istanbul, Hemingway and John Dos Passos have interesting and insightful things to say about the "first world" geopolitics of the time.

Cross-referencing American literature and Turkish studies therefore allows us to put into practice Said's prescription for the willed double perspective necessary to anyone wishing to write as honestly as possible about a culture not his or her own. It may not be possible. And if honesty is not necessarily what separates fiction from fact, but what renders any writing honorable, then all we can ask for is that heightened self-consciousness that made Mary Montagu's eighteenth-century account of Turkey, for the most part, an important travel narrative.

American Writers in Istanbul

1

Herman Melville in Istanbul

Ishmael, Urban Naturalist

> General thoughts about Constantinople. As for the mud, mere wet pollen of a flower.

HERMAN MELVILLE's last voyage abroad was an eight-month excursion that took him through Europe and the Levant from October 11, 1856, to May 6, 1857. He had the manuscript of *The Confidence Man* in his bags, the last book of prose he would publish in his lifetime. He was thirty seven years old and suffering from rheumatism, sciatica, and bad eyesight. The stress of intense writing, the waning of his literary reputation in the public eye, and his subsequent growing melancholia had alarmed his friends and family. They had therefore encouraged him to take to the sea again in hopes that some wandering in foreign regions would prevent his enthusiasm for things both seen and unseen to lead him even closer toward a pending madness. Like Ishmael's hazy hopes for his journey aboard the *Pequod,* as many who write of Melville's last voyage like to note, the wish of those who cared about him was that a trip East of Western Europe, a place he had always dreamed of going, would work toward "driving off the spleen, and regulating the circulation" of the weary writer (Melville 1851, 23).

The journal, which Melville kept as a record of his travels, reveals that he did experience periods of pleasure or heightened curiosity, but that for the most part the Middle East, Egypt, and Palestine in particular, left him anxious though unmoved. The highlights of the journals, both from an aesthetic and conceptual point of view, are his entries about Constantinople, which he visited for six days, from December 12 to 18. Out of a recording of staccato impressions of England and Greece, rawly sketched to be teased later into more comprehensive forms, the journal entries concerning the capital of the Ottoman Empire momentarily

1. The Sea of Marmara and General View of Constantinople, 1878. From Edmund Ollier, *Cassell's Illustrated History of the Russo-Turkish War,* London, 1878.

expand into full paragraphs and extended meditations on some of Melville's pet preoccupations: the relation of man and nature and the intimations of things that lie beyond human ken. In Istanbul Melville finds further evidence of the complex of linked analogies and paradoxes that inform his fictional worlds. What will disarm or disturb other visiting writers to Istanbul will ultimately excite and attract Melville because he brings to the complicated city a sensibility prepared for its manifold contrasts.

Observing the arrival of an Austrian steamer into Salonica, Greece, from Constantinople, Turkey, Melville notes the mayhem of the cosmopolitan crowd aboard. The initial misgivings one reads in his word choices will give way in later pages to a rhetorical enthusiasm—even for the things he dislikes—once he crosses over to the city itself. There is a sense in this first description, however, that the well-traveled Melville is seeing something familiar yet new in the crowd, a sensation that will accompany him on his first passage into the threshold of Western Europe and the Middle East.

> A great host of poor deck passengers, Turks, Greeks, Jews &c. Came ashore in boats, piled up with old dusty traps from which the Plaigue seemed shaken. Great uproar of the porters & contention for luggage.—Imagine an immense accumulation of the rags of all nations, & all colors rained down on a dense mob all struggling for huge bales & bundles of rags, gesturing with all gestures & wrangling in all tongues . . . Upon the uproar at the landing Olympus looked from afar cold & snowy. (Melville 1955, 73)

Though the syntax is truncated here like most of his journal entries, the description nonetheless brings to mind the collection of nations in the streets of New Bedford as described in the chapter "The Street" in *Moby Dick* (1851). The exotic diversity of the Ottoman crowd is dramatized only to be put into relief by a local detail whose contrast suggests that strangeness is not only a relative concept, but a concept strange only to those for whom mingling with the "rags of all nations," including Americans, is not an everyday reality.

> In thoroughfares nigh the docks, any considerable seaport will frequently offer to view the queerest looking nondescripts from foreign parts. Even in Broadway and Chestnut streets, Mediterranean mariners will sometimes jostle the affrighted ladies. Regent Street is not unknown to Lascars and Malays; and at Bombay, in the Apollo Green, live Yankees have often scared the natives. (Melville 1851, 59–60)

Like New Bedford itself, the mythological mountain Olympus, witness to the comings and goings of international groups of wanderers, is ultimately unmoved in the face of so much diverse, worldly activity. Melville's initial disapproving descriptives, "dusty," "Plaigue," "uproar," "mob," terms typical in the texts of new arrivals to the Levant, are terms he self-consciously checks with Mt. Olympus's distant calm.

This fusion of exception and acceptance will permeate the pages dedicated to the topography and population of labyrinthine, crowded Istanbul. Descriptions of the congested streets are often as morbid as they are animated.

> Came through the vast suburbs of Galata &c. Great crowds of all nation—money changers—*coins of all nations circulate*—Placards in four or five languages. [(Turkish, French, Greek, Armenian) Lottery.] ad-<vertisements> of

> boats the same. *You feel you are among the nations.* Great curse of Babel; not being able to talk to a fellow being . . . The horrible grimy tragic air of these streets. The rotten & wicked looking houses. So gloomy & grimy seems as if a suicide hung from every rafter within. (Melville 1955, 84–85)

Diversity and dilapidation come hand in hand in the paragraphs, and Melville's attraction to the first never seems tempered by his discomfort with the latter. On the contrary, the "curse of Babel" that makes the global experiment that is mid-nineteenth-century Istanbul untidy is also what gives the city its particular resonance. Civilizations come and go, the streets seem to say, nodding their weathered rafters, and Melville's journal records this transience in the texture of the city's surface in terms we recognize from his earlier work. His recurrent effort to render in his fiction the struggle between man and nature from the side of nature finds an unlikely analogy in a metropolis of one million five hundred people, "a moderate estimate, judging from the swarms," he notes (Melville 1955, 101). The confusion of the city, the maze-like quality of its thoroughfares and dead ends will be repeatedly compared to phenomena in the natural world.

MELVILLE spent a good part of his time lost in the city. His arrival, hampered by a night and day of fog that kept the ship anchored in the Sea of Marmara, "very thick, & damp & raw. Very miserable for the Turks and their harrems," foreshadows Melville's preoccupation with forces of nature that seemed to him to pervade the city, even account, in his terms, for its inscrutable thus alluring character.

> The fog only lifted from about the skirts of the city, which being built on a promontory, left the crown of it hidden wrapped in vapor. Could see the base & wall of St. Sophia but not the dome. It was a coy disclosure, a kind of coquetting, leaving room for the imagination & heightening the scene. Constantinople, like her Sultanas, was thus veiled in her "ash-mack." (Melville 1955, 77)

While this employment of eroticized, Orientalist rhetoric is typical in the texts of Western observers, this will be the only time Melville borrows from the discourse of his predecessors. Once he is in the city, his analogies become less predictable. When nature is not of direct interest in his descriptions or discussion, Melville consistently summons the language of nature in various metaphorical guises to represent the seemingly random quality, or mysterious geometry, of Istanbul's streets and structures.

> Started alone for Constantinople and after a terrible long walk, found myself back where I started. Just like getting lost in a wood. No plans to streets. Pocket-compass. Perfect labryth [labyrinth]. Narrow. Close, shut in. If one could get *up* aloft, it would be easy to see one's way out. If you could get up into tree. Soar out of the maze. But no. No names to the streets no more than to natural allies among the groves. No numbers. No anything. (Melville 1955, 79)

Rather than representing the city as a mistake of nature, an errant miscalculation of the forms Western civilization creates to reflect the rational structures of nature, Melville, unlike many of his post-Enlightenment contemporaries, will associate his confusion with man's general inability to read the signs of nature. His inability to locate himself, his discomfort over the failure of his technological mechanisms, his compass, to lead him out of the confusion is not just a tourist's complaint. It is a comment on man's fundamental relationship to his environment. As the journal progresses, Constantinople as a whole, and places and structures within, will be repeatedly referred to as forests or trees. By suggesting that just as there are no "natural allies among the groves," no signs on the streets, Melville intimates in this early observation a subject he often contends with in his fiction and poetry: there is much about the city that reflects, or is emblematic of, the natural lawlessness, or natural detachment in the relationship between man and nature. The city, like nature, tends to its own rhythms heedless of the passage of generations. Even the destructive effects of men's actions, the chaos that ensues after a fire, a crusade, or an invasion, are taken in stride like other natural disasters. And it is for this reason that Melville's writing about Istanbul is neither Romantic in its praise nor chauvinistic in its criticism.

Alongside Melville's recurrent references to chaos and lawlessness are repeated observations of a further parallel he notes in the relationship between nature and human structures in Istanbul. He will compare architectural shapes to corresponding forms in the trees and vegetation that grow about them, and the effects of these resemblances on his imagination appeals invariably to his metaphysics:

2. An Old Istanbul Street, 1883, by C. Biseo, from Edmonde de Amicis, *Constantinople,* Paris, 1883.

> No wonder the Czars have always coveted the capital of the Sultans. No wonder the Russian among his firs sighs for these myrtles.—Cedar & Cypress the only trees about the capital.—The Cypress a green minaret, & blends with the stone ones. Minaret <perhaps> derived from cypress shape. The intermingling of the dark tree with the bright spire expressive of the intermingling of life & death. (Melville 1955, 94)

While other observers will emphasize the exotic or picturesque quality of minarets on the Constantinople skyline, a way of seeing mosques that emphasizes their difference, thus contingent relationship to the topography and the philosophy of Christian terrains, Melville's vision of minarets ignores the exclusions of orthodox faith. His familiar play with the symbolic potential of juxtaposed particulars in the world, whichever the world, leads him to apply minarets and cypresses to the question of existence, a question that transcends, because it does not exclude, disparate avenues of inquiry, of faith.

The heaven-directed reach of minarets, like steeples, speak to Melville's troubled experiment with the transcendental, a life-long journey that his friend and mentor Hawthorne witnessed from the distance of age and a more secure trust in the potential of Christian faith: "It is strange how he (Melville) persists—and has persisted ever since I knew him . . . in wandering to and fro over these deserts . . . he can neither believe nor be comfortable in his disbelief; and he is too honest and courageous not to try to do one or the other" (Kazin 1997, 91). In Istanbul Melville carries on his search for traces of the infinite in the finite, a Calvinist tendency he shared with Hawthorne. There is "nothing finer," he claims, than the "six towered mosque of Sultan Achmet soaring up with its snowy spires into the pure blue sky, like light houses" (Melville 1955, 80). If the dark cypresses seem signs of death—or life (the parallelism may or may not be consciously inverted)—the minarets as "bright spires" are also "light houses," a sailor's or wanderer's guide to safety. Mosques are treated with the usual fusion of respect and irreverence that Melville's reserves for houses of worship:

> The Mosque is a sort of marble marquee of which the minarets (four or six) are the stakes. In fact when inside it struck me that the idea of the edifice was borrowed from the tent. Though it would make a noble ball room. Off shoes & went in. This custom more sensible than taking off hat. Muddy shoes but never muddy heads. (Melville 1955, 83)

Like the pulpit in *Moby Dick* that is not "without a trace of the same sea-taste" that decorates the rest of the chapel, and as "earth's foremost part" is "the bow" that must "bear the earliest brunt," Melville moves easily from the description of a religious custom or a customary religious object to an expanded reading of its potential significance on a broader philosophical level (Melville 1851, 69–70). The physical and the metaphysical interact in his paragraphs like subgenres of similar orders, close enough in kind to not require separate attention or separate space on the page.

Melville's interest in the "linked analogies" between the physical world, metaphysics, and man's mind is a preoccupation he held in common with the American Transcendentalists. "Every appearance in nature," says Melville's contemporary, Ralph Waldo Emerson in his essay "Nature," "corresponds to some state of the mind, and that state of the mind can only be described by presenting that natural appearance as its picture . . . Light and darkness are our familiar expression for knowledge and ignorance; heat for love. Visible distance behind and before us, is respectively our image of memory and hope" (Emerson 1981a, 20). The primary theme of *Moby Dick* is man's struggle with nature's portion in his fate. The White Whale, like an idol, functions as a medium for the contemplation of the potential correspondences that exist between the earthly and unearthly, and the understanding of this relationship varies from character to character. For Ahab, according to the omniscient narrator, this particular Leviathan is emblematic of the agony of man's existential condition: "The White Whale swam before him as the monomaniac incarnation of all those malicious agencies which some deep men feel eating in them, till they are left living on with half a heart and half a lung" (Melville 1851, 246). Ahab's internal experiences are inexplicably echoed in external phenomena: "O Nature, and o soul of man! How beyond all utterance are your linked analogies! Not the smallest atom stirs or lives on matter, but has its cunning duplicate in mind" (Melville 1851, 406). Ishmael's momentary lapse of consciousness at the helm in the chapter "The Try-Works" leads him to sermonize against the "unnatural hallucination of the night" and the false illumination of fire which displaces the healthy radiance of the sun: "Give not thyself up, then, to fire, lest it invert thee, deaden thee; as for the time it did me. There is a wisdom that is woe; but there is a woe that is madness" (Melville 1851, 543). Man must be selective when communing with the elements; the powers we become enthralled to can mean the difference between sense and insanity, life and death.

F. O. Matthiessen, however, argues rightly that while Melville may have been as partial as Emerson and the Transcendentalists to the "doctrine of the 'linked analogies' between nature and man's mind, and that of the symbolic significance of every natural fact," he "diverge[d] from the Transcendental conclusion that its effect on man was necessarily beneficent" (Matthiessen 1941, 406). Ahab and Ishmael's soliloquies are the performance of this diversion in Melville's fiction. Some of Melville's observations of the intermingling of architecture and nature in Istanbul also reflect his particular anti-Romantic naturalism, most pointedly when he talks of architecture located underground—subaltern spaces such as the Cistern of Philoxenus, one of nineteen known reservoirs that exist deep under the city's surface like the "sunless seas" in Coleridge's "Kubla Khan":

> Then to the Cistern of 1000 columns. You see a rounded knoll covered with close herbage. Then a kind of broken cellar way, you go down, & find yourself on a wooden, rickety platform, looking down into a grove of marble pillars, fading away into utter darkness. A palatial sort of Tartarus. Two tiers of pillars one standing on t'other; lower tier half buried. Here & there a little light percolates through from breaks in the keys of the arches; where bits of green straggle down . . . At whatever point you look, you see lines of pillars, like trees in an orchard arranged in the quincus style.—Came out. Overhead looks like a mere shabby common, or worn out sheep pasture. (Melville 1955, 81–82)

The cistern is represented as an organic space: the entrance, "a rounded knoll" in a "common," a "sheep pasture," opens to a chthonian underworld where "marble pillars" are in "groves," are "like trees in an orchard." But this architecture couched in similes of meadows and forests, is not read in pastoral terms. The effect, Melville suggests, is "Tartarean," the same adjective he applies to the "shapes of the pagan harpooners" stirring the "hissing masses of blubber into the scalding pots" in the Try-Works on the *Pequod* (Melville 1851, 539–40). And like the hellish scene in which the ship "freighted with savages, and laden with fire, and burning a corpse, and plunging into that darkness of darkness, seemed a material counterpart of her monomaniac commander's soul," the cistern, where silk-spinning boys "flit about like imps," and where it would be a "terrible place to be robbed or murdered in," seems to correspond to the dark, irrational underside of the city's consciousness (Melville 1955, 82). If Emerson, as a Romantic Naturalist, believed that the integration of nature is the purpose of man's existence, and that through an understanding of nature man can enter into rapport with it, Melville took a less positive view of this symbiotic relationship. The cistern, like the light and vegetation that permeates it, is both of this world, and not of it, and Melville notes this ambiguity in his description.

While some commentators will focus on Melville's references to the fear of internment in Istanbul, concluding that Melville did not find the "spiritual uplift" he was looking for on his journey, this is a reading of the journal which does not take into account Melville's complex attraction to "the obverse side of the Transcendental dream" (Kazin 1997, 97; Matthiessen 1941, 406). Descending into the cistern, "as into a ship's hold," Melville is both frightened and fascinated. There is something supernatural about the human activity, the "twisting silk" and "spinning jennies," that goes on in the awful darkness. Yet his symbolic references to nature suggest that this strangeness reflects nature's own inexplicable ways. Like meadows and forests, this ancient structure is impermeable to interpretation.

3. Underground Cistern: Sultan Ahmet, 1835, by William Henry Barlett, from Julia Pordoe, *The Beauties of the Bosphorus,* London, 1835.

Melville, like Emerson, believed that man's reading of the world depended largely on his character and mood. Emerson asks, "Have mountains, and waves, and skies, no significance but what we consciously give them when we employ them as emblems of our thought. The world is emblematic" (Emerson 1981a, 23). The narrator in Melville's 1852 novel *Pierre* echoes Emerson's subjective hermeneutics: "Say what some poets will, Nature is not so much her own ever-sweet interpreter, as the mere supplier of that cunning alphabet, whereby selecting and combining as he pleases, each man reads his own peculiar lesson according to his own particular mind and mood" (qtd. in Matthiessen 1941, 406). Matthiessen goes on to note that Melville, in his copy of *Hamlet,* marked, "Here is forcibly shown the great Montaigneism of Hamlet" next to the lines spoken by Hamlet to Rosencrantz: "There is nothing good or bad but thinking makes it so" (406). Interpretation and value are relative concepts. Although Montaigne flirted with Christian revelation, he tended to agree with the Skeptics that any information we profess to gain about the world beyond that available to the immediate senses must make no claim to truth, though this did not mean that wandering the cosmos via one's imagination was a misuse of time. Melville's defense of subjectivity should be read in these terms, and not as Emersonian positivism. To Hawthorne Melville writes that "what plays the mischief with the truth is that men will insist upon the universal application of a temporary feeling or opinion" (qtd. in Matthiessen 1941, 407). The result of Melville's skeptical conception of the limits of man's ability to do much more than project his own moods onto the "cunning alphabet" provided to us by nature allows a certain autonomy to the outside world. Even as he acknowledges the influence of the human psyche over the lessons we take away from experience, this authority is manifold and paradoxical: the gold doubloon that Ahab has hammered to the mast to be given to the first man that spots the White Whale becomes a cabalist sign that each man pauses before and studies. To Ahab, "This round gold is but the image of the rounder globe, which, like a magician's glass, to each and every man in turn but mirrors back his own mysterious self. Great pains, small gains for those who ask the world to solve them; it cannot solve itself" (Melville 1851, 551). Ahab's morbid mood may read in the gold coin the lesson that "'t is fit that man should live in pains and die in pangs," but he also acknowledges the solipsism of the world.

Melville, like his Promethean anti-hero Ahab, not only doubted a transcendent power's will to communicate with human beings through nature, he also doubted the very possibility of an empathetic nature. And it is within this recurrent theme of the indifference of nature that further observations of Istanbul may be considered.

> Passed between wall & Golden Horn through Greek & Jew quarters, and came outside the land wall in view of Sweet Waters, which run inland & end in beautiful glades. Rode along the land wall. By this wall Constantinople was taken by the Turks & the last of the Constantines fell in their defense. Four miles of massiveness . . . In many parts rent by earthquakes. The towers especially. Great cracks & fissures . . . the riven parts stand toppling like inverted pyramids. Evergreen vines mantling them . . . The strength of the masonry shows, that when by earthquake the summit of a tower has been thrown down, it has slid off retaining its integrity—not separating, but rubbing like a rock-slide. In the wide tracks, they cultivate them—garden spots—very rich & loamy—here fell the soldiers of Constantine—sowed in corruption & raised in potatoes. (Melville 1955, 86–87)

What is often recounted in the West as a tragic tale—the overpowering of the Byzantinians by the Ottoman Turks in 1453—is offered here with an objective distance that borders on disinterest, at least in the historical, human drama itself. Things are simultaneously destroyed and reborn in this entry, with Melville as keenly interested in the destruction as the rebirth. While wars and earthquakes have brought down much of the man-made walls, it appears to Melville less tragic than interesting due to the composition of the damage. Just as there is beauty in the landscape surrounding the walls, so there is an aesthetic quality to a structure that has been beaten, but not entirely, by forces of nature. The toppled masonry is like "inverted pyramids," "has slid off retaining its integrity . . . like a rock-slide." Whatever the disaster, human or natural, there is a sense of inevitability in these lines.

Melville feels compelled to record places not so much for their historical significance, and not always for their uniquely symbolic or emblematic significance, but for, as Harold Bloom notes, "a love of surfaces and their details, and a contrasting search for deeply lodged, inner truths underneath those shining outside" (Bloom 1999, 12). The "inner truth," if there is a search for one here, comes in the final phrases where we see Byzantine soldiers represented as fertilizer for mid-nineteenth-century vegetable gardens. While the line "sowed in

4. Old City Walls at Topkapı, Yarikhisar, 1835, by William Henry Barlett, from Julia Pordoe, *The Beauties of the Bosphorus*, London, 1835.

corruption & raised in potatoes" is a parody of St. Paul's words in 1 Corinthians 15:52 concerning the resurrection of the dead: "It is sown in corruption; it is raised in incorruption"—a favorite biblical pun of Melville's, the editor of Melville's *Journal* Howard C. Horsford notes—it is also a passing commentary on the significance or place of man in the cycles of nature (Horsford 1955, 22). Like all natural thus corporeal beings, man and his structures are not exempt from the bylaws of time. Just as things are born and die in nature, so do civilizations rise and fall, and one man's destruction is another man's sustenance, Melville wryly asserts. "Through all her provinces, nature seems to promise immortality to life but destruction to beings," says the character Babbalanja in Melville's third novel *Mardi* (1849). "Nature is not for us" (qtd. in Matthiessen 1941, 406). Thus, the disinterest in Melville's observation is not necessarily callous toward medieval Greeks so much as it is receptive to the indifference of nature to its own particulars. His detailed description of the wall's surfaces and final pun reflects his mixed posturing toward human earnestness in the face of his own mortality.

What seems to attract his eye and imagination the most in Istanbul is the urban capital's uncanny coexistence with a disinterested nature. It is a city that in its very sinews seems to reflect Melville's own complex views of this relationship. Observations of ruin and dilapidation are more often than not preceded or followed up by observations of sudden beauty.

> Looked at the burnt column [of Constantine] again. Base bedded in humus. It leans, is split & chipped & cracked. Of a smoky purple color. Is garlanded round with laurel (chisseled) at distances. (Croton water pipes on end)—Street scenes. Gilded carriages of style of Hogarths carriages. *Yellow boots daintily worn by the ladies in the mud*— Intricacy of the place. (Melville 1955, 93)

The column, like the walls, bears its history paradoxically and thus honestly in its attractive, cracked lines. What could be read as the neglect of those responsible for urban renewal is admired instead not for its Romantic dilapidation, but for the enduring sophistication of its design. Yellow boots are worn "daintily" in the mud, and the overall effect is one in which people and their tired, inherited monuments coexist stoically, if not rather cheerfully, with an uncompromising nature.

Melville will initially relate this propensity for accepting the things one cannot control to Islamic fatalism. Stranded on his arrival in the fog just beyond Istanbul near the Princess Islands, Melville records the following conversation with a person he calls "Old Sinop" because of the old man's participation in the Crimean War: "I said to him 'This is very bad' he answered 'God's will is good,' & smoked his pipe in cheerful resignation" (Melville 1955, 76). Dorothee Metlitsky Finkelstein in her book, *Melville's Orienda,* maps out the general vogue for Near Eastern literature, culture and travel in the mid-nineteenth century, a movement that Melville joined at its zenith. Not only did this popular trend lead to a exodus of Western travelers to the Holy Land and its neighboring vicinities, it also lead to an enthusiasm for mystical, pre-Islamic religions, for Sufism in particular, which was transmitted through the translations of Persian poets. The "Orientalizing tendency was taken for granted as standard literary equipment—an attitude persistently reflected in the most popular American magazines of the time" (Finkelstein 1971, 18–19). "Authoritative" articles on Turkish life and literature written by J. P. Brown, a well-known American Orientalist, dragoman, and eventual consul-general in Constantinople, appeared in the New York-based *Knickerbocker*

Magazine continually from June 1842 to August 1857 (Finkelstein 1971, 19). Finkelstein writes that Melville's early writing, his fragments, *Mardi,* and later, his long verse poem *Clarel* (written in 1876, but left unfinished at his death in 1891) reveal his familiarity with Eastern texts, both fictional and nonfictional. The list of texts would include *The Arabian Nights, Vathek, Saadi's Gulistan,* and other translations of the Sufi poets of medieval Persia in Sir William Jones's *Poems, Consisting Chiefly of Translations from the Asiatick Languages,* Omar Khayyam's *Rubaiyat,* and Herbelot's *Bibliothèque orientale,* plus hundreds of travel narratives. Thus, well versed in Occidental translations of the Ottoman territories on his mid-life voyage to Istanbul, Melville arrived with a lifetime of learned assumptions about the disposition of the culture, particularly an expectation of the "cheerful resignation" he would meet with among the faithful. Melville, Finkelstein suggests, believed that although "Islam failed, like other religions, to arrive at 'ultimate truth,'" it nevertheless "taught its followers to submit, to compromise with reality in its doctrine of resignation, tolerance, liberality, serenity" (Finkelstein 1971, 276).

The journal reveals, however, that as Melville enters further into the city's recesses he begins to read unanticipated, less prescribed characteristics in the Ottoman character and environment. He notes a certain capacity for living, and with style, in uncertainties, but he does not appeal solely to Islam, or mysticism, to explain this aptitude away. He repeatedly notes, for example, the ability of Ottoman women to transcend the unpleasantness of their immediate environment:

> *Street sights.*—The beauty of the human countenance. Among the women ugly faces rare.—Singular these races so exceed ours in this respect. Out of every window look faces (Jew, Greek, Armenian) which in England or America would be a cynosure in a ball room.—Wretched looking houses & and filthy streets. *Tokens of pauperism without the paupers.* Out of old shanties peep lovely girls. like lillies *& roses* growing in *cracked flower-pots.* (Melville 1955, 90)

Just as he remarks the paradoxical charm of "*yellow boots daintily worn by the ladies in the mud,*" he here notes the superior beauty of Ottoman women to English or American women despite the unbecoming conditions of their "presentation." Seeing beyond material circumstances that would perhaps paralyze an upper-middle-class American's ability (or those able to afford foreign travel) to judge female beauty objectively, Melville's signature anti-Romantic approach to people and their places comes through in these sections. Aware of the centrality of the rose, or gül, in the literary tradition of the medieval Sufi poets, Melville adopts this image in order to make a non-Western observation about the nature of beauty. As "*roses* growing in *cracked flower-pots,*" among "*tokens of pauperism without the paupers,*" the girls are emblems of a higher order of beauty, but they are not exceptional. They exist daily within the imperfect world. Peering out the windows of shanties, like roses in cracked pots, the beautiful girls reveal the natural order of things: an intermingling and coexistence of elements that may appear contradistinctive to the untrained or unenlightened eye.

Like the integrated, regal beauty of the women in a poor neighborhood, Melville notes the cultivated quality of facades exposed to the weather:

> Holyday aspect of the Bospherus—the daisies are tipped with a crimson dawn, the very soil from [which] they spring has a ruddy hue.—Kiosks & fountains. One is amazed to see such delicate & fairy-like structures out of doors. One would think the elements would visit them too rudely; that they would melt away like castle of confectionary. Profuse sculpture & gilding & painting.—The bays sweep round in great ampitheatres. (Melville 1955, 94)

Again, nature and architecture are offered side by side in the same entry, each reinforcing the exposé of the other. The diminutive details of nature, the daisies, encounter the larger elements, just as the "delicate" engravings on the kiosks and fountains confront the ecosystem. Thus, not only do the organic flowers and the reflections of them carved in marble relief share more than a surface resemblance; they also share a fundamental deportment vis-à-vis a potentially hostile environment: they bravely, if off-handedly, face a higher nature that may be for or against them depending on its mood. The language of enchantment, "fairy-like," and refinement, "confectionary," in this description suggest the dreamy, artificial rhetoric of the picturesque. This effect is furthered by the final framing or staging of the scenes in windows or amphitheatres, as if all were a display arranged for the traveler's viewing pleasure. But while Melville's syntactical yoking of nature and architecture, like his earlier linking of nature and beautiful women, may nod to such formal conventions of the picturesque in nineteenth-century travel writing from time to time, they do not bend in any consistent way.

In their introduction to *The Anthropology of Landscape,* Eric Hirsch and Michael O'Hanlon offer ways of understanding social and historical attitudes of men to nature that may be applied to Melville's approach to Istanbul landscapes in order to distinguish it from that of his contemporaries. In landscape painting, for example, and particularly in the nineteenth century, there is a relationship between the foreground in painting and the background which exemplifies a relationship "between an ordinary, workaday life and an ideal, imagined existence, vaguely connected to the everyday" (Hirsch and O'Hanlon 1995, 3). Background can be conceived of as "the perceived potentiality" of a place "thrown into relief by our fore grounded existence (the way we might be)." Social life, they go on to say, "can never achieve the timelessness of a painting, although . . . this is often what is striven for in particular cultural contexts (in most cases, without the use of canvases as such)." If we consider Melville's descriptions of Istanbul as "literary tableaus" we find that he challenges this assessment of the contrast between foreground and background in commonplace representations of landscape "without the use of canvases" (or writing) precisely because his illustrations, while they may direct the viewer to temporal issues, do so by nonconventional means and for nonconventional ends. "Imperial history," argues P. Carter in *The Road to Botany Bay,* is a form of history which "'reduces space to a stage' upon which actors enact significant historical events" (qtd. in Hirsch and O'Hanlon 1995, 3). In other words, and in the case of travel writing, as the authors note, "what the travel writer writes is not the physical country, but the enactment of a historical space" that is more informed by one's own history than actual local events (Hirsch and O'Hanlon 1995, 4). Melville, unlike most travel writers in the Ottoman Empire, seems to abandon the perception of history or culture specific "background potential" once the fog has lifted. If and when he uses "the stage" as a metaphor, it is borrowed not to frame the landscape in Western metaphors of contained exoticism, but for its topographical accuracy: the "bays" that "sweep round" the shores of the Bosphorus do strike one as "great ampitheatres" due to their steep, terraced incline. Ottoman women may be like flowers, but they are not eroticized beyond human recognition. The Walls of Constantine are not gazed upon as memento mori in the usual sense (the ironic use of St. Paul disallows this), and they are not read as tragic codes signifying the kind of infidel threat to Western history and culture that enflame crusades in their various guises to the Middle East. And while Melville does add, as mentioned earlier, that the Cistern of 1000 Columns would be a "terrible place to be robbed or murdered in," the menace has more to do with the "Tartarean" effects of the darkness and the depth of the space than with any real or imagined intentions of the people he actually encounters there. If landscape, or the picturesque, is a "restrictive way of seeing which privileges the 'outsiders' point of view" as Hirsch and O'Hanlon argue, Melville avoids this hegemonic tendency by decreasing the distance between himself as an outsider and the people and spaces inside the city through offering them as nearly pure foreground. His discussion may not be free of his desire to examine certain kinds of background potential in Istanbul—he takes his fascination with the correspondences between man, nature, and metaphysics everywhere he goes. But because the nature of his search is free-floating, manifesting itself in careful, tactile descriptions of the surfaces of things not only for their aesthetic qualities but for what they might tell him about the always mysterious, always illusive nature of being, he avoids the clumsiness of other travel writers who stumble around the city in search of home.

Even Emerson, despite his Transcendentalism, enacts the kind of historical space depicted by Hirsch and O'Hanlon on his "real" trip to England: "England is a garden . . . Nothing is left as it was made. Rivers, hills, valleys, the sea itself, feel the hand of the master" (Emerson 1981b, 399). The "master," in this case, is no higher spirit than the industrious Englishman. From here, Emerson unleashes the culturally specific and culturally exclusive flip side of his Romantic Naturalism: "The Russian in his snow is aiming to be English. The Turk and Chinese also are making awkward efforts to be English. The practical common-sense of modern society, the utilitarian direction which labor, laws, opinions, religion takes, is the natural genius of the British mind" (Emerson 1981b, 400). Emerson avoids the pretty and pathetic in this particular discussion of landscape by replacing it with a Romanticized pragmatism—though he does so at the expense of others. When Melville's travel journal entries become critical of landscape in any sustained way—and they certainly do in Cairo and Jerusalem—they tend to avoid imposing the kind of fixed ideas of other cultures as Emerson does above. Of the environs of the pyramids, Melville says:

> Line of desert & verdure, plain[er] than that between good & evil. An instant collision of alien elements. A long <billow> of desert forever hovers as in act of breaking, upon the verdure of Egypt. Grass near the pyramids, but will not

> touch them—as if in fear or awe of them. Desert more fearful to look at than ocean. (Melville 1955, 119)

Melville does not regain his enthusiasm for landscape after leaving Turkey on December 23 until he quits the Mediterranean and reaches Italy in mid-February. While he may have misgivings about the pyramids and the desert of Egypt, his next stop after Turkey, his reservations continue nevertheless to be couched in language that intermingles the abstract and concrete in ways that deepen the enigmatic potential of surfaces. However, the journal suggests that the time spent between in the Middle East is more work than pleasure and his health problems return. His journal entries become more and more cursory and cold the closer he gets to Bethlehem:

> Over Olivet by St: Stephens Gate to Bethany—on a hill—wretched Arab village—fine view—Tomb of Lazarus, a mere cave or cell—On down into vallies & over hills—all barren—Brook Kedron—immense depth—black and funereal—Valley of Jehohophat, grows more diabolical as approaches Dead Sea. (Melville 1955, 134–35)

Later in early February, the Greek Islands seem to him equally desolate, "rocky, naked & barren. Patches of verdure on some . . . A fine sail upon the whole. But the scenery is all outline. No filling up. Seem to be sailing upon gigantic outline engravings" (Melville 1955, 166). While the quality of the writing deteriorates during the rest of his Mediterranean leg of the voyage, the result of his health, perhaps, more than anything, Melville nevertheless does not intrude on these countries and cultures with the kind of American or Eurocentric arrogance we see in Emerson above. His criticisms, like his compliments in Turkey, concentrate, for the most part, on how the foreground, the land and the edifices, seem to reflect the private philosophical concerns that he impresses indiscriminately on all he sees.

In Istanbul Melville delights in scenes that even overturn or trump his own expectations of space and place. These moments, again, often manifest themselves in the interplay between nature, or nature's beings, and man's constructions. He is fascinated by the pigeons of Istanbul that seem to ignore the fact that their place is outside with other creatures of the air:

> The Propontis, the Bosphorus, the Golden Horn, the domes the minarets, the bridges, the men of war, the cypresses.—Indescribable.—Went to the Pigeon Mosque [of Bayezid II, 1497–1505]. In its court, the pigeons covered the pavement as thick as in the West they fly in hosts. A man feeding them. Some perched upon the roof of the colonnades, & upon the fountain in the middle& on the cypresses.—Took off my shoes, & went in. Pigeons inside, flying around in the dome, in & out the lofty windows. (Melville 1955, 83)

Equally at home on colonnades, in cypresses, and inside mosques, the pigeons draw his attention by their disregard for the frontiers between the outside and the inside. In another mosque, he notes a further confusion of place that makes room for the sacred and the profane simultaneously, a narrative that concludes again with birds.

> A Verandah without, a colonnade within. A fountain in the middle. Columns of variously colored marbles & mosaic. Heaps of old traps, old capotes being cut up by beggars. bales with marks. Pile of old hoops rusting. Pile of old haversacks and belts & spoons & kettles [Grated windows look between the double galleries. Beautiful effect. Outside, under gallery, rows of penstocks, with stone footstool below, for worshippers to wash feet & c. Within, four vast pillars supports to the dome, like towers (white marble). Most perfect specimen of the mosque. Regular square fountains. Birds perched among the chandeliers, flying about. (Melville 1955, 96)

Not particularly worried about the mess, he admires, as he interfuses, the contrasting physical details that all together animate, by including life in what otherwise might be a solemn, solemnized, or emptied-out space. Melville does not ignore the non-Romantic particulars in order to offer the scene's background potential in its purest form, that is "emptiness itself" (Hirsch and O'Hanlon 1995, 4). Rather, he registers them in equal measure with "the most perfect specimen" itself. The mess is not charming: it is real urban debris; the enclosed but exposed inner square is not physically empty, uninhabited, or distant "from the populations for which [it] hold[s] significance," as sacred sites often are depicted according to traditional expectations of the picturesque. Melville neither cleans up nor dirties down the scene through cultural critique. Instead, he offers the elegant, sacred structure together with the shabby, irreligious clutter—both the products of human labor—and the result is yet one more example of Melville's identification with the city's penchant for mixed metaphors.

"Perched among the chandeliers, flying about" are the ubiquitous birds, which today still surprise one: a sparrow pausing in a ray of filtered light on a gallery railing, a pigeon rousting high up in a gap left by a fallen brick. The beautiful and the ugly are equally visited by these emissaries of nature and their unexpected presence indoors is always a surprise to a visitor used to the impenetrable inner sanctuaries of most houses of worship. Despite the logical explanation for their existence inside—the large doors covered in the daytime by huge leather curtains only, and the fact that most mosques remain open to worshippers and tourists every day—there is always something uncanny about the presence of the birds. Melville seems to have felt this too, and added the phenomenon to his bag of metaphysical questions concerning the interpenetration of the natural and the mystical. Offering the wild birds as he does, however, as improbable yet incorporated facts of the urban space, he acknowledges that while men, the natural world, and the sacred might at times seem to exist side by side in Istanbul, this does not necessarily mean that they are in communication. Beings seem to coexist with little dramatic regard for one another. This is indifference but with a difference: it is not so much a tragic or apathetic state of affairs as it is an arrangement whereby parties pursuing their sundry industries within close proximity of one another leave doors open to commerce with the other. In contrast to Captain Ahab's abstract nihilism, the narrator of *Moby Dick* asks the following questions, and then offers the following warning, about the possibilities of intercourse between a higher power, nature, and man, in what may appear to be an uncommunicative universe.

> Oh busy weaver! Unseen weaver!—pause!—one word! whither flows the fabric? what palace may it deck? wherefore all these ceaseless toilings? Speak weaver!—stay thy hand!—but one single word with thee! Nay—the shuttle flies—the figures float from forth the loom; the freshet-rushing carpet for ever slides away. The weaver-god, he weaves; and by that weaving is he deafened, that he hears no mortal voice; and by that humming, we, too, who look on the loom are deafened; and only when we escape it shall we hear the thousand voices that speak through it. For even so it is in all material factories. The spoken words that are inaudible among the flying spindles; those same words are plainly heard without the walls . . . Ah, mortal! then, be heedful; for so, in all this din of

> the great world's loom, thy subtlest thinkings may be overheard afar. (Melville 1851, 573–74)

He who plies the loom and he who looks on may not be able to talk over the noise that is creation. The deity whose spirit permeates the mosque and the men whose tapings and clanging echo within the dome may speak past each other. But according to the narrator of *Moby Dick,* who in this case is much like the bird who passes back and forth between realms in the journal, one may enter the domain of the other: he himself simulates the journey on a daily basis.

The material source for the mediation in the quotation above is the skeleton of a sperm whale that has taken dominion on a South Pacific Isle. The whale "himself all woven over with the vines; every month assuming greener, fresher verdure," has also been adopted and adorned as an idol by local people. Despite his trappings, however, the spent whale is "but himself a skeleton" (Melville 1851, 574). "Life folded Death; Death trellised Life," says the fascinated narrator. Melville witnesses another simulation of the folding of the biological into the metaphysical, the provision for the otherworldly in the material, in the ancient cemeteries of Constantinople. Immediately after the discussion of fallen soldiers and vegetable gardens, Melville adds the following scene and commentary on the role of the city walls: "These walls skirted by forrests of cemetery—the cypress growing thick as firs in a Scotch plantation. Very old—a primal look—weird. The walls seem the inexorable bar between the mansions of the living & the dungeons of the dead" (Melville 1955, 87). The editor notes that Melville initially had written, "The 'haggard' walls seem the 'stern' inexorable bar between the mansions of the living & dungeons of the dead," but lined the adjectives out on second thought. The deletion is interesting because not only would "haggard" contradict the integrated beauty of his earlier impression of the walls, but also "stern" would have exaggerated the division between the living and the dead. Instead, he opts for an abstract qualifier that suggests an inevitability, but not necessarily a threatening one.

Melville's remarks on cemeteries involve nature even further in the spiritual temperament of the metropolis. Unlike the old churchyards of Europe or the burial grounds of America—sometimes, but not always, annexed to a place of worship—the older, larger cemeteries of Istanbul seem to reside as distinct ideas in the city. The Jewish, Armenian Christian, Greek Orthodox, or Muslim dead have separate quarters, but in all cases, the organization of cemeteries in

Istanbul contrasts greatly with those further West. There is less attention to symmetry. Graves lie together at wild angles to conserve space. Their surfaces are small garden spaces where spring irises, autumn chrysanthemums, or the evergreen weed sprout inside marble fences. Most striking, however, are the trees, which are allowed to grow out of the dead. Ancient Oaks or young Judas trees sometimes crowd a fifteenth-century marble marker with turbaned head and Ottoman script, but the process has been so slow and gentle that the trees do not topple so much as embrace the gravestones. Ottoman cemeteries are forests of trees and marble that hang on to each other at dramatic angles.

Like so many other travelers to the Ottoman Empire, Flaubert too noted the maze-like streets and the cemeteries on his visit to Constantinople in November of 1850: "One gets lost in the streets, which seem to have no beginning or end. The cemeteries are like forests in the middle of the city" (Flaubert 1954, 113). These sudden urban woods harboring the dead strike Flaubert in much the same way as they will Melville six years later. The French writer is also attracted to their integration into the life of the city.

> The oriental cemetery is one of the most beautiful things about the East. It does not have that profoundly exasperating quality of cemeteries at home—no wall, no ditch, no separation or enclosure of any kind. It is situated anywhere, in the country or in a town, here and there and everywhere, like death itself alongside of life, and given no attention whatever. You walk through a cemetery as you walk through a bazaar. All the graves are alike; they differ only in age, as they grow old they sink and disappear, like one's memory of the dead. The cypresses planted in the cemeteries are gigantic, and give the places a green light full of peace. (Flaubert 1954, 113)

Death and life exist unabashedly together. Cypresses rise aloft as graves descend, and the inhabitants of Constantinople do not overlook this natural fact, which is also the story of their individual mortality, but seem to agree to it on a daily basis. Melville also remarks on the functional or surrogate role of the Istanbul cemeteries: "Up early; went out; saw cemeteries where they dumped garbage. Sawing wood over a tomb. Forrests of cemeteries. Intricacy of the streets" (Melville 1955, 79). Taken aback by what may seem like disrespect for the dead, Melville records other unorthodox activities in the cemeteries: "Went toward the cemeteries of

Pera. Great resort in summer evenings" (Melville 1955, 89). These offhanded but hardly condemning observations that tell us, as Flaubert does, of the practical or less reverent uses of burial grounds, are accompanied in the journal by another story of human grief that echoes the existential questioning one sees throughout the pages of *Moby Dick*.

> Saw a burial. Armenian. Juggling & incantations of the priests—making signs & c.—Nearby, saw a woman over a new grave—no grass on it yet. Such abandonment of misery! Called to the dead, put her head down as close to it as possible; as if calling down a hatchway or celler; besought—"Why don't you speak to me? My God!—It is I!—Ah, speak—but one word![″]—All deaf.—So much consolation.—This woman & her cries haunt me horribly. (Melville 1955, 89)

The journal, like the novel, shifts registers mid-paragraph. Yoked to the juggling and ceremony—"*Armenian Funerals winding through the streets. Coffin covered*

5. Dolmabahçe from the Beyoğlu Cemetery, 1835, by William Henry Barlett, from Julia Pordoe, *The Beauties of the Bosphorus*, London, 1835.

with flowers born on a bier. Wax candles born one each side in daylight. Boys & men chanting alternately. Striking effect, winding through the narrow lanes" (Melville 1955, 89)—is this moment of profound sorrow and distress. In this dramatic monologue that Melville imagines for the woman faced with the death of a loved one resonates Ahab's anguish and metaphysical isolation in the face of an indifferent God, or the Indefinite. Her unheeded appeal endows her, as it does Ahab, with an emblematic status—she is everyman demanding an explanation at the doors of fate. Yet in this cemetery where one woman wails the condition of man, a condition that haunts Melville's fiction and poetry, in others people saw wood, dump garbage, have picnics.

Like Constantinople itself, its cemeteries and their seemingly incompatible inner dramas appeal to Melville's Shakespearean fondness for fusing the profound and the absurd. The city performs the Byzantine interplay between the realistic and abstract, the confounding of the high and the low, that Melville (as well as Shakespeare) was criticized for in his fiction by contemporaries.

> Ought Mr. Melville to write such books? [*Mardi, Moby Dick, Confidence Man*] Will he continue to write such books always? We do not hesitate to return an emphatic "No!" to both these questions . . . We desire him to give up metaphysics and take to nature and the study of mankind. We rejoice, therefore, to know that he is, at this moment, traveling in the Old World, where, we hope, he will enjoy himself heartily, look about him wisely, and come home ready to give us some pictures of life and reality. (O'Brien 1857, 366)

It is precisely the metaphysical trajectories in Melville's adventure writing that distinguish it from popular high-sea fiction, a genre certainly more marketable in the mid-nineteenth century and more palatable to critics of the kind above who hampered Melville's career in his lifetime and wished him god speed on his journey to wellness in 1857. Melville confessed to Hawthorne that in *Moby Dick* he had written a "wicked" book and simultaneously confirmed his innocence. The novel's wickedness lies, among other things, in its unorthodox metaphysical speculation, and this is a characteristic the novel shares with the *Journal*. "It is Melville's quality of relating everything which he did and saw to 'everything that lies beyond human ken' which distinguishes the *Journal* [and his later poem *Clarel*] from other travel writing," suggests Dorothy Finkelstein (Finkelstein

1971, 281). Thus, because Melville must include death and nature in his pictures of life and reality, his excursion by boat to visit the largest and most renowned cemetery of Constantinople located in "Scutari," now modern Üsküdar, seems a necessary part of his Old World journey. His enthusiasm for the textures of the city is visible in the excited rush of places and impressions on the page, expressions of sustained delight we see nowhere else in the journal.

> In morning took caique, & crossed the Bosphorus to Scutari. Luxurious sailing. Cushioned like ottoman . . . Calm of water. Tide-rips. Sun shining on Sultan's Palaces. Sunrise opposite the Seraglio. *As Constantinople is finest site for capital, so Seraglio for pleasure grounds, in the world.*—Great barracks at Scutari. Noble view of Constantinople & up the Bosphorus. Cemeteries like Black Forest. Thuringian look. Roads passing through it. Beautiful daisies. The quays. The water mosque. The hills & beach.—*General thoughts about Constantinople. As for the mud, mere wet pollen of a flower.* (Melville 1955, 104)

Melville, like Flaubert, considered Constantinople a singular world city.

> Of Constantinople, where I arrived yesterday morning, I shall tell you nothing except to say that I have been struck by the idea of Fourier, that some day it will be the capital of the world. It is really a fantastic human ant-hill. You know that feeling of being crushed and overwhelmed what one has on a first visit to Paris: here you are penetrated by that feeling, elbowing so many unknown men, from Persian and Indian, to the American and the Englishman, so many separate individualities which, in their frightening total, humble your own. And then the city is immense. (Flaubert 1954, 113)

Melville's thoughts about Istanbul's unique character, like Flaubert's, emerge from his observations of the city's paradoxical intermingling of the aesthetic and the unsightly, its cosmopolitan mayhem and delicate beauty. It is this coexistence of opposites that make it a modern tower of Babel, a place perhaps doomed, but heroic as a transnational experiment. Again, the cemeteries appear in Melville, here like dark, "Thuringian" German forests. The daisies are charming, however, and finally the squalor, the earthy reality of the city, is the source of its organic beauty: "*As for the mud, mere wet pollen of a flower.*"

Despite his critic's hope that Melville will "enjoy himself heartily" and "look about him wisely," that is, optimistically and pragmatically, the writer will include his impressions of the forested cemeteries and the emblematic role of the Bosphorus Straits in his metaphysical musings on the folding of life in death, death in life, in a manuscript poem entitled "The Continents."

> From bright Stamboul Death crosses o'er;
> Beneath the cypress evermore
> His camp he pitches by the shore
> of Asia old.
> Requiting this unsocial mood
> Stambouls's inmyrtled multitude
> Bless Allah and the sherbert good
> And Europe hold.
> Even so the cleaving Bosphorus parts
> Life and Death.—Dissembling hearts!
> Over the gulf the yearning starts
> To meet—infold!
>
> MELVILLE 1955, 104

Published posthumously, the poem recalls the caique crossing to Üsküdar on December 16, 1856. It echoes many strains in the journal: the forests of cypress and myrtle; a cemetery, this one on the Asian side of Istanbul where he believed Turkish Ottomans preferred to be buried; the wailing Armenian woman's desire for communication with the other world. More importantly, however, the poem captures in twelve lines what the journal in twenty-eight edited pages seems to say: Istanbul with its minarets like the mystical fountain of the whale spout seems a place of the world that can represent Melville's typological understanding of existence. Enfolding death and life, the city embodies complex and irreducible ontological uncertainties with a certain amount of grace. Neither a worldly paradise or hell, it allows room for intimations of both, and thus invites belief in the possibilities of the communion of men, nature, and the transcendental, yet never promises consummation. Melville, looking at the "noble view of Constantinople & up the Bosphorus," like Ishmael gazing on the "semi-visible steam" of the whale spout, sees and admires the agnostic potential of the phenomenon. As Ishmael concludes by thanking God for allowing him intuitions as well as "doubts and denials," so might Melville conclude his journal entry on Constantinople with the lines, "Doubts of all things earthly, and intuitions of some things heavenly; this combination makes neither believer or infidel, but makes a man who regards them both with equal eye" (Melville 1851, 480).

If the city lives with a death wish, a yearning for the infinite, this desire likewise parades itself in style. The shores of Asia and Europe, which are "cleaved" by the Bosphorus, are compared in another entry to partners in a refined dance.

> At 8 ½ A.M. took steamer up the Bosphorus to Buyukdere.—Magnificent! The whole scene one pomp of art & nature. Europe & Asia here show their best. A challenge of contrasts, where by the successively alternate sweeps of shores both sides seems to retire from every new proffer of beauty, again in some grand prudery to advance with a bolder bid, and thereupon again & again retiring, neither willing to retreat from the contest of beauty.—Myrtle, Cypress, Cedar—evergreens.—Catch glimpse of Euxine from Buyukdere. The water clear as Ontario—the banks natural quays, shelving off like those of a canal. Large vessels go close along shore.—The palaces of the Sultan—the pleasure houses—palaces of embassadors—The white foam breaks on these white steps as on long lines of coral reefs. One peculiarity is the introduction of ocean into inland recesses. Ships anchor at the foot of ravines, deep among the green basins, where the only canvass you would look for would be tents.—A gallery of ports & harbors, formed by the interchange of promontory & bay. Many parts like the Highlands of the Hudson, magnified. Porpoises sport in the blue; & large flights of pigeons overhead go through evolutions like those of armies. The sun shining on the palaces. View from the heights of Buyukdere. A chain of Lake Georges. No wonder the Czars have always coveted the capital of the Sultans. (Melville 1955, 94)

Melville resorts to painterly discourse to represent the interplay of topography and water along the Bosphorus, and his geographical references are repeatedly North American, but again rather than enacting a historical space that privileges an outsider's point of view, Melville seems to abandon his imagination to the immediacy of the place. Istanbul, with its "challenge of contrasts," appeals to Melville's aesthetics, which are ultimately an extension of his metaphysics. And nature is an integral part of the city's urban pomp and finally its irreducible irony. The assimilation or acceptance of the wild into the urban suggests that in the case of Istanbul what may appear to be "man's insanity" may very well be a reflection of "heaven's sense" (Melville 1851, 530).

Melville left Istanbul for Smyrna (modern Izmir) the day after his visit to the Asian side cemetery. He would then proceed on to Cairo.

> At 4 P.M. sailed in steamer Acadia for Alexandria, via Smyrna. It was sunset are [ere] we rounded Seraglio Point. Glorious sight. Scutari & its heights, glowed like sapphire. Wonderful clearness of air. As a promontory is covered with trees, terraced up clear to its top, so Constantinople with houses. Long line of walls.—Out into Sea of Marmora. (Melville 1955, 105)

If the city radiates like the jewel of the East, a common epithet for the capital of the Byzantine and Ottoman Empires alike, Melville appends his own leitmotif to his parting words: Istanbul, its sloped hills forested with houses like headland trees, is fenced in by the city walls. Nature and architecture are syntactically intertwined as they face the sea, that other country Melville, neither believer nor infidel, regarded with an equal eye.

2

Mark Twain in Istanbul

A Liability Abroad

> This great city contains a million inhabitants, but so narrow are its streets, and so crowded together are its houses, that it does not cover much more than half as much ground as New York City. Seen from the anchorage or from a mile or so up the Bosphorus, it is by far the handsomest city we have seen. Its dense array of houses swells upward from the water's edge, and spreads over the domes of many hills; and the gardens that peep out here and there, the great globes of the mosques, and the countless minarets that meet the eye everywhere, invest the metropolis with the quaint Oriental aspect one dreams of when one reads books of eastern travel. Constantinople makes a noble picture. (Twain 1911, 2:66)

AND SO BEGINS Mark Twain's initial approach to Istanbul, not the first or last "Oriental" city he will visit aboard the steamship *Quaker City.* Mark Twain's first broad literary success, *The Innocents Abroad, or The New Pilgrims' Progress; Being Some Account of the Steamship Quaker City's Pleasure Excursion to Europe and the Holy Land,* published in 1869, was the consequence of a measure of restlessness, and some wanderlust. Working as a New York-based correspondent for a San Francisco newspaper, the *Daily Alta California,* Twain desired a journalistic adventure that New York had initially promised the provincial writer but had not delivered to his satisfaction. He convinced the paper to subsidize a five-month pleasure cruise that would take him to Mediterranean Europe, North Africa, and the Middle East in exchange for regular travel letters for the paper under the title "The Holy Land Excursions. Letter from 'Mark Twain.'" When Twain boarded the steamer in 1867 at the age of thirty-two, along with seventy other "pilgrims," it was in the wake of an American vogue for European travel that had started after the European wars that grew out of the French Revolution and the

6. Galata Bridge, 1890.

Napoleonic Wars (Edwards 2001, 6). By 1818, there was already regular transatlantic maritime service between New York and Liverpool (Edwards 2001, 7). By 1840, American travel abroad could be called an industry. By 1850 an estimated thirty thousand Americans were traveling to Europe each year.

International tourism and a national taste for travel narratives evolved together. As a genre, American travel writing aimed, among other things, to turn tables on the critical gaze of the old country. Royall Tyler would initiate the genre in 1808 with *Yankee in London,* "answering the charge of cultural depravity in the New World" by "out-Britishing the British" (Wonham 2003, 111). The American writers who emulated Tyler's reverse subjectification of European culture in their discourse were responding to not only a national urge for cultural independence from Europe but also a new-felt political and economic confidence vis-à-vis the fatherland. By the time Twain embarked on his first international voyage with the aim of chronicling his adventures, the American travel narrative as a genre was thus already well established. American humorists had discovered the value, commercial and other, of tapping into American resentment and suspicion of the British and the French, former colonial powers that by the mid-nineteenth century had evolved into rival imperial powers.

Upon returning to San Francisco Twain spent the first part of 1868 "rewriting" the fifty-one travel dispatches he had posted to the *Daily Alta* and seven others printed in two New York papers. The result would be *The Innocents Abroad,* the book that would remain his best seller throughout his lifetime, selling seventy thousand copies in its first year alone. The book met with positive reviews. William Dean Howells, who would later become Twain's friend and regular correspondent, admired the cheeky revisionism of *The Innocents Abroad* in a December 1869 review in *Atlantic Monthly:*

> It is always good-humored humor, too, that he lavishes on his reader, and even in its impudence it is charming; we do not remember where it is indulged at the cost of the weak or helpless side, or where it is insolent, with all its sauciness and irreverence. The standard shams of travel that everybody sees through suffer possibly more than they ought, but not so much as they might; and one readily forgives the harsh treatment of them in consideration of the novel piece of justice done on such a traveller as suffers under the pseudonym of Grimes. (Howells 1869, 1)

Bret Harte in a January 1870 review for *Overland Monthly* also enjoyed the author's impudence, the "humor that seems to have had very little moral or esthetic limitation," the "suggestive hint of the lawlessness and audacity in which the trip is treated" (Harte 1870, 1). When Twain decided after completing the manuscript to reenact his Old World voyage in a lecture tour throughout the United States in 1868, audiences responded enthusiastically, and Twain's public persona as the irreverent Yankee humorist was firmly launched.

Due to his initial success and then career as a satirical wit, Twain would be criticized for losing his hallmark sense of humor in later essays collected under the title *The Dammed Human Race.* Bigelow Paine, Twain's biographer and first literary executer, would choose to edit out Twain's later political passages, particularly those condemning U.S. foreign policy, in order to maintain the "traditional Mark Twain" that the American public was comfortable with and cheered up by (Zwick 2002, 247). Yet the exaggerated disdain that would characterize Twain's later political satire is present in his first book of nonfiction. In early letters to friends and family, he lamented the role he had created for himself as public jester, a role that circumscribed his political voice and prevented his public from heeding his critiques of the national and international problems he keenly witnessed. And it is in this light, generated by Twain's lifelong preoccupation with international politics, that we can begin to approach one of the least humorous chapters in *The Innocents Abroad*, that of his visit to Constantinople.

THE DESCRIPTION of the initial approach to Istanbul that ends "Constantinople makes a noble picture" drops, but with little trace of bathetic irony, to the following ill-humored phrases in the next paragraph: "But its attractiveness begins and ends with its picturesqueness. From the time one starts ashore till he gets back again, he execrates it" (Zwick 2002, 259). And execrate is what Twain will do relentlessly in his chapter narrating his visit to the capital of the Ottoman Empire.

> Ashore, it was—well, it was an eternal circus. People were thicker than bees, in those narrow streets, and the men were dressed in all the outrageous, outlandish, idolatrous, extravagant, thunder-and-lightning costumes that ever a tailor with the delirium tremens and seven devils could conceive of. There was no freak in dress too crazy to be indulged in; no absurdity too absurd to be tolerated; no frenzy in ragged diabolism too fantastic to be attempted. (Twain 1911, 2:67)

While contemporaries such as Bret Harte find Twain's "grotesque rage at every thing and every body amusing . . . his mock assumption of righteous indignation . . . the real power of the book, and the decided originality of Mr. Clemen's humor," later critics agree that when Twain left the eastern frontiers of Christendom he temporarily lost the better part of his sense of humor (Harte 1870, 1). Passages such as the above are perhaps amusing in isolation; however, two consecutive chapters of high-pitched harangue distance the reader quickly. Despite this general agreement of a narrative weakness in *The Innocents Abroad,* the abrupt plunge from light comedy in Athens and the Crimea to acerbic complaint in Istanbul has not been accounted for in all its complexity. Chapters 33 and 34 are glossed over in general commentaries on Twain and the Middle East because Constantinople cannot be prescribed within geographical or mythological representations of the Holy Lands, the ultimate destination for the ship of pilgrims as well as the primary geographical focus for critics who discuss Twain's travels outside of Europe. Thus, Istanbul inspires a predictable silence on the part of critics.

Those who do comment on Twain's chapter on Istanbul sublimate the city's identity within a larger anti-Orientalist critique. Muhammad Raji Zughoul offers useful historical background on the reign of Abdul Aziz, the Sultan in power at the time of Twain's visit. The essay is dedicated primarily to the comparison of Twain's descriptions and assessments of Napoleon III and Abdul Aziz as leaders and men, the former in a consistently positive light, the latter in a negative light fraught with Orientalist stereotypes that Zughoul depicts rightly as defamatory. Zughoul's conclusions, however, do not reach beyond his own outrage at Twain's chauvinism and reduce Twain's enigmatic maliciousness to a single source: Twain as representative of the West's "Islamophobia." Twain is one more "champion" of the kind of "Anti-Islamic propaganda" we can trace to the eighth century:

> The text shows that Twain's perception of the Sultan, the Turks and consequently the Muslims, and the Ottoman Empire were by no means the product of "Innocence" . . . the Emperor and the Sultan in Mark Twain represent stereotypical European perceptions of the East strongly marked by distrust, condescension, phobia and above all hatred. (Zughoul 2000, 6)

Passages such as the one on the great Bazaar, which concludes chapter 33, serve to "demolish and devastate the whole structure and the character of the Ottoman capital," "strip the city out of its pride, and contribution to human civilization" (Zughoul 2000" 5):

> We went to the great Bazaar in Stamboul, of course, and I shall not describe it further than to say it is a monstrous hive of little shops, thousands I should say—all under one roof, and cut up into innumerable little blocks by narrow streets which are arched overhead . . . It is full of life, and stir, and business, dirt,

> beggars, asses, yelling peddlers, porters, dervishes, high-born Turkish female shoppers, Greeks, and weird-looking and weirdly dressed Mohammedans from the mountains and the far provinces—and the only solitary thing one does not smell when he is in the Great Bazaar, is something which smells good. (Twain 1911, 2:75–76)

Zughoul's own rhetorical response to Twain's contempt for "every thing and every body" he encounters in the Turkey is useful. The adjectives Zughoul unleashes to protest Twain's character equals the target writer's own animated scorn: Twain is "insolent," "rude," "abusive," disdainful," discourteous," "acrimonious," "shameless," "sick humored." Twain reveals a "conspicuous hatred," "much disrespect," an "outrageous manner . . . beyond all limits of cultural sensitivity." Insolence is of course one of Twain's primary modes of expression, and Turkey is not the first or last country to be the target of his trademark lack of courtesy: if chaotic defines the streets of Istanbul in *The Innocents Abroad,* slothful qualifies the Italian countryside:

> *They* have nothing to do but eat and sleep and sleep and eat, and toil a little when they can get a friend to stand by and keep them awake. *They* are not paid for thinking—they are not paid to fret about the world's concerns. They are not respectable people—they are not worthy people—but in their breasts, all their stupid lives long, resteth a peace that passeth understanding! How can men, calling themselves men, consent to be so degraded and happy. (Twain 1911, 1:209)

The Greeks are equally disreputable:

> The fleets that were the wonder of the world when the Parthenon was new, are a beggarly handful of fishing-shacks now, and the manly people that performed such miracles of valor at Marathon are only a tribe of unconsidered slaves today. The classic Illyssus has gone dry, and so have all the sources of Grecian wealth and greatness. The nation numbers only eight hundred thousand souls, and there is poverty and misery and mendacity enough among them to furnish forty millions and be liberal about it. (Twain 1911, 2:62–63)

No other place that Twain describes suffers more sustained criticism, however, than Istanbul, and certainly no other "Oriental" city, whether it be Tangiers or Jerusalem. It is precisely the exaggerated rhetoric of Twain's discontent, the relentless amassing of negative noun phrases and adjectives, with little or no intermittent recourse to comic relief, however, that gives us pause. It is certainly true that Twain's narrative reiterates negative European perceptions of the East, but his inflated, monomaniacal discourse cannot be called stereotypical, either of his own writing or the writing of preceding or contemporary travel literature about the Middle East Orient. It is simply too excessive. Thus, his contempt for the capital of the Ottoman Empire requires a closer look and a more multifarious explanation than classical allegations of "Anti-Islamic propaganda" can provide.

> Drifting noiselessly about are squads of Turkish women, draped from chin to feet in flowing robes, and with snowy veils bound about their heads, that disclose only the eyes and a vague, shadowy notion of their features. Seen moving about, far away in the dim, arched aisles of the Great Bazaar, they look as the shrouded dead must have looked when they walked forth from their graves amid storms and thunders and earthquakes that burst upon Calvary that awful night of the Crucifixion. A street in Constantinople is a picture which one ought to see once—not oftener. (Twain 1911, 2:68)

Christian references are suspect in Twain's secular travel narrative, and so this comparison of Turkish women to the dead at Calvary must be taken with a certain grain of salt. But the passage's moody imagery and then dismissive conclusion is typical of what takes the place of Twain's regular use of anticlimax or bathos in the service of cultural satire.

Most of Twain's humor in *The Innocents Abroad* is the result of situational irony: the narrator as a traveling foreigner finds himself in compromising, humorous, and paradoxical situations because he is obliged to negotiate vaguely understood cultural norms. He will often begin an anecdote seriously, "After dinner we felt like seeing such Parisian specialties as we might see without distressing exertion, and so we sauntered through the brilliant streets and looked at the dainty trifles in variety stores and jewelry shops" (Twain 1911, 1:106). He will then proceed to undermine the normalcy of the narration with a joke aimed as much at himself, or the American tourist whom he represents, as at the foreigner or foreign situation at hand: "Occasionally, merely for the pleasure of being cruel, we put unoffending Frenchmen on the rack with questions framed in the incomprehensible jargon of their native language, and while they writhed, we impaled them, we peppered them, we sacrificed them, with their own vile verbs and participles" (Twain 1911, 1:106). The joke is on the unworldly, monolingual, yet shameless American rather than on the French language the sentence pretends to offend. It is the subject's credibility that falls, not the object's.

What disappears in the Istanbul chapter is the speaker's playful ability to mock himself. When there are any jokes at all, and there are few, they are no longer on Twain or the American. While the final ungrammatical "oftener" compromises the credibility of the speaker in the passage on the "shrouded dead" above, it is aimed less at self-mockery than deflating the momentarily grave contemplation of the Istanbul women: Twain must dismiss whatever weight the biblical reference has lent them; they must not be allowed to drift away enriched by any metaphorical sophistication, however momentarily gained. Because people tend to lose their ability to laugh at themselves when they feel threatened, Twain experienced a certain menace in Istanbul that frustrated any ironic relationship he might have established with the city. In Istanbul Twain is confronted with challenges his robust black humor failed to match, a failure only partially explained by the fear and suspicion of the East he has inherited from a thousand years of anti-Islamic European propaganda against the Turks. It is not Twain's custom to recirculate unexamined historical and cultural clichés, and yet he does precisely that in Constantinople. The story of the "Terrible Turk" is "tired and a touch familiar," as Elizabeth Bishop says of such emptied-out narratives of foreign travel in her poem "2000 Illustrations and a Complete Concordance," yet Twain consistently falls back on such tropes (Bishop 1994, 57).

What he does best in his political writing is critically examine the bigotry and pride that govern foreign policy, whether U.S. expansionism in the Philippines or European colonialism in Africa. Thus, his failure of imagination goes deeper than a general theory of racism will allow. It is failure that has other political as well as cultural roots. It is also a failure that seems to threaten his art, a possibility he cannot simply laugh off. For all his disparagement he takes Istanbul very seriously, and his consolidated disparity of tone shows a consistency he does not even lavish on the French. Consistency, however, undermines the machinations of irony. Without a playful anticlimactic falling, an absurd reversal in the sentence's logic, Twain's writing loses its character.

Twain's own struggles with representation, or the failure thereof, are particularly ironic when read alongside his project to invalidate previous travel narratives to the Ottoman capital. In his short 1869 preface, Twain announces that he, like Mary Wortley Montagu and many revisionist travel writers before him, will not rely on rumor or intertext, but on empirical experience that will prove his predecessors false. He claims a commitment to veracity, or what would pass as authenticity in an American idiom, motivates the book:

> Yet not withstanding it is only a record of a pic-nic, it has a purpose, which is, to suggest to the reader how *he* would be likely to see Europe and the East if he looked at them with his own eyes instead of the eyes of those who travelled in those countries before him. (Twain 1911, 9)

His purpose is not didactic, and any departure from received forms only underscores his desire to offer a fresh and objective look at scenes that have become nearly immune to reinterpretation due to overexposure.

> I make small pretense of showing any one how he *ought* to look at objects of interest beyond the sea—other books do that, and therefore, even if I were competent to do it, there is no need. I offer no apologies for any departures from the usual style of travel-writing that may be charged against me—for I think I have seen with impartial eyes, and I am sure I have written at least honestly, whether wisely or not. (Preface)

While a Twain text may have honorable ends, honest is not how one would characterize the details that constitute its means. Yet for all his improbable manipulation of facts in the text as a whole—what Henry Wonham (2003) calls Twain's tall tale Yankee humor—in Istanbul Twain cannot quite leave received opinion behind. A leitmotif that runs through the Istanbul chapter—and we will see it even more often in the sections on the holy land—is a condemnation of travel narratives that raise false expectations with Romantic, fanciful Orientalist discourse. His references are the accounts of such eighteenth-century travel writers as Charles Farrar Browne, better known as Artemus Ward; the guidebooks of Harpers and Appleton for Americans abroad; Bayard Taylor's *Views A-Foot* (1855); and books specifically about travel for the Christian pilgrim, such as William Prime's *Tent Life in the Holy Land* (1857); and William M. Thompson's *The Land and the Book* (1858). Twain has this to say of these men who have gone before him into a Turkish bath:

> When I think how I have been swindled by books of Oriental travel, I want a tourist for breakfast. For years and years I have dreamed and dreamed of the wonders of the Turkish bath; for years and years I have promised myself that I would yet enjoy one. Many and many a time, in fancy, I have lain in the marble bath, and breathed the slumbrous fragrance of Eastern spices that filled the air . . . The cadaverous, half nude varlets that served in the establishment had nothing of poetry in their appearance, nothing of romance, nothing of Oriental splendor. They shed no entrancing odors—just the contrary. (Twain 1911, 2:87)

Even though Twain has announced in his preface that he would look "with his own eyes instead of the eyes of those who traveled in those countries before him," he nevertheless has allowed these other eyes to guide him through the city. His subjects—the bath, the street dogs, the narghile or Turkish water pipe, the coffee, St. Sophia—are the standard topics of interest prescribed by any guide book, past and present. While Twain may depart "from the usual style of travel-writing," he nevertheless allows those texts to control his agenda and condition his expectations.

He mocks his fellow passengers for their own slavish dependency on the images that have inspired their dreams of the holy land:

> These men have been taught from infancy to revere, to worship, the holy places where on their happy eyes were resting now. For many and many a year this very picture had visited their thoughts by day and floated through their dreams by night . . . What wonder that the sordid lights of work-day prudence should pale before the glory of a hope like theirs in the full splendor of its fruition? Let them squander millions! (Twain 1911, 2:225)

Yet when he comes to Istanbul he finds himself depending on the same books he claims to revile, if only because the observations and rhetoric of the Constantinople chapters are based on an oppositional logic that depends on received Oriental images for their very existence. If traditional Romantic Orientalism finds splendor and luxury in Constantinople, Twain finds filth and decay. If it notes music in the call to prayer and spice in the air, he experiences noise and stench. He systematically reduces to rubble any expectations of charm created by his predecessors:

> Everywhere was dirt, and dust, and dinginess, and gloom; everywhere were signs of a hoary antiquity, but nothing touching or beautiful about it; everywhere were those groups of fantastic pagans; overhead the gaudy mosaics and the web of lamp-ropes—nowhere was there any thing to win one's love or challenge his admiration.
>
> The people who go into ecstasies over St. Sophia must surely get them out of the guide-book (where every church is spoken of as being "considered by good judges to be the most marvelous structure, in many respects, that the world has ever seen"). (Twain 1911, 2:72)

Or, of Smyrna on the Aegean coast of Turkey:

> Superior to the call to prayer, the noises in the streets, the interest of the costumes—superior to every thing and claiming the bulk of attention first, last, and all the time—is a combination of Mohammedan stenches, to which the smell of even a Chinese quarter would be as pleasant as the roasting odors of the fatted calf to the nostrils of the returning Prodigal. Such is Oriental luxury—such is Oriental splendor! We read about it all our days, but we comprehend it not until we see it. (Twain 1911, 2:123)

Replacing idealized fictions with tactile "facts" Twain will often lament his boyhood fascination with the wild tales of the Arabian Nights even as he argues that such tales are responsible for misinforming the adult tourist and preventing him from seeing clearly the unromantic realities of a place when faced with them. Thus, a certain nostalgia hangs about the fringes of Twain's empiricist project as he deconstructs the Oriental metanarratives that haunt his text.

Bruce Michelson, in "Mark Twain the Tourist," suggests that fatigue, "the unpleasant landscape, and the necessity for constant piety" might account for the aesthetic decline in the travel narrative (Michelson 1987, 183). Michelson argues for a reading of the narrative structure of *The Innocents Abroad* as "paidia" or "play of the free and improvisatory sort," the object of which is to "sustain an imaginative engagement and thereby to transform a various and sometimes tedious real world into a world of novelty, fantasy, and adventures" (Michelson 1987, 172). Twain may very well have labored to avoid the obligatory response required by a Romantic reading of the ancient seat of the Byzantine Empire. However, problems arise when we suggest that the topography of

Istanbul in the mid-nineteenth century was "unpleasant" or "tedious" and thus could not stimulate Twain's imagination. Nor can we say, as Henry Wonham in a similar vein argues, that Istanbul inspires the kind of "interpretive drama" and "performance of a tale" that make the vignettes that pepper the rest of the text so engaging (Wonham 2003, 117). Though Michelson may not have had the Istanbul chapters specifically in mind, his proposal is condemning. His proposal is also true, though perhaps not for the reasons he offers. The overturning of Orientalist stereotypes does not lead to transformation in *The Innocents Abroad.* After having destroyed all the Romantic tropes he can muster, Twain finds he has nothing with which to replace them. Rather than forging new novelties, fantasies, and adventures, the narrative point of view reduces the complex realties of the city to a myopic caricature of Middle Eastern squalor. Twain ultimately undermines what he set out to do—write impartially and honestly about a foreign country.

Situational irony, as well as bathos, requires certain terms of agreement as stylistic devices. In order for a narration to perform the contradictions necessary to create the effect of dissembling or sinking, there must be information in the text that is shared by the reader and writer. There must be agreed-upon norms, the violation of which gives rise to humor. In order to "suggest to the reader how *he* would be likely to see . . . the East if he looked at [it] with his own eyes," Twain as a Yankee humorist must know what his audience will expect from an Orientalist text. Twain has chosen, however, to reject the knowledge that circulates in the culture. Having systematically destroyed expectations, he finds himself faced with a void that was once filled, however vaguely and erroneously, with shared narratives about Constantinople or the Ottoman Empire. Having performed this revisionist move he finds himself face to face with a void he cannot fill in any fresh way. Although he catalogues his impressions furiously, he cannot seem to make pragmatic, American sense of the ancient, illogical city where Anatolian customs and public practices endure despite Western European encroachment:

> Crowding the narrow streets in front of [the shops] are beggars, who beg forever, yet never collect any thing; and wonderful cripples, distorted out of all semblance of humanity; almost; vagabonds driving laden asses; porters carrying dry-goods boxes as large as cottages on their backs; peddlers of grapes, hot corn, pumpkin seeds, and a hundred other things, yelling like fiends; and

> sleeping happily, comfortably, serenely, among the hurrying feet, are the famed dogs of Constantinople. (Twain 1911, 2:68)

Catalogues and cursory descriptions replace vignettes as the narration's modus operandi. Though street dogs, newspapers, and the Turkish bath receive some extended attention, there is less "interpretive drama" and "performance of a tale" than we see in other chapters. Istanbul is not a stage for the kind of shenanigans we see in Athens. The city is certainly performing, but Twain cannot understand the players, their language, or their stage directions. Unable to read the city, Twain replaces dialogue with monologue, and the narrative possibilities that arise when people encounter other people are reduced to surly voyeurism. In other countries Twain is often amused by encounters that seem to trump his expectations; "preferable fictions" like the French barbershop, for example, delight him because, as Wonham argues, Twain's "allegiance is neither with cherished traditions nor with the reality that undermines them; his interest is in a perpetual sequence of contrasts" (Wonham 2003, 127). However, this is not the case in Istanbul. The city offers an overabundance of contrasts, contrasts that are unreadable, impenetrable, and finally uninterpretable to the American travel writer. If Twain enjoys contrasts in other cultures, here he sees only chaos.

Twain takes no pains to present himself as an informed cultural tourist. Like many American travel writers and journalists, "He arrives in Europe with only a yarn spinner's shrewdness to compensate for an abundance of ignorance" (Wonham 2003, 115). Foreign reviewers of *The Innocents Abroad* would criticize the lack of savoir-faire in Twain's "greenhorn" Yankee persona, yet they would also find it seductive, as did the British writer of this unsigned review in the October 8, 1870, issue of the *Saturday Review:*

> He parades his ignorance of Continental languages and manners, and expresses his very original judgments on various wonders of art and nature with praiseworthy frankness. We are sometimes left in doubt whether he is speaking in all sincerity, or whether he is having a sly laugh at himself and his readers . . . To do him justice, however, we must observe that he has a strong tinge of the peculiar national humor.

It is Twain's ignorance of Ottoman history and culture that is partially responsible for his inability to read Istanbul. If he can fabricate his way through

Mediterranean Europe and the Holy Land, places lavishly documented in annals available in America, his dearth of actual information on the Eastern Empire becomes a handicap he cannot write well without.

Because Twain rewrote and supplemented the *Alta* letters after his voyage, we cannot read them chronologically. Yet his description of the Ottoman Sultan, Abdul Aziz, whom he sees at the Paris exposition before coming to Istanbul, suggests to us that his anti-Turkish sentiments were well in place before he ever experienced the empire directly:

> A short, stout, dark man, black-bearded, black-eyed, stupid, unprepossessing—a man whose whole appearance somehow suggested that if he only had a cleaver in his hand and a white apron on, one would not be at all surprised to hear him say: "A mutton-roast to-day, or will you have a nice porter-house steak" (Twain 1911, 1:120)

> Abdul Aziz, Sultan of Turkey, Lord of the Ottoman Empire! Born to a throne; weak stupid, ignorant, almost, as his meanest slave; chief of a vast royalty, yet the puppet of his Premier and the obedient child of a tyrannical mother . . . and when he is surfeited with eating and sleeping and idling, and would rouse up and take reins of the government and threatens to *be* a Sultan, is charmed from his purpose by wary Fuad Pacha with a pretty plan for a new palace or a new ship—charmed away with a new toy, like any other restless child, a man who sees his people robbed and oppressed by the soulless tax-gatherers, but speaks no word to save them; who believes in gnomes, and genii and the wild fables of the Arabian Nights, but has small regard for the mighty magicians of today, and is nervous in the presence of their mysterious railroads and steamboats and telegraphs; who would see undone in Egypt all that great Mehemet Ali achieved, and would prefer rather to forget than emulate him; a man who found his great empire a blot upon the earth—a degraded, poverty stricken, miserable, infamous agglomeration of ignorance, crime, brutality, and will idle away the allotted days of his trivial life, and then pass to the dust and the worms and leave it so! (Twain 1911, 1:121–22)

Although Twain may lack knowledge of Ottoman history and culture, he can nevertheless present himself as versed in contemporary, topical Ottoman events and figures. Yet his references to the troubles in the empire, and the men he chooses to vilify or praise, parrot or swell the common European point of view of the period. Abdul Aziz's reign is an infamous one according to Turkish and European historians alike. The sources of his troubles are historical, however, rather than natural, as Twain would have his reader believe. Faced with enormous financial debts after the Crimean War, uprisings and revolts in different parts of the empire (incited as often as not by European and Russian-backed parties), visionary but expensive social reforms called the Tanzimat program, and elaborate royal projects such as the building of Beylerbey Palace (as indicated by Twain above), Abdul Aziz amassed enormous foreign debt. If the nineteenth-century Ottomans would become known abroad as "the sick man of Europe," it was an economic and political ailment, rather than a timeless condition of the Orientalized East, as many Occidental writers including Twain suggest.

Despite these mid-nineteenth-century troubles, and the fact that many countries that were once a part of the Ottoman Empire would come under the control of European powers in the late nineteenth century, we cannot speak of European colonialism in Turkey proper. Turkey had been admitted to the Concert of Europe upon the signing of the Treaty of Paris in 1856 after the Crimean War, and European member nations had agreed to "respect the independence and the territorial integrity of the Ottoman Empire" (qtd. in Freely 1996, 277). This agreement was a source of political and economic frustration for European powers, who despite their political promises were waiting impatiently for the redistribution of territories that they believed would fall to them when the "Muslim" empire dissolved. The fact that the empire had not ceded all its fronts, or had not completely collapsed, is partially at the root of Twain's own colonial rhetoric. Like that of his contemporaries, his disparagement belies a frustration with Ottoman "obstinacy" in the face of Western expansionism. Although the Ottomans would not behave like colonials, colonial forms of Eurocentric discourse could still represent them as such to a hostile Western audience.

Twain, again, reverts to Orientalist rhetoric to signify a state of affairs he cannot, or will not, investigate beyond the confines of received opinion. Abdul Aziz as vulgar meat vendor is reduced to a form of immigrant servitude that an urban American reader would recognize in the marketplaces of New York City. He is superstitious, fatuous, and infantile in the eyes of the enlightened, technologically advanced, adult traveler. He ignores those who would save him: Mehemet Ali of Egypt, for example, who dreamed of founding a new dynasty independent of the

Ottoman Empire and launched repeated military campaigns to do so, much to the discomfort of the Sublime Porte. Twain sees the poverty in Constantinople in mythological rather than historical terms. The "degraded, poverty stricken, miserable, infamous agglomeration of ignorance, crime, brutality" he notes everywhere is not accounted for in any complex material context—as consequences, for example, of multiple fires that had ravaged the city, or of the influx of immigrants from throughout the empire to Istanbul in the years after the war. It is timeless Oriental idleness, not challenges in time, that Twain's biased eye records.

TWAIN'S DISAPPROVAL of the policies and politics of empire is not confined to the Ottomans. When critics say that Twain lost his sense of humor in his later work they are referring to essays such as "To the Person Sitting in the Darkness," in which Twain lambastes the hypocrisy of American military intervention in Cuba and the Philippines: "And as for a flag for the Philippine Province, it is easily managed. We can have a special one—our States do it: we can have just our usual flag, with the white stripes painted black and the stars replaced by the skull and crossbones" (Twain 1976, 473). While policy makers would argue they were sending American troops to support wars of independence in Cuba and the Philippines, their refusal to acknowledge the new republics as sovereign powers and their subsequent moves to control them (the United States paid Spain $20 million for the Philippines) were vehemently criticized by Twain until his death in 1910 (Zwick 2002, 237). The Christian church, the American Congress and state legislatures, and big business, the "Trinity of our national gods," were seen as mutually implicated in the suppression and abuse of other nations (Twain 1976, 473). Although the average American may have benevolent instincts, Twain would argue that he is trained by these powers to advocate violence abroad in the name of domestic peace and comfort.

> Everything is prosperous, now; everything is just as we should wish it. We have got the Archipelago, and we shall never give it up. Also, we have every reason to hope that we shall have an opportunity before very long to slip out of our contract with Cuba and give her something better in place of it. It is a rich country, and many of us are already beginning to see that the contract was a sentimental mistake. But now—right now—is the best time to do some profitable rehabilitating work—work that will set up and make us comfortable, and discourage gossip. (Twain 1976, 472)

Involved in various organizations that supported human rights in the face of imperialism, Twain in 1891 was a founding member of the American Friends of Russian Freedom, a group that supported the Russian Revolution. Later he served as vice president of the Anti-Imperialist League's New York branch, a group that also included William James, John Dewey, William Dean Howells, and Andrew Carnegie (Zwick 2002, 239). He would become a leading American voice against imperialist expansion at home and abroad.

Thus while Twain resorts to negative Orientalist discourse to disparage the Ottoman Empire, it must be noted that the language he uses when speaking of empires, or imperialism in general, is rarely complimentary, particularly in his later essays. He will refer to American colonialism in Hawaii as "the disease of civilization" (Zwick 2002, 230). American soldiers who massacre Muslim women and children in the southern Philippines in 1906 are "Christian butchers" (Zwick 2002, 243). "In America—as elsewhere—free speech is confined to the dead" he writes in a private notebook after *Harper's Bazaar* refuses to publish "The War Prayer" about Christian fervor for American wars abroad and "King Leopold's Soliloquy" about brutal Belgian rule in the Congo (Zwick 2002, 246). It is certainly true that by reverting to Orientalist tropes this early text reinforces an age-old mode of cultural and religious racism. It is also true that Twain tended to feel disinclined to pull his punches, however low, in all his anti-imperialism writing. Moving further East in *The Innocents Abroad* Twain lets fly the following hyperbolic fantasy of imperial destruction:

> If ever an oppressed race existed, it is this one we see fettered around us under the inhuman tyranny of the Ottoman Empire. I wish Europe would let Russia annihilate Turkey a little—not much, but enough to make it difficult to find the place again without a divining-rod or a diving-bell. (Twain 1911, 2:164)

He then goes on to specify—in material terms that appeal to an American laissez-faire theory of economics—the nature of Syrian oppression under Ottoman rule:

> The Syrians are very poor, and yet they are ground down by a system of taxation that would drive any other nation frantic. Last year their taxes were heavy enough, in all conscience—but this year they have been increased by the addition of taxes that were forgiven them in times of famine in former years. On top

> of this the Government has levied a tax on *one-tenth* of the whole proceeds of the land. This is only half the story . . . the people are naturally good-hearted and intelligent, and with education and liberty, would be a happy and contented race. They often appeal to the stranger to know if the great world will not some day come to their relief and save them. The Sultan has been lavishing money like water in England and Paris, but his subjects are suffering for it now. (Twain 1911, 2:164–65)

Because Twain never identifies his sources, it is impossible to know from whom and from where he gets what he offers as on-site data. The language in the passage above smacks as much of missionary zeal as of secular social progressiveness, suggesting he may have relied on the word of Protestant missionaries who were the largest group of active Americans living in the Ottoman empire at the time. Not completely trusted, they were nevertheless tolerated by the Sublime Porte.

Twain's early criticism of the Ottoman Empire must be read in the larger context of his emergent anti-imperial discourse. As one of America's most caustic anti-imperialist public voices at the turn of the century, Twain's Oriental rhetoric, however chauvinistic it may be, reflects his fundamental censorship of a subject that eventually transcends race, religion, and cultural affiliation. Twain argues a universal "Descent of Man" in his ironic refutation of Darwinian theory in "Man's Place in the Animal World" (1896): "Man is a Reasoning Animal. Such is the claim. I think it is open to dispute. Indeed, my experiments have proven to me that he is the Unreasoning Animal" (Twain 1976, 211). And his experiment is an intercultural one in which he confines an international group of human beings in a cage to see how they interact in comparison to peaceful, diplomatic rabbits and geese. His case study includes "an Irish Catholic from Tipperary," a "Scotch Presbyterian from Aberdeen," a "Turk from Constantinople; a Greek from Crete; an Armenian; a Methodist from the wilds of Arkansas; a Buddhist from China; a Brahmin from Benares. Finally, a Salvation Army Colonel from Wapping" (Twain 1976, 212). After two days "there was but a chaos of gory odds and ends of turbans and fezzes and plaids and bones and flesh—not a specimen left alive. These Reasoning Animals had disagreed on a theological detail and carried the matter to a Higher Court." Twain's critique of the political dangers of religious orthodoxy is democratic: whatever the creed—the church, the mosque, the temple—organized religions work in collusion with nationalist objectives and work against each other, the end of which is the undermining of world peace.

IT IS DIFFICULT, nevertheless, to locate anything not prejudicial against Muslims and Ottomans in Twain's response to Christian massacres in Damascus in 1861:

> All the Christians who could get away fled from the city, and the Mohammedans would not defile their hands by burying the "infidel dogs" . . . How they hate a Christian in Damascus!—and pretty much all over Turkeydom as well. And how they will pay for it when Russia turns her guns upon them again!
>
> It is soothing to the heart to abuse England and France for interposing to save the Ottoman Empire from the destruction it has so richly deserved for a thousand years. It hurts my vanity to see these pagans refuse to eat of food that has been cooked for us; or to eat from a dish we have eaten from; or to drink from a goatskin which we have polluted with our Christian lips, except by filtering the water through a rag which they put over the mouth of it or through a sponge! I never disliked a Chinaman as I do these degraded Turks and Arabs, and when Russia is ready to war with them again, I hope England and France will not find it good breeding or good judgement to interfere. (Twain 1911, 2:187)

The reactionary nature of Twain's diatribe here is not an isolated case in the text. Despite Twain's own anti-Christian stance—one that is made clear in *The Innocents Abroad*—he will often defend Christians in the face of what he sees as Muslim prejudice or disrespect. His bigotry, as with all forms of chauvinism, is thus not wholly the result of a confident sense of superiority over others but rather the result of an anxiety that arises when naturalized definitions of the self are challenged. Twain mocks his Presbyterian shipmates for their narrow-mindedness and ignorance throughout the text and in doing so minimizes, or distances, the role of the Judeo-Christian tradition in his own American identity. Yet his Christian "vanity" suddenly emerges when confronted by the Ottomans and the Chinese, the latter famous, according to Twain, for their bad treatment of Christian missionaries. His injured pride triggers a crusader rhetoric with heavy nationalist overtones that aims to neutralize the insult or challenge that is ultimately very personal. Despite his satirical treatment of his fellow believers, Twain identifies with his Christian heritage enough to borrow from its discourse when he feels threatened by the other.

We see a similar Christian reaction to Ottoman-Muslim pride in Twain's treatment of the famous St. Sophia, the fifth-century Byzantine church turned fifteenth-century mosque. In *The Innocents Abroad,* the insult to Twain's heritage takes the form of a denigration of the monument, particularly the changes it has undergone since the fall of Constantinople to the Ottomans: "I do not think much of the Mosque of St. Sophia. I suppose I lack appreciation. We will let it go at that" (Twain 1911, 2:71). Of course he does not, and the next page is an extended countering of the "ecstasies" visitors are taught to experience from guidebooks:

> It is the rustiest old barn in heathendom . . . The inside of the dome is figured all over with a monstrous inscription in Turkish characters, wrought in gold mosaic, that looks as glaring as a circus bill; the pavements and the marble balustrades are all battered and dirty; the perspective is marred every where by a web of ropes that depend from the dizzy height of the dome, and suspend

7. St. Sophia Mosque, 1890s, by Ch. De Billy, from Gustave Schlumberger, *Un empereur byzantin au dixième siècle,* Paris, 1890.

> countless dingy, coarse oil lamps, and ostrich eggs, six or seven feet above the floor. (Twain 1911, 2:71–72)

Twain's aversion, however, is not purely aesthetic. The rituals of Muslim worship come in for equal criticism:

> Squatting and sitting in groups, here and there and far and near, were ragged Turks reading books, hearing sermons, or receiving lessons like children, and in fifty places were more of the same sort bowing and straightening up, bowing again and getting down to kiss the earth, muttering prayers the while, and keeping up their gymnastics till they ought to have been tired, if they were not. (Twain 1911, 2:72)

Twain makes no attempt to appreciate the outward trappings of religious differences. Aiming straight at the dignity of Muslim rites, his mocking tone has the cold distance of sarcasm rather than conspiratorial proximity of irony.

An entry in the travel notebook that does not make it directly into the final text helps make historical sense of this "Islamophobic" section in *The Innocents Abroad:* "It seems curious to see these eastern devotees going through with their extravagant ceremonies in a church that was built for Christian worship, & this strikes one more than anything else" (Twain 1975, 398). A sense of an appropriated heritage fuels the aesthetic critique and helps explain the negative depiction of the Muslim devotees. Again, condescension, rather than pure cultural elitism, is a reaction to a cultural challenge that Twain does not admit to in the revised text. St. Sophia, no longer the jewel of the Eastern Christian Empire, must be razed rhetorically in a discourse of dispossession. Although he will allow in the final version that "all the interest that attaches to [St. Sophia] comes from the fact that it was built for a Christian church and then turned into a mosque, without much alteration, by the Mohammedan conquerors of the land," the sentiment of cultural loss evident in the notebook is replaced by an attitude of cultural domination in the final text (Twain 1911, 2:71). The only interest the monument might have for the Western tourist is its Christian history. The story of the humiliating Christian defeat by Muslim conquerors disappears into the recesses of guidebook detachment.

Connected to this challenge to Twain's Christian identity is a similar perceived affront to his American national identity by the Ottoman Turks. Again, despite Twain's own anti-nationalist rhetoric and his increasing disdain for misguided American patriotism, we find him defensive in the face of what strikes him as Ottoman disregard for the American traveler. And it is again in the notebooks, rather than in the revised text, where this is made clear. In a rare moment of self-mockery in the Istanbul chapters, Twain inflates the importance of the Pilgrims' visit to a Grand Duke, the Russian Emperor's third brother, while in Yalta:

> Our imperial visit has had a good effect. It worries the Sublime Porte a good deal. It is well, for the offensive resolutions of Congress concerning the Cretan insurrection have just been received, & it may prevent an offensive reply—may even avert war—who knows? (Twain 1975, 412)

Americans are not popular with the Ottomans in 1867. The U.S. House of Representatives, in sympathy with the people of Crete, had a month before Twain's arrival in Istanbul endorsed a Cretan rebellion against the Turks. In 1866, aid to Cretan refugees had become a popular American cause: musical and literary benefits were organized to raise money (Richards, Elliott, and Hall 1915, vol. 1). In this humorous reference to these tensions, the Russians are once again seen as those best placed to oversee the breakup of the Ottoman Empire. The ironic humor in the notebook entry arises from the fact that contrary to the grand reception the American pilgrims received in Odessa and Yalta, the Sublime Porte seems to have never acknowledged their brief presence in Constantinople. Though Twain will suggest in the notebooks that the Sultan was not pleased with their visit to the Czar because the "Americans show no disposition to visit him,". other entries suggest that Twain was disappointed by the slight and slighted American presence in Istanbul (Twain 1975, 413). "All foreign consulates fine but American—bad—people in Europe & Asia respect style" (402). Having no fixed residence, American representatives in Constantinople were obliged to move frequently around the city—so much so that Edwin A. Grosvenor, Istanbul resident and teacher (and father of the first editor of consequence of *National Geographic* magazine, Istanbul-born Gilbert Grosvenor), suggests that "the appropriate emblem" for the American contingency "is a carpet-bag rather than an eagle" (qtd. in Twain 1975, 402). Thus, in the face of Twain's own disregard for the integrity of the empire is an equal and opposite one from the Ottomans vis-à-vis his fatherland.

One of Twain's better moments in the chapters referring to Turkey plays with the dubious reputation of Americans abroad.

> We brought not a relic from Ephesus! After gathering up fragments of sculptured marbles and breaking ornaments from the interior work of the Mosques; and after bringing them at a cost of infinite trouble and fatigue, five miles on muleback to the railway depot, a government officer compelled all who had such things to disgorge! He had an order from Constantinople *to look out for our party,* and see that we carried nothing off. (Twain 1911, 2:149)

Exaggerating what was probably a much smaller, but still serious bit of looting, Twain implicates the Americans in a comedic game of power relations. The situational irony is simultaneously self and subject directed. Twain's refers again to his national vanity and pride as he challenges with inflated arrogance what is first thought to be an Ottoman order:

> I never resist a temptation to plunder a stranger's premises without feeling insufferable vain about it. This time I felt proud beyond expression. I was serene in the midst of the scoldings that were heaped upon the Ottoman government for its affront offered to a pleasuring party of entirely respectable gentlemen and ladies. I said, "We that have free souls, it touches us not." (Twain 1911, 2:149)

Stealing the language of passive resistance, Twain mocks the Americans' paradoxical attitude of entitlement. At once avaricious, altruistic, and proud, Twain suggests, though without confessing guilt, that whatever national or cultural sins the Ottomans might commit, the Americans too can compete in a race of ignobility. When they find out it has been the British Embassy that requested they be watched, Twain openly declares the nature of his scapegoat Orientalism: "This was bad—very bad. Coming solely from the Ottomans, it might have signified only Ottoman hatred of Christians, and a vulgar ignorance as to genteel methods of expressing it" (Twain 1911, 2:150). Orientalist representations are based, he lets slip, on assumptions. Malevolence, ignorance, lack of sophistication, tropes that find a receptacle in anti-Ottoman discourse, are ready-made for the Western traveler who might appeal to them when convenient.

Yet despite Twain's anti-Ottoman sentiments that are born partly from these challenges to his identity as a Christian and an American, from time to time he notes correspondences between American and Ottoman culture, or at least allows comparisons to be made that simultaneously incriminate the U.S. in the Oriental transgressions he identifies at hand. Polygamy is not exclusively a Turkish custom, and Americans who are scandalized might think twice before judging: "They say the Sultan has eight hundred wives. This almost amounts to bigamy. It makes our cheeks burn with shame to see such a thing permitted here in Turkey. We do not mind it so much in Salt Lake, however" (Twain 1911, 2:77). Rather than describing the slave market in the shocked, accusatory terms used by many foreigners, Twain offers a "Slave Girl Market Report," a commercial advertisement as it would appear in an American metropolitan newspaper in all its cold, capitalist pragmatism: "Sales of one lot of Circassians, prime to good, 1852–1854, at [$]240 @ 242½, buyer 30; one forty-niner—damaged—at [$]23, seller ten, no deposit. . . . There is nothing new in Nubians. Slow sale" (Twain 1911, 2:78). If he condemns the slave markets of Istanbul, he reminds his American audience that not only does the United States have a history of trade in humans but it has been a particularly efficient and profitable one. In an 1868 lecture drawn from the Quaker City materials, Twain draws a parallel between Ottoman and American abuse of political office: "One of [the sultan's] great officers come into office without a cent, & went out in a few years & built himself a palace worth 3 million. It brought tears to my eyes in that far foreign land—It was so like home" (Twain 1975, 414). Moments such as these remind us that despite the chauvinism that Twain gives full rein to in the Turkish texts, he does not lose a self-conscious sense of social injustice at home.

There is a sense in the notebooks and journals, the final revised text, and the lectures that followed that despite the great past of the Ottomans and the hopeful future of the Americans, both in the mid-nineteenth century are the poor relations of Western Europe. The dirt and poverty Twain notes in the labyrinthine backstreets of Istanbul remind him of the backstreets of old U.S. towns and of the badly maintained houses of rural America. But whatever associations Twain might draw between his homeland and this "far, foreign land" pale in comparison to the differences he notes. The shabbiness of the shores in parts of the Golden Horn may remind him of the docks of New York, but Twain is ultimately ill at ease in Constantinople's cosmopolitan confusion. If the people startle him, he is no less surprised by other wildlife that dwells side by side with the beggars and dwarfs in the city:

8. Constantinople street dogs, late 1900s.

> In one narrow street (but none of them are wide) I saw three dogs lying coiled up, about a foot or two apart. End to end they lay, and so they just bridged the street neatly, from gutter to gutter. A drove of a hundred sheep came along. They stepped right over the dogs, the rear crowding the front, impatient to get on. The dogs looked lazily up, flinched a little when the impatient feet of the sheep touched their raw backs—sighed and lay peacefully down again. No talk could be plainer than that. (Twain 1911, 2:82)

The city that he attempts to control through traditional Orientalist tropes, like the street dogs, does not notice the American tourist's passage. The city goes on without him, beyond the reaches of his inventive Yankee discourse. When Twain decides to make the excursion to Russia, other passengers decide to stay on in Istanbul. "I guess Dan is well tired of Constantinople by this time" he muses in his notebook about his cabin mate Dan Slote (Twain 1975, 405). When back in Constantinople the ship is delayed due to fueling problems, there are three days that are unaccounted for in Twain's journal. The editor of the notebooks cites a letter Twain writes to his family on September 1, his last evening in Constantinople: "I am staying in the ship, tonight. I generally stay on shore when we are in port. But yesterday I just ran myself down. Dan Slote, my room-mate, is on shore. He remained there while we went up the Black Sea, but it seems he has not got enough of it yet" (Twain 1975, 412). Thus ends the original version of his visit to Istanbul, though once again the revised text would guard no traces of this final dearth of detail. Twain, unlike his roommate, may have had enough of the city, but this closing paralipsis is odd. After all that he would commit to print about his unpleasant visit to Istanbul, he leaves no record of this part of his excursion. In the end, Twain disappeared silently into the city he claimed to have little interest in, and what he was up to we will never know.

3

Dispatches from Constantinople

Ernest Hemingway on the Greco-Turkish War

> A writer's job is to tell the truth. His standard of fidelity to the truth should be so high that his invention, out of his experience, should produce a truer account than anything factual can be. For facts can be observed badly.
>
> —HEMINGWAY, *Men at War*

IN A 1920 *Toronto Star Weekly* piece entitled "How to Be Popular in Peace Though a Slacker in War," Hemingway advises his readers on the best way to appear to be a war veteran: "Buy or borrow a good history of the war. Study it carefully and you will be able to talk intelligently on any part of the front. In fact, you will more than once be able to prove the average returned veteran a pinnacle of inaccuracy if not unveracity [*sic*]" (Stephens 1968, 363; brackets in original). It is certain that he followed his own advice when in 1922, at the age of twenty-three, Hemingway took the Simplon-Orient Express from Paris to Istanbul to cover the Greco-Turkish war as a foreign correspondent for the *Star.* Except for articles and stories printed in his high school weekly newsletter in Chicago, he had not yet published anything of significance. Rather than entering medical school, he had taken a job as a cub reporter on the *Kansas City Star* until volunteering as an ambulance driver in Italy during World War I. Upon his return to the United States, he secured a freelance assignment with a Toronto-based newspaper, where from February 14, 1920, to September 13, 1924, his pieces would appear in the *Toronto Star Weekly* and the *Toronto Daily Star.* Eventually sent by the *Star* to Europe, in 1922 Hemingway was based in Paris as a postwar foreign correspondent. Against the wishes of his first wife, Hadley, he had wired his editors in Canada to send him on assignment to Constantinople to report on the last phases of the Greco-Turkish war (1920–1922): "WONDERFUL ASSIGNMENT BUT IF

9. Ottoman and foreign officers and troops, with Golden Horn and Galata Tower in the background, early 1900s.

WAR HASTE NECESSARY STOP IF NO WAR GREAT SERIES NEAR EAST ARTICLES ANYWAY" (Mellow 1992, 193). Mustafa Kemal's Nationalist troops were making their way toward Istanbul; Greek and Armenian quarters in Smyrna (modern Izmir) had been set to flames two weeks earlier, and refugees were beginning to make their way through Thrace toward Greece.

Hemingway arrived in Istanbul in mid-September of 1922. Probably reading a borrowed history on the long train ride down through Eastern Europe, the voice of the dispatches, from the outset, is characterized by an insider's loose confidence in his subject. Constantinople would be "Constan," as Gibraltar would later be just plain "Gib." Initially making up with posturing what he lacked in expertise, Hemingway in a very short time, nevertheless, would begin to send back dispatches that are noteworthy for their objectivity as well as literary value. While the writer has been criticized for his naïve reporting of others' national struggles, often by those who do not share his prejudices, he nevertheless seems to have developed a remarkable understanding of the historical and political complexities that had led to this particularly terrible moment in the history of Turkish-Greek relations. And to this he would add to his articles his growing concern over the dangerous role of Western powers in the conflict. He would miss the fighting between the Greeks and Turks in Anatolia but would arrive in time to report on the rumors circulating in the city as to the possible defeat or victory of the Nationalist forces. He would then report on the tensions in the city as everyone awaited the inevitable arrival of Kemal Pasha. Later he would cover the Convention of Mudania where, after the victory of the Turkish Nationalists, Kemal Atatürk, newly renamed and elected first president of the Republic, and the Allied Powers came to terms: the Allies returned Eastern Thrace to Turkey while Turkey accepted the neutralization of the Bosphorus Straits under international control. Hemingway would report at length on the Greek evacuation, the result of the infamous exchange of population, whereby eventually some 1.3 million Greeks were forced to leave their native lands in Asia Minor and go to Greece while a half a million Turks were similarly forced to leave their homes in Greece and make their way to Turkey. As Robert O. Stephens suggests in *Hemingway's Nonfiction: The Public Voice,* Hemingway's general knowledge of war up to this point in his career, including his experience in Italy, was limited primarily to the "knowledge of retreats and evacuations" (Stephens 1968, 258). Later he would cover the Lausanne Conference, where on July 24, 1923, the final terms of the peace treaty between Turkey and Greece would be decided and signed.

It is often said of Hemingway that he went to school to journalism to learn how to write fiction. In a 1950 *Paris Review* interview with George Plimpton, he himself said, "On the *Star* you were forced to learn to write a simple declarative sentence. This is useful to anyone. Newspaper work will not harm a young writer and could help him if he gets out of it in time" ("The Art of Fiction," qtd. in Stephens 1968, 8). He would say in 1956 that journalism, "when done on your knees," had its own kind of integrity; it was "that writing of something that happens day by day, in which I was trained when young, and which is not whoring when done honestly with exact reporting" (Stephens 1968, 6; qtd. in Stephens 1968, 3). While much of his early journalism would be recycled in his later stories, Hemingway nonetheless responded angrily to interviewers, critics, and biographers who insisted later in his career on mentioning his newspaper work and fiction in the same breath: "If you have made your living as a newspaperman, learning your trade, writing against deadlines, writing to make stuff timely rather than permanent, no one has the right to dig this stuff up and use it against the stuff you have written to write the best you can" (qtd. in Stephens 1968, 4). As early as March of 1922, before his assignment in Istanbul, he complained in a letter to Sherwood Anderson that "this goddam newspaper stuff is gradually ruining me" because it was interfering with his real work, his poetry and fiction (Hemingway 1981, 63). The best advice Gertrude Stein ever gave him, he would repeat in various places and at various times in his life, and never without a trace of malicious irony, was to quit journalism if he ever hoped to be a serious writer. His relationship with newspaper agencies was never smooth. When the International News Service's New York bureau, to whom he was simultaneously and secretly sending European dispatches under the pseudonym John Hadley, refused in mid-December of 1922 to cover Hemingway's expenses unless he sent receipts, Hemingway cabled: "SUGGEST YOU UPSTICK BOOKS ASSWARDS" (Mellow 1992, 213). Two months before he officially resigned from the *Toronto Daily Star* in December of 1923 he would write to Ezra Pound about the problem of leaving cats indoors and his sentiments vis-à-vis his newspaper work: "Later in the evening I will track down the piece of Merde by the smell and will carefully wipe it up with the aid of a copy of the Toronto Star" (Hemingway 1981, 97).

Whatever qualms Hemingway had with his early journalism career, however, he would continue to write essays and articles for newspapers and magazines for the rest of his life: his writing during World War II, for example, would be confined primarily to nonfiction. There is little question that his early apprenticeship at the *Star* played as much a role in his stylistic development as a creative writer as did the early mentorship of Stein and Ezra Pound. His undemanding vocabulary, his preference for nouns and the economy of the declarative sentence, his telling of what happened while simultaneously managing to communicate an emotion "aided by the element of timelessness" were "tricks" he had learned as much in newspaper writing as he did, for example, from Stein's theory of concentration: "the necessary effort a true writer made to find the exact word or words that matched his or her emotional experience of an event" (qtd. in Mellow 1992, 204). It can also be argued that Hemingway's early ambitions to be a writer, rather than a "mere" journalist, are manifest in the language and narrative organization of his *Star* dispatches. Lincoln Stephens, an acquaintance at the Lausanne Conference, was struck by the literary quality of Hemingway's cable concerning the Greek exodus from Thrace: "It was so vivid . . . I was seeing the scene and said so" (qtd. in Mellow 1992, 205). The cable led him to predict that Hemingway would become an important voice among a new generation of writers in Europe (Mellow 1992, 205).

While critics note that he used journalism to practice his developing art, less is said of what specific shapes this rehearsal took, and more importantly, the effect his emergent commitment to certain aesthetic principles had on the nature of his news reporting. A dispatch about traveling through the Balkans on his way to Istanbul (cabled on October 16, nearly one month after his arrival) offers an early example of Hemingway's application of certain fictional techniques, or ways of writing he was developing in the service of the "human interest" story. He would extend these techniques to his coverage of the war in Asia Minor:

> The typewriter carriage is bent; stuck tight, and will have to be freed in Constantinople.
>
> So this is being scrawled in pencil while the long, brown Orient Express crawls its way across Europe, over imaginary borders, through mountains, and across the level harvest fields toward Constantinople and Scutari, where a short, bronze-faced, blond Turk with a seasoned army of 300,000 men and a united nation at his back dictates terms to the Allies who two years ago hunted him as a bandit. (Hemingway 1985, 286)

There is an associative movement to the lines. A seemingly intimate conversation with his reader about the conditions of his "scrawl" elides mid-line into the echoing "crawl" of the train through frontiers that are as unreal in his imagination, he seems to suggest, as they are on the maps of warring politicians. Rather than naming Mustafa Kemal, he describes what he looks like in terms that might confound a Western audience trained to envision a "terrible Turk" advancing from the East as a dusky, criminal figure. Highlighting Kemal's golden features, thus his resemblance to a Western ideal of the hero, Hemingway then offers a compressed version of the military and political landscape he is traveling toward. The opposition—at this early point in the dispatches referring to Kemal Pasha and the Nationalists, no friends of the Canadians, Americans, or the Triple Entente—is experienced and large; there is solidarity in Anatolia and it is not for the ineffective Sultan in Constantinople who is negotiating with the Allied Powers. He then sums up the segments of the sentence, separate but connected like cars of a train, with a twist that emphasizes the instability of constructed meaning: reversals in power relations mean exchanging subject pronouns for objective pronouns to indicate who is dictating to whom; bad now means good; "bandit" now means national icon. Within six lines the speaker describes a landscape and a "war hero" while simultaneously setting a scene that has the dramatic potential of fiction without straying from the political realities of the situation at hand. And yet the lines do not read like provocation, like a young journalist out to contradict the establishment with an alternative reading of people and events for the sake of novelty. It reads like fiction, like an attempt to create vivid and real pictures in the mind of a reader intelligent enough to distrust the caricatures and historical clichés usually fed to him by the popular press.

This was not the case with Hemingway's first cables out of Istanbul written before he developed his sea legs and local contacts. Initial cables are brief and dry and rely on the evasive passive tense:

> BRITISH ORDER KEMAL TO QUIT CHANAK
>
> *Constantinople.*—With the British and Turks on the verge of war in the neutral zone, General Harrington, Commander-in-chief, dispatched a new demand to Mustapha Kemal today that he evacuate the Chanak area.
>
> It was understood that no time limit was set.
>
> The dispatch of the fresh ultimatum followed the receipt of an ultimatum from Kemal, in which he demanded that the British evacuate the Asiatic side of the Straits.
>
> Kemal's note was considered decidedly hostile.
>
> One high British official stated that the note had closed the door to peace. (September 30, 1922; Hemingway 1985, 277)

While Hemingway, after two weeks in Istanbul, still writes a decidedly British point of view, his cable appears relatively neutral when compared to a *New York Times* story written on the same exchange of demands two weeks prior:

> THE NEW TURKISH PERIL
>
> England, France and Italy have notified the Turks that an attack on the Straits will be resisted by all three powers, and if the Turks can be persuaded that the Allies mean business then will there will be no attack. But the French solicitude for Turkey's "legitimate susceptibilities" is disquieting. What is chiefly to the point now is whether there will be a continuance of French indulgence toward illegitimate susceptibilities. (September 15, 1922; *New York Times*, 1922)

Rather than reporting the demands of both sides, the *New York Times* report focuses on infighting among the Allies and relegates the highly qualified ("illegitimate") Turkish demands to an "indulgence" of the French. The ambiguous, noncommittal nature of the narrative voice that would characterize Hemingway's early fiction is perhaps not clearly present yet in these first dispatches, but a certain balanced objectivity reveals itself when compared to similar dispatches in other papers of the time.

Within a month and a half, Hemingway's cables would shed their British bias and demonstrate more and more the kind of "five finger exercise" he would practice in his "serious writing": "Remember what the noises were and what was said . . . Find what gave you the emotion; what the action was that gave you the excitement. Then write it down making it clear so the reader will see it too and have the same feeling that you had" (Hemingway to an "aspiring writer," qtd. in Mellow 1992, 204). In a November 10 cable entitled "Kemal's One Submarine" by the editors in Toronto, Hemingway offers three war vignettes that suggest that he was already observing the five finger exercise in his attempts to make destroyer flotilla patrols come alive in the minds of his readers and create images of soldiers, Turkish and other, as participants in the absurd human drama that is war. After describing the departure of a Russian submarine to Turkey, a gift to Mustafa Kemal, Hemingway recounts how the captain, caught between the British and the Russians, pursues an alternative career on the Black Sea coast:

> He turned up next off Trebizond [Trabzon] as a full-fledged pirate, halting ships, searching the passengers and crew and doing a very good business. He is still under the name "Jolly Roger" and the captain is laying away plunder enough to

10. Armies preparing for Mustafa Kemal, early 1900s.

> enable him to retire if he escapes the gallows that are waiting for him in Odessa and the six lean grey destroyers [that] cruise up and down the Bosphorus waiting for him to appear. (Hemingway 1985, 320)

The following story from the same dispatch also reads like a moment of comic relief but adds an ear for the tragi-comical in the bold yet flat and thus almost burlesque declaration of a Turkish soldier:

> At one time, during the Mudania Conference, a destroyer was running a night patrol along the Asiatic side of the Straits. No one knew whether there was going to be peace or war . . . As the boat neared the beach [near Beykos], it was fired upon. It kept going and after the first ragged volley there was no shooting. As the boat landed on the beach a horseman rode out of the black shadow at the side of the searchlight beam and spoke in French.

> "We are a squadron of Kemalist Cavalry," he said, and the officer in charge could see the horses huddled back of the little hill. "We have come here to show we could if we want to. Now we are going back."
>
> There was nothing for the British officer to do. The cavalry were some thirty miles in the neutral zone—but all the British army and navy's efforts in those days were directed to avoiding war instead of accepting provocations for it. The officer went back with his boat to the destroyer. (Hemingway 1985, 320–21)

With a similar eye for travesty, Hemingway records another act of Turkish infiltration:

> Another night a destroyer patrol near the suburb of Bebek stopped a boatload of Turkish women who were crossing from Asia Minor after the ferries were stopped [by British order]. On being searched for arms or contraband it turned out all the women were men. They were all armed—and later proved to be Kemalist officers sent over to organize the Turkish population in the suburbs in case of an attack on Constantinople. (Hemingway 1985, 321)

The brief vignettes are offered free of any interpretation beyond their immediate military consequences, yet the war news resembles folklore. The reason for writing these "slices of life" is not to belittle, or in the case of the last story, to feminize the Turkish soldiers as is often the case in Orientalist discourse; rather, Hemingway looks for action and events that make good fiction as he simultaneously fictionalizes the news. People become characters: pirates with names, French-speaking revolutionaries in the shadows, cross-dressers. While Hemingway would write about the realities of war all his life, his realities would always have an absurdist edge. War, finally, was a ridiculous but inevitable human project and if one were to write as honestly of war as one tried to of love, heroism was often replaced with failure, or luck, or something in between.

"A writer, if he is any good," he tells George Plimpton, "does not describe. He invents or *makes* out of knowledge personal and impersonal and sometimes seems to have unexplained knowledge which could come from racial or family experience" (qtd. in Stephens 1968, 205). Hemingway's journalism is more invention than description in that it reenacts historical information through fictional means. Truth is not to be confused with fact in such an enterprise, because truth must communicate something beyond the pretense of data, something that remains when allegiances and luck shift. A Hemingway mantra, the "true sentence," was the only responsibility a writer had, to himself and to his reader. And true sentences were made up of words selected for their fidelity to a thing, a place, a moment—a fidelity that was the consequence of an intricate as well as idiosyncratic synchronization of experience, history, emotion: everything and anything that participated in the translation of phenomena into words (Hemingway 1964, 12). This was a responsibility he had discovered early in his writing career under the guidance of older writers, especially Ezra Pound: "Here was a man I liked and trusted the most as a critic then," Hemingway says of Pound in the early Paris days, "the man who believed in the *mot juste*—the one and only correct word to use—the man who had taught me to distrust adjectives as I would later learn to distrust certain people in certain situations" (Hemingway 1964, 134).

The *mot juste* had many purposes, and one was the desired participation of the reader: "A writer's problem . . . is always how to write truly and having found what is true, to project it in a way that it becomes a part of the experience of the person who reads it (Hemingway, "The Writer and War," in Stephens 1968, 208). Hemingway labored in his early journalism to involve his reader in events unfolding on the other side of the world, and it is his aesthetic approach to "what is true," his fictional treatment of fact, that leads to reporting on the Greco-Turkish war that is distinctive. In the following October 19 dispatch, originally entitled by the copy-editors "Constantinople Cut-Throats Await Chance For Orgy," Hemingway attempts to project the psychology of a city whose history is about to change as Mustafa Kemal's Nationalist forces approach Istanbul. In order to do so he builds up associations that would be familiar to his Canadian audience, in this case baseball, horse races, and hospitals, underscoring quite consciously the fictional nature of the reader's, and writer's, relationship to actual events.

> *Constantinople.*—There is a tight-drawn, electric tension in Constantinople such as only people who live in a city that has never been invaded can imagine.
>
> Take the tension that comes when the pitcher steps into the box before the packed stands at the first game of the world series, multiply it by the tension that comes when the barrier snaps up, the gong's clang, and they're off at the King's Plate at the Woodbine [Toronto racetrack], add to it the tension in your mind when you walk the floor downstairs as you wait frightened and cold for

> someone you love, while a doctor or a nurse are doing something in a room above that you cannot help in any way, and you have something comparable to the feeling in Constantinople now.
>
> It is we correspondents who have nothing at stake that get the selfish world series thrill. (Hemingway 1985, 294)

The cable begins with adjectives that give physicality to a feeling that paradoxically can only exist, he writes, in the absence of experience. He thus suggests that the reader, the citizen of Toronto who knows nothing of invasions, is more capable of empathizing with the citizen of Constantinople than he might believe. He then compares the "invasion" to the launching of not any game or race, but to specific ones with particular compositions, mechanisms, and sounds that would be familiar to his audience, again making something concrete and palpable out of the unimaginable. The address is familiar and personal: it directs the reader to "take," "multiply," "add," and uses the plural possessive pronoun "your" to indicate a shared experience. Although he will conclude the passage with a reference to the decadent ease of the journalist as voyeur, Hemingway does not compare a military action to a spectator sport alone. He concludes his variations on a theme of tension with a detailed dramatization of waiting that suggests the final hospital scene of *A Farewell to Arms.* He forces the reader to envisage and thus contend with the threat of death. Because finally, though this may seem like a game to those watching from a distance, it is no game; it is war. Hemingway knows that facts alone cannot communicate the reality of the Greco-Turkish war to most readers. Applying the same aesthetic principles to many of the dispatches as he would to his fiction, Hemingway animates the facts through fictional means in the service of telling a truth.

"All you have to do," Hemingway urged a young writer during the Spanish Civil War, "is write the truth and be there where you can write it. If no honest man is in Madrid to write about what really happens if it ever falls, it will be one of the tragedies of history" (qtd. in Stephens 1968, 204). Truth, among other things, meant being an objective witness of war in the context of Hemingway's journalism. This was a particularly difficult undertaking in the case of the Greco-Turkish war for many reasons, not the least of which was the centuries-old accumulation of representations of the Muslims of Asia Minor as "invaders." Western sympathies had always lain with the Christian inhabitants of Constantinople and still did in 1922. While Hemingway overwhelmingly represents the fears of the Christian community in Istanbul—his choice of "invasion" above to inscribe what others might call "liberation" is only one small case in point—he nevertheless writes about the conflict with a relatively equal eye for the challenges and atrocities experienced and committed by both Turks and Greeks. His failure to endorse the usual Western narrative of the Turks solely as barbarian aggressors and the Greeks solely as civilized victims even motivates one writer to argue recently that Hemingway represents the Turks as victims in the war (Lecouras 2001, 1). His coverage, like his novels of war, tends to highlight the effects of the political and military disputes on the ground, regardless of loyalty to any side. Like all correspondents, he reports on the activities of international powers during the war. But unlike most correspondents, and like many contemporary critics, he records not only the interests of the British, the Italians or the Russians, but notes their interference in and manipulation of the conflict.

The outcome of the war had much effect on how the war would be represented historically. The diaspora of Greeks and Armenians, many of whom immigrated to Europe and America, meant that certain points of view, the views of those who lost their country, would be voiced abroad more regularly. Because much of what transpired in Turkey in the early part of the twentieth century has never been fully resolved among the original parties, thus preventing the wounds of war from healing, it remains difficult to gain an impartial view either of the events leading up to the war or a balanced account of what transpired during and after. Emotions remain high. Hemingway, having no apparent allegiances to either the Greek or the Turkish positions, seems to have been interested in these emotions on a human level, but his dispatches take no consistent political side. His only loyalty, when he was writing well, was to his art, as Lecouras rightly argues. Though this argument accuses Hemingway of dehistoricizing the war in the service of art in the case of "The Quai at Smyrna," this loyalty to certain aesthetic principles, I will argue, is precisely what makes his reports on the war historically valuable.

In the new 1998 introduction to his 1973 book *Ionian Vision,* Michael Llewellyn Smith, former British Ambassador to Greece, explains the political maneuvering that would eventually lead to the Greco-Turkish war that began formally in 1920. Eleftherios Venizelos, prime minister of Greece, and Lloyd George, prime minister of Britain, began negotiations concerning the future of Ottoman territories in 1915. Independence movements in distant Ottoman territories coupled with the general parceling of Ottoman lands by Western powers had begun in earnest during World War I, a war that the Ottomans, as allies of the Germans, would lose. While there is debate as to which party first proposed the idea of "annexing" the west coast of Asia Minor to Greece, both the British and the Greeks had an interest in Turkey. The British, according to Llewellyn, felt that Asia Minor "was the only territory, except Cyprus, which Britain could realistically offer" in exchange for Greece's participation in the war on the side of the Entente (Llewellyn 1998, xiii). Venizelos, who believed that Asia Minor historically "'belonged' to Hellenism," assumed that the Turkish Nationalist movement would "dissolve" with the Ottoman State, writing in a "well known memorandum" that "our Muslim subjects will be excellent and law abiding citizens" (Llewellyn 1998, xviii, xvi).

Venizelos received a mandate from the Supreme Council at the Versailles Peace Conference to occupy Smyrna and the surrounding zones for "peace keeping purposes" on May 1919 (Llewellyn 1998, xviii, xvi). Taking advantage, like all European powers, of a weakened and ineffectual Ottoman State, Venizelos and Lloyd George nevertheless miscalculated the support for Mustafa Kemal in Asia Minor and the growing success of his Nationalist movement. The Kemalist troops, in defiance of the Treaty of Sèvres (August 10, 1920) that assigned further Turkish territories to Greece, and in defiance of the Ottoman government in Constantinople who supported the treaty, went to war with the Greek troops in Anatolia. When it eventually became clear that the Kemalists would replace the Sultan as the official voice of Turkey, European powers, and especially the British, in their desire to establish working relations with Ankara, the new capital of the Turkish Republic, withdrew support for their Greek allies. Greek troops, already deep into Anatolia and abandoned by their European Allies, began their retreat burning Turkish villages on the way. Turkish troops and unenlisted groups attacked Greek communities, particularly in Smyrna, where thousands of Greeks died in the horrifying flagration that is the subject of Hemingway's "The Quai at Smyrna."

Everyone, including Hemingway, had predicted an "orgy" upon the arrival of Kemal's troops in Istanbul. However, the fear seemed to be as much of outsiders as of the Nationalist troops themselves:

> It is the collection of cutthroats, robbers, bandits, and Levantine pirates who have gathered here from Batum to Baghdad, and from Singapore to Sicily, that are getting the Woodbine thrill. They are waiting for the looting to begin. And they are ready to begin it on their own account as soon as the triumphal entry

> of Mustapha Kemal Pasha's troops start the riotous orgy of celebration that will permit them to fire the wooden tenement quarter which will burn like a gasoline-soaked matchbox.
>
> If the Allied and Turkish police prevent the orgy . . . it will be the finest achievement in the world because the tough element of all the Near East, of the Balkans, and of the Mediterranean are gathered in Constantinople like jackals waiting for the lion to make his kill.
>
> The people who are getting the sickening, cold, crawling fear-thrill are the Armenians, Greeks, and Macedonians, who cannot get away or who have elected to stay. Those who stay are arming themselves and talking desperately. (October 19, 1922; Hemingway 1985, 295)

Hemingway acknowledges the dangerous position of minority groups in Istanbul: "The Armenians, Jews and Rumanians are clearing out of Constantinople. They are selling their property at any sacrifice and getting out. The government issues statements urging them not to be foolish, assuring them that all measures of protection for the inhabitants will be taken, that patrols are being reinforced, that there is no danger" (Hemingway 1985, 292). In a passing reference to Turkish violence in Smyrna, he recognizes the historical breadth of minority fears: "But the Armenian Jews and the Jewish Rumanians have heard all that before" and "cannot forget Smyrna. So they go with a history of a thousand years of massacre behind them, it is hard for the racial fear to be quieted, no matter who makes the promises." He goes on, however, to implicate the Greeks in their present political and social catastrophe:

> The Greeks are in a different position. They have a guilty national conscience. It is an uncontested fact that the Greek army in its retreat across Anatolia laid waste and burned the Turkish villages, burnt the crops in the fields, the grain on the threshing floors and committed atrocities. These facts are testified to by American relief workers and Christians who were in the country before, during and after the Greek retreat. (Hemingway 1985, 292)

He concludes the section by following his later advice to the young journalist in Spain to "write the truth and be there where you can write it." The truth, in this case, means the gathering of information from all sides in the service of honest witnessing. "I will take up the question of Greek atrocities later when I have the evidence and testimony of both Christians and Turks and will try and give a complete presentation of the matter to the *Star* readers" (Hemingway 1985, 293). And finally, he leaves the reader with a meditation on the universal "logic" of wartime violence, though he specifies Mediterranean countries: "The fact is that atrocities are always followed by counter-atrocities in these countries and have been since the siege of Troy. And it is the innocent who suffer. The victim of the revenge is rarely the perpetrator of the original outrage. It is this that is emptying Constantinople of Greeks" (Hemingway 1985, 293).

Hemingway's leanings toward objective realism in his early journalism, as well as his developing trust in the power of an invented or made knowledge to project that reality to an audience, allow him as a Western reporter to write an unusually balanced yet vivid account of an "Eastern" war. While in his dispatches both Greeks and Turks, the people of "those countries," are culturally distanced, he attempts, in the short time he is there, to understand the historical, political, and social contexts of their fight and pass it on to his readers. Unlike other news reporters he does this by not subscribing to many of the common tropes that position East against West. He makes a point, for example, to differentiate between positions toward Islam within the Turkish population itself, once he has understood that difference. While he often references Christians, rarely differentiating between Greek, Armenian, or European forms of Christianity, his allusions to Islam are more historicized. His first mention of Islam in Turkey comes in the context of Western rumors of Kemal's prohibition of alcohol, which prove to be false. The remaining discussions come in the context of Kemal's secularism.

> TURKS DISTRUST KEMAL PASHA
>
> *Constantinople.*—Mustapha Kemal Pasha a few months ago was regarded as a new Saladin of the Moslem world. He was to lead Islam into battle against Christianity and to spread a holy war though all the East. Now the East is beginning to distrust him. Mohammedans I have talked to say: "Kemal has betrayed us." There is no more talk of holy war. (October 24, 1922; Hemingway 1985, 302)

The Kemalists would prove as opposed to the power of the Caliphate, or religious authority in the Ottoman Empire, as they were to the power of Sultans. Basing their Republican model on a European ideal of elected rather than inherited leadership, they likewise supported the complete separation of "church" and state. In November of 1922 the Grand National Assembly in Ankara abolished the Sultanate, giving the role of Caliphate to the last Sultan, a role purely religious with no political power (Freely 1996, 247). The Caliphate would eventually be dissolved in March of 1924, and "all members of the Ottoman line" would be "forbidden to reside within the boundaries of the Turkish Republic," legislation that would eliminate the last connections that "linked Turkey with the Ottoman Empire" and mark the official end of six centuries of Ottoman Empire (Freely 1996, 251).

Hemingway became quickly aware of the schism between the secular Nationalists and the religious community. His information was based, he claims, on the reports one gets as "gossip when the Mohammedans talk politics" (TDS, 303). Contrary to rumors in the West, the heads of the Turkish Nationalist movement were "atheists and Freemasons rather than good Mohammedans" and Mustafa Kemal Pasha was hardly "a conquering messiah for the Mohammedan peoples" (Hemingway 1985, 303). This split between supporters of religious rule and secular rule in Turkey, rather than a weakness in the resistance movement, could prove, Hemingway suggests, the only hope for the Allied forces. While the new secular leader of Turkey moved the country toward a form of government that a modern Europe could, in theory, admire, he nevertheless posed a potential problem for them in their own race for control of the natural resources of other countries. While "Pan-Islamites" might be "disappointed in Kemal the Saladin because he shows no inclination to plunge into a fanatical holy war," they may, however, still get their war, Hemingway suggests, "from Kemal the business man" (Hemingway 1985, 303–4). The new Turkish government was interested in the oil fields of Mesopotamia, oil, Hemingway notes, that "Great Britain wants to keep" (Hemingway 1985, 304). Hemingway ultimately understands that the Greco-Turkish war is a geo-political war and not a continuation of the religious wars, the Crusades (though also geo-political wars), a correlation that inevitably crops up in the discourse of other writers on the subject.

Hemingway does not recirculate clichéd symbolisms of holy war. Nor does he offer patent ideological readings of the political struggle. Applying fictional elements to his news reporting as formal techniques only, ideological allegories, like forced symbolisms, appear neither in his journalism nor, I would argue, in his fiction.

Paraphrasing Hemingway in an August 1965 interview, Robert O. Stephens writes, "Intellectually imposed symbols in a writer's work were usually failures . . . meanings, including symbolic ones, came out of a created, real experience. If the experience was true, he insisted, the symbols would be there without the writer's trying for them ("Hemingway in Cuba," *Atlantic Monthly* 216 [August

1965]: 104; qtd. in Stephens 1968, 208). Writing later about the social pressures of Marxism on the modern writer, "Everyone tries to frighten you now by saying or writing that if one does not become a communist or have a Marxist viewpoint one will have no friend and will be alone," Hemingway says in a 1935 letter to Ivan Kashkin, "A writer is like a gypsy. He owes no allegiance to any government . . . He can be class conscious only if his talent is limited. If he has enough talent all classes are his province. He takes from them all and what he gives is everyone's property" (Hemingway 1981, 419). As he will later in Spain, Hemingway drifts between political adversaries in Turkey, attempting to grasp what he can of the manifest human problems at hand and to reinvent them in language loyal to his experience. His reports are not ideologically sound, and the stories within the reports do not adhere to politically motivated plots or themes. News reporting shaped by a writer's "individual sense of reality" may be considered unreliable as well as dangerous both from a professional and socio-political point of view (Hemingway, preface to *The Fifth Column;* qtd. in Stephens 1968, 117). In Hemingway's case, however, an engaged "indifference" has certain merits.

Hemingway's description of the exodus of Greek refugees from Eastern Thrace is particularly powerful, again because he uses fictional techniques to communicate the horrible reality of the mass departure. This is not an abstract immigration: we see particular people, animals, and objects in specific weather and landscape. There is a voiced, third person narrator rather than a voiceless commentator. And commentary on the political context of the march, as well as the existential implication of the horrors of it, winds among and directs the graphic images like the cavalry in charge.

> A SILENT, GHASTLY PROCESSION WENDS WAY THROUGH THRACE
>
> *Adrianople.*—In a never-ending, staggering march the Christian population of Eastern Thrace is jamming the roads towards Macedonia. The main column crossing the Maritza River at Adrianople is twenty miles long. Twenty miles of carts drawn by cows, bullocks and muddy-flanked water buffalo, with exhausted, staggering men, women and children, blankets over their heads, walking blindly along in the rain beside their worldly goods.
>
> This main stream is being swelled from all the back country. They don't know where they are going. They left their farms, villages and ripe, brown fields and joined the main steam of refugees when they heard the Turk was coming.

> Now they can only keep their places in the ghastly procession while mud-splashed Greek cavalry herd them along like cow-punchers driving steers.
>
> It is a silent procession. Nobody even grunts. It is all they can do to keep moving. Their brilliant peasant costumes are soaked and draggled. Chickens dangle by their feet from the carts. Calves nuzzle at the draught cattle wherever a jam halts the stream. An old man marches bent under a young pig, a scythe and a gun, with a chicken tied to his scythe. A husband spreads a blanket over a woman in labor in one of the carts to keep off the driving rain. She is the only person making a sound. Her little daughter looks at her in horror and begins to cry. And the procession keeps moving. (October 21, 1922; Hemingway 1985, 297)

Eight dispatches later, and on his way back to Paris, Hemingway returns to the scene in Adrianople. This time he includes images of Turks who share a similar fate with their Greek counterparts as victims of war.

> REFUGEE PROCESSION IS A SCENE OF HORROR
>
> *Sofia, Bulgaria.*—In a comfortable train with the horror of the Thracian evacuation behind me, it is already beginning to seem unreal. That is the boon of our memories.

11. Population exchange: Turkish Greeks (Rums) being sent to Greece, 1923.

> I have described that evacuation in a cable to *The Star* from Adrianople. It does no good to go over it again. The evacuation still keeps up. No matter how long it takes this letter to get to Toronto, as you read this in *The Star* you may be sure that the same ghastly, shambling procession of people being driven from their homes is filing in unbroken line along the muddy road to Macedonia. A quarter of a million people take a long time to move.
>
> . . . All the stream of slow big-wheeled bullock and buffalo carts, bobbing camel trains and sodden, fleeing peasantry were moving west on the road, but there was a thin counter stream of empty carts driven by Turks in ragged, rain-soaked clothes and dirty fezzes which was working back against the main current. Each Turk cart had a Greek soldier in it, sitting behind the driver with his rifle between his knees and his cape up around his neck to keep the rain out. These carts had been commandeered by the Greeks to go back country in Thrace, load up with goods of refugees and help the evacuation. The Turks looked sullen and very frightened. They had reason to be.
>
> At the fork of the stone road in Adrianople all the traffic was being routed to the left by a lone Greek cavalryman who sat on his horse with his carbine slung over his back and accomplished the routing by slashing dispassionately across the face with his quirt any horse or bullock that turned toward the right. He motioned one of the empty carts driven by a Turk to turn off to the right. The Turk turned his cart and prodded his bullock into a shamble. This awoke the Greek soldier guard riding with him, and seeing the Turk turning off the main road, he stood up and smashed him in the small of the back with his rifle butt.
>
> The Turk, he was a ragged, hungry-looking Turk farmer, fell out of the cart on to his face, picked himself up in terror and ran down the road like a rabbit. A Greek cavalryman saw him running, kicked spurs into his horse and rode the Turk down. Two Greek soldiers and the cavalryman picked him up, smashed him in the face a couple of times, he shouting at the top of his voice all the times, and he was led, bloody-faced and wild eyed, not understanding what it was all about, back to his cart and told to drive on. Nobody in the line of march had paid any attention to the incident. (November 14, 1922; Hemingway 1985, 322, 324–25)

As James Mellow notes, Hemingway illustrates here that "misery travels in both directions on the Karagatch road" (Mellow 1992, 198). In the second dispatch, he begins by emphasizing the distancing effects of memory while simultaneously closing that distance for his audience: "As you read this *Star,*" no matter the post-date, "a quarter of a million people" are still stumbling in the mud and rain toward the unknown. The effect is immediate and visceral. The reader is not allowed the comfort of distance, even as the writer self-consciously observes the escapist processes of his own memory. An individual story of arbitrary brutality emerges within a larger narrative of disinheritance. This time the victim is a Turkish farmer, commandeered and abused by Greek soldiers. As in his novels of war, the narrator relies on action to dramatize an idea—in this case, as is the case, for example, in *A Farewell to Arms,* the chaos and subsequent brutality that are the social and psychological effects of war, be it in Turkey or Italy or Austria. The impulsive and violent reactions of the exhausted Greek soldiers to the nervous Turkish farmer and his bewildered, terrified response to their contradictory orders show us rather than tell us about the chaos and brutality of the march. The rather lengthy narrations of the procession, the active accounts, the embedded narratives, terminate with terse, apathetic lines that function as conclusions: "Her little daughter looks at her in horror and begins to cry. And the procession keeps moving"; "Nobody in the line of march had paid any attention to the incident." These summaries drive home a twofold consequence of war for those not directly responsible yet immediately affected: the concrete, dehumanizing results of war for the vulnerable and the poor, regardless of, in this case, "fluctuating" nationalities, and the subsequent reduced humanitarian feeling of all parties on the ground, military and civilian, same side or opposed, vis-à-vis each other.

Besides applying fictional techniques to reconstruct groups of people and anonymous yet representative individuals in the service of "realism"—or what the writer, dismissive of critical labels in his own time and ignorant of philosophical and philological debates to come, calls "truth"—Hemingway appeals to the profile, or more precisely, to the fictional device of characterization to bring to life public and private personalities for his distant readers. In the dispatch above in which he recreates the evacuation in Thrace through the disquieting distance of memory, he also introduces his readers to a "character," Madame Marie, the owner of an inn in Adrianople who corroborates the cable's leitmotif of how the miseries of war cut across nationality or national borders. Continuing with the first person, and using direct rather than reported speech, the cable is a voiced account of the atmosphere and experience of war from multiple points of view as Hemingway writes himself into the dialogue:

> Madame Marie, a big, slovenly Croatian woman, gave us some coffee and sour black bread in the bare room that served as dining-room, hotel office and parlor.
>
> "Our room was lousy, madame," I said cheerfully, to make table talk.
>
> She spread out her hands. "It is better than sleeping in the road? Eh, monsieur? It is better than that?"
>
> I agreed that it was, and we went out with madame standing looking after us.
>
> Outside it was drizzling. At the end of the muddy side street we were on I could see the eternal procession of humanity moving slowly along the great stone road that runs from Adrianople across the Maritza valley to Karagatch and then divides into other roads that cross the rolling country into Western Thrace and Macedonia. (Hemingway 1985, 323–24)

Hemingway, with a "Constantinople-acquired malaria" chill, returns to Madame Marie to write a cable for the *Star* after a day of witnessing the procession, including the incident of the Turkish farmer.

> The fever was strong and Madame Marie brought me a bottle of sickly sweet Thracian wine to take my quinine with.
>
> "I won't care when the Turks come," Madame Marie said, sitting her great bulk down at the table and scratching her chin.
>
> "Why not?"
>
> "They're all the same. The Greeks and Turks and the Bulgars. They're all the same." She accepted a glass of the wine. "I've seen them all. They've all had Karagatch."
>
> "Who are the best?" I asked.
>
> "Nobody. They're all the same. The Greek officers sleep here and then will come the Turk officers. Some day the Greek officers will come back again. They all pay me." I filled up her glass.
>
> "But the poor people that are out there on the road." I couldn't get the horror of that twenty mile long procession out of my mind, and I had seen some dreadful things that day.
>
> "Oh well." Madame Marie shrugged. "It is always that way with the people. Toujours la même chose. The Turk has a proverb, you know. He has many good proverbs. 'It is not only the fault of the axe but of the tree as well.' That is his proverb."
>
> That is his proverb all right. (Hemingway 1985, 325–26)

Madame Marie is a rounded character. She has bulk and attitude and weary cunning. She is dynamic, as opposed to static: a couple glasses of wine change her from an impassive proprietress to a confidante on the subject of military occupation. A fallen but pragmatic sibyl, she predicts the future based on what she has seen, and she has seen enough to convince her that taking sides is futile, particularly when business is concerned. "They're all the same . . . They've all had Karagatch." When the narrator teases out the latent sexual gist of her words, associating power over a place with the right of access to its women, "Who are the best?" her answer, "Nobody," plays along yet also directs the exchange back to the arbitrary and unstable nature of power.

The dialogue is staccato and stark like the dialogue of the early novels and similarly gains its power through paralepsis, the silences that emphasize a point by passing over it: "It is better than sleeping in the road? Eh, monsieur? It is better than that?" I agreed that it was . . ." and he goes outside where he sees at the end of the street the passing refugees who have been walking all night, or sleeping along the muddy road. Nothing more need be said. Madame Marie's character encompasses the stoicism and moral lassitude of the land she stubbornly clings to as time washes over its victors and victims. The Turkish proverb she shares—and she insists that her taste for good proverbs transcends cultures and national borders—is a Sufic proverb. The interdependency of all experience that the proverb suggests becomes wisdom too tough to take for the reporter, who, unlike Madame Marie, is witnessing this kind of disaster for the first time. His ironic response, "That is his proverb all right," is a retort we will see often in Hemingway's later fiction, usually from the mouths of world-weary, or war-weary men. "Some business" repeats the charter fisherman narrator in *To Have and Have Not.* He has just found out that men who smuggle Chinese from Cuba to Key West, "Plenty big business," often get killed. The irony is grim.

Another character puts in a brief but poignant appearance at Madame Marie's. "Shorty," the taller of two American movie men, has been gathering footage of the exodus.

> "Got some swell shots of a burning village today," Shorty pulled off a boot. "Good show—a burning village. Like kicking over an ant hill." Shorty pulled off the other boot. "Shoot it from two or three directions and it looks like a regular town on fire. Gee I'm tired. This refugee business is hell all right. Man

> sure sees awful things in this country." In two minutes he was snoring. (Hemingway 1985, 323)

Hemingway does not pass open judgment on the inappropriate slang, "swell," and the anthill simile, or the offensive, flippant attitude toward another people's tragedy. Rather, as a fiction writer preferring, like Aristotle, the power of action to set tragedy in motion, he allows the man's actions, the banal removal of his boots one by one and his falling immediately to sleep, to contrast with the horrendous content of his uninterrupted "chitchat." The contrast requires no third-person glossing to make Hemingway's point clear. When a "disinterested" aesthetics serves the market—"Good show," "Shoot it two or three directions"—rather than an ethic of artistic integrity committed to telling, or creating, the truth, the result is Shorty, a man jaded and dehumanized by the "business" of war. When market strategies command the newsroom, the result is sensationalism. The intertextual vignette is short but smart: couched between dispatch paragraphs whose restrained realism only increases the reader's empathy, Hemingway makes a declaration of sorts about the difference between popular journalism and what he hopes he is doing.

Another characterization, which like Madame Marie's simultaneously animates an individual while sketching a cultural or political landscape or idea, is one of Hamid Bey, "next to Kemal, perhaps the most powerful man in the Angora government" (Hemingway 1985, 281). Again the characterization is heterogeneous; Hamid Bey trumps the expectations a Western audience might have of a man who had until recently been a high-ranking member of an outlaw Nationalist movement. But he proves in the course of the characterization and dialogue, however, to be precisely what one would expect of a professional politician.

> HAMID BEY WEARS SHIRT TUCKED IN WHEN SEEN BY STAR
>
> *Constantinople.*—Bismarck said all men in the Balkans who tuck their shirts into their trousers are crooks. The shirts of the peasants, of course, hang outside. At any rate, when I found Hamid Bey—next to Kemal, perhaps the most powerful man in the Angora government—in his Stamboul office where he directs the Kemalist government in Europe, while drawing a large salary as administrator of the Imperial Ottoman Bank, a French capitalized concern—his shirt was tucked in, for he was dressed in a grey business suit.

> Hamid Bey's office is at the top of a steep hill beyond an old seraglio and houses the Red Crescent—equivalent to our Red Cross—of which Hamid Bey is one of the leaders and where attendants in Red Crescent khaki carry out the order of the Angora government.
>
> "Canada is anxious about the possibility of a massacre of Christians when Kemal enters Constantinople," I said.
>
> Hamid Bey, big, bulky, with grey moustaches, wing-collared and with a porcupine haircut, looked over his glasses and spoke French.
>
> "What have the Christians to fear?" he asked. "They are armed and the Turks have disarmed. There will be no massacre. It is the Greek Christians who are massacring the Turks now in Thrace. That's why we must occupy Thrace now—to protect our people." (October 9, 1922; Hemingway 1985, 281)

Hemingway introduces the "character" by way of an anecdote on the correlation between a man's dress and his honor. After offering Hamid Bey's curriculum vitae, which identifies him as a politician with international banking connections, Hemingway intensifies the folkloric wisdom of the anecdote by putting the man in "Western" dress, a "grey business suit" that suggests the "Angora" or Ankara government is as sophisticated, thus as potentially mendacious, as any Western authority. The dubious role of the Red Crescent office (the Red Cross), whose reports Hemingway has identified in a previous dispatch as propaganda for the occupation of Thrace, is again put in question through the attire of its staff: military khaki. The agency, like its leader, can be judged by appearances: a military project posing as a "neutral" humanitarian relief organization. Again, rather than the conventional reported speech of journalism, Hemingway chooses dialogue punctuated with character description. Hamid Bey is well fed, fashionable, and educated: he speaks French, the language of diplomacy, that only the Turkish elite would know. This preamble to the heart of the dispatch—Hamid Bey's reassuring response to "Canadian" fears that there will be no mass killing of Christians once the Kemalists arrive in Constantinople—puts his answer in question. In this case, characterization does the work of the "objective" commentary of journalism: Hamid Bey's credibility as a character directly reflects on the credibility of Turkish and Allied promises that there will be no "patriotic orgy" upon the "triumphant entry."

A third characterization, that of İsmet Pasha, modern Turkey's first prime minister, contrasts with that of Hamid Bey in that Hemingway offers his audience a Turkish politician they can like because he appears to gainsay, at least in Hemingway's hands, much that one expects of a politician regardless of nationality. İsmet Pasha would become İsmet İnönü after the river Inonu where Greek forces were halted by Kemal's army during the October 1920 offensive that had threatened Ankara (Freely 1996, 245). He would also, as commissioner for foreign affairs, be the head of the Turkish Peace Delegation at Lausanne where Hemingway, along with other Western journalists, jostled to gain access to the Turkish commission: "This conference is very dull and secretive," Hemingway tells a friend in a December 1, 1922, letter, "and everybody follows everybody else around—the Turks today are just like wood chucks when you wanto find them their in their holes and then they pop out as soon as your gone" (Hemingway 1981, 76). Hemingway's characterization of İsmet Pasha, like that of Hamid Bey, shows a man who is as he seems; only in this case the verdict will ultimately be relatively positive. Included in a January 23, 1923, dispatch sent from Lausanne under the title "Mussolini, Europe's Prize Bluffer, More Like Bottomley than Napoleon," the characterization of İsmet Pasha, besides being interesting in itself, also functions as a foil for a particularly damning portraiture of Mussolini who "in contrast to Ismet . . . is the biggest bluff in Europe" (Hemingway 1985, 330). While the characterization begins by describing what appear to be unflattering details of the diminutive man's physical features, Hemingway will surprise the reader by associating these features with a particular kind of personal, and by extension political, integrity.

> *Lausanne, Switzerland.*—Everyone wants to see Ismet Pasha but once they have seen him they have no desire to see him again. He is a little dark man, absolutely without magnetism, looking as small and uninteresting as a man can look. He looks more like an Armenian lace seller than a Turkish general. There is something mouselike about him. He seems to have a genius for being unrecognized. Mustapha Kemal has a face that no one can forget, and Ismet has a face no one can remember.
>
> I think the solution is that Ismet has a good movie face. I have seen him, in pictures, look stern, commanding, forceful and, in a way, handsome. Anyone who has seen in real life the weak, petulant face of any one of a dozen movie stars who look beautiful on the screen, knows what I mean. Ismet's face is not weak or petulant, it is simply plain and characterless. I remember seeing Ismet

in the first days of the conference come into the Hotel Savoy as a crowd of newspaper correspondents were coming out from one of Tchitcherin's famous "mass interviews." Ismet, waiting for the lift, stood in the midst of this crowd of men who had been trying to get appointments to speak with him for days, and not one of them recognized him. He was too unobtrusive.

It was too good to spoil, but I stepped up and greeted him.

"It is very funny, this, Excellency," I said as a couple of correspondents crowded him away from the door of the lift.

He smiled like a schoolgirl, shrugged his shoulders and raised his hands to his face in a mock gesture of shame. He giggled.

"Get an appointment to come and talk to me," he said, shook hands, stepped into the lift and grinned at me. The interview was over.

When I did interview him we got along very well, as we both spoke such bad French. Ismet conceals his defective knowledge of French, which is a disgrace to an educated Turk, as in Turkey a knowledge of French is as much a social necessity as it is in Russia, by pretending to be deaf. He appreciates a joke, Ismet does, and he smiles delightedly to himself as he curls back in his chair and has the remarks of the great shouted into his ear in Turkish by his secretary.

The next time I saw Ismet, after I had interviewed him, he was sitting at a table in a jazz dancing place in Montreux smiling delightedly at the dancers, a pair of large, grey haired Turks sitting at his table with him and looking morosely on while he ate quantities of cakes, drank three cups of tea, and made countless jokes in bad French with the waitress who brought the tea. The waitress seemed delighted with Ismet and Ismet with her, they were having a wonderful time. Not a soul in the place recognized him. (Hemingway 1985, 327–30)

What poses as a critique evolves into something of a tribute, though certainly an unconventional one for a future prime minister. Hemingway initially qualifies İsmet Pasha with an abundance of adjectives, a suspect move from a writer who preferred the solidity of nouns. The adjectives progress from the uncomplimentary "uninteresting," "mouselike," "characterless," and generally the forgettable, to "unobtrusive," a change that is subtle but not unimportant. Not only will this contrast with the description of Mussolini, who because of "the weakness in his mouth" (Hemingway 1985, 330) often scowls and sneers, it creates a portrait of a politician whose manifest qualities are in direct contradistinction to that of a Fascist whom Hemingway scorns. İsmet Pasha does not insist that those around him become an extension of him. In fact, he seems to enjoy not being recognized.

This lack of ego, at least on a superficial level, registers as a good sign for the reporter: although a general, İsmet Pasha is not what one expects of one. If anything, this man of war appears to be over civilized.

Often taken to task for his machismo, Hemingway plays with the reader's prejudices vis-à-vis conventional expectations of a manly leader. İsmet Pasha's feminine qualities—he is like a "schoolgirl," he giggles, he playfully covers his face in mock shame, he smiles "delightedly"—are precisely what make him attractive to the correspondent as a man and a politician. Again, there is no homoeroticism or Oriental feminization of the Turkish male—İsmet Pasha appears to be sexless. Rather, the characterization of İsmet Pasha suggests that a politician with "soft" qualities is a vast improvement over a bully. Unlike Hamid Bey, a competent Francophone and a ward of French banking interests in the Empire, İsmet Pasha, like Hemingway, speaks bad French. Functioning as a sign of borrowed or adopted civility in the two dispatches, fluency in French is a liability in the hard-knocks ethos of the dispatches precisely because it is "a social necessity." İsmet Pasha and Hemingway get along very well because their shared "defective" French suggests that neither have been completely culturally colonized. Although Hemingway suggests that İsmet Pasha attempts to

12. İsmet İnönü.

hide his linguistic weakness by playing deaf, his deafness, caused by years of artillery noise, was in fact no disguise. And compared to Mussolini's misogynistic behavior—he is nasty to "unattractive peasant women in their Sunday clothes," though gives rare interviews to attractive American female journalists (though James Mellow suggests that Hemingway was simply jealous because he had been granted no such favor)—İsmet Pasha chats with, rather than chats up, waitresses (Mellow 1992, 214). He drinks tea rather than whiskey, likes cake, and responds "delightedly" three times in the space of two pages. Hemingway ties up his characterization of İsmet Pasha by circling back to the beginning. If the Pasha has threatened to appear too precious in the course of the dispatch, Hemingway reminds us of his initial "thesis": "Not a soul in the place recognized him." Hemingway notes virtues in the necessity of character that another might not see.

These characterizations, because they provide his distant readers with rounded rather than flat characters, make more real what otherwise could remain very abstract public personalities. They give resonance to what might otherwise be hermeneutically limited types. The reality and resonance of Hemingway's early journalism stems from his evolving aesthetics that value fictional invention as a legitimate way to communicate knowledge beyond the limitations of data. While fictional techniques in his journalism certainly aestheticize the Greco-Turkish war, they also serve to historicize it in a way conventional journalism does not. Like a good omniscient narrator, Hemingway the correspondent travels indiscriminately through events and personalities, teasing out what is shared and what is particular. His approach to the political strategies, the military solutions, and, most importantly, their human consequences is not partisan because ideology does not motivate the form and content of the dispatches.

It is important, however, not to romanticize Hemingway's personal commitment to the political or social plights of the Greeks and Turks in 1922. Hemingway's ethics are primarily aesthetic, and it is a mistake to confuse the loyalty of the man with the loyalty of the writer. He may have written remarkably empathetic accounts of the Greek emigration, but he also took time away from coverage of the tragic march to shoot twenty-two quail that "seemed easy to hit" in the "nice open country with sort of sage brush" (qtd. in Mellow 1992, 197). He tends to list his assignment in Turkey along with other European "adventures" and spectacles:

> Came down the Rhine from Frankfurt to Cologne and visited Chink and came back to Paris—and saw Siki nearly kill Carpentier and I got a cable from the Star to go to Constantinople and went and was with the Greek Army in the big retreat—and three weeks in Constan itself—very fine weeks when just as it was getting light you'd all get into a car and drive out to the Bosphorus to see the sun rise and sober up and wonder whether there was going to be a war that would set the whole world on fire again—and there damn nearly was. And then rode across Thrace in a car, horseback, and walked and then went through Bulgaria and Serbia and finally hit Triest and had a wonderful meal and was damn glad to talk wop again and got the train straight back to Paris and Hadley. (Hemingway 1981, 86)

In the same July 17–18, 1923, letter to his friend William Horne who had also driven an ambulance in Italy during World War I, Hemingway speaks of the necessity of carrying on after the trauma and drama of such an experience. Just as bullfighting will replace the thrill of war "like having a ringside seat at the war with nothing going to happen to you," Hemingway's wartime assignment in Turkey might also fall under the category of "new kicks" (Hemingway 1981, 88).

> Horney we've got to go on. We can't ever go back to old things or try and get the "old kick" out of something or find things the way we remembered them and they are fine and wonderful and we have to go on and have other things because the old things are nowhere except in our minds now. I suppose this sounds like all sorts of Merde from the old manure spreader. I'm not meaning to talk moral . . . Your [sic] probably tired of the narrative by this time [referring to the list of adventures above]. But I'm trying to give you the dope and destroy our status as classic myths. (Hemingway 1981, 86)

Hemingway consumed experience as much for its narrative potential as to assure that his mythic status as an adventurer and writer did not become obsolete, if only in his own mind. Action, however, was much easier than writing, he maintained, though one was unthinkable without the other.

Whatever his personal "failures" as a crusader in the moral battles of war, his dispatches from Turkey rehearse two particular political beliefs he would express through his writing or in personal interviews all his life: the necessity of national sovereignty and the general failure of politicians to serve people justly due to their pride and folly. Hemingway makes a point of directing much of the responsibility for the chaos in Istanbul in 1922 to the foreign occupation of the city and other "outside" elements rather than to intrinsic qualities of the local Greeks or Turks themselves. In a retrospective dispatch written after his departure he writes about the "most exciting" nightlife of Istanbul as compared to the "the most civilized and amusing" nightlife of Paris, the "most sordid, desperate and vicious" of Berlin, and the "dullest" of Madrid (Hemingway 1985, 517). Excitement in a Hemingway text often means a night out on the town that promises lots of drink and some violence, and the tensions in the city resulted in both, though in this account the terms are comical.

> Constantinople before the Mudiana Armistice was probably the most hectic town in the world. Mustapha Kemal had announced that when he came into town it was going to be shut tight up—and everybody believed him. He had done everything he ever said he would up till then.
>
> Nobody slept much during the day and nobody slept at all during the night . . . the followers of the prophet spent their waking hours trying to make absolutely sure there would be none of the product of Constantinople's Bavarian breweries left to dump into the Golden Horn when Kemal arrived.
>
> The breweries tried to keep pace with the Moslem demand. It was a great race. Along toward evening, the crews of British, American, Spanish, Italian and French fleets would come ashore and rush to the aid of the Mohameddans in their struggle with the breweries. In spite of their small numbers, their organization was better.
>
> As the evening advanced fights would break out among the sailors of the different nationalities in the various Galata beer emporiums. This no doubt slowed up their efficiency . . . All of Constantinople was in a feverish sort of wildness. It had nothing of the sullen ugliness of the Berlin pleasure resorts. (Hemingway 1985, 517–22)

Couched in the logistics of war, the mock-heroic battle unifies Muslims and Christians in their assault on the breweries. The bedlam that is Istanbul results from the efforts of an international, interreligious coalition. Later a captain of a "neutral nation" will give a 3:00 AM order to "commence firing on the city" after drinking "douzico straight" (Hemingway 1985, 323). "Somebody had sense enough to grab him and take him below. Constantinople had been a little too much for him."

While this is a comical rendering of the atmosphere of a city under foreign occupation waiting for Nationalist forces to assault or liberate the capital, depending on one's point of view, other accounts by Americans living in Istanbul at the time, such as the following by one Dr. Gates, also speak of the hectic atmosphere of the city and put the responsibility in the hands of the occupiers.

> The occupation of Constantinople by the Allies brought them no credit. The British, French, and Italians all exercised authority; there was no adequate division of territories or delineation of control, and the result was they worked at cross purposes. They were jealous of one another, each power fearing that the others might gain some advantage in the way of trade or influence. The rivalry of nations found illustration in this situation. Some of the foreign officials were corrupt, bribery was frequent and vice increased. The soldiers—tired of the

13. Occupying forces patrolling Beyoğlu, 1920s; Turkish, Italian, French, and English soldiers under a French officer.

> war—gave themselves to the pleasures of the city, and collisions often took place between soldiers of different nations. The administration of public affairs was worse than it was under the Turks, and the spectacle was saddening to us all. We had hoped for better things. (qtd. in Freely 1996, 230)

Istanbul's suffering is exacerbated, not lessened, under foreign occupation. Hemingway's emphasis on the dangers posed by outside elements is aimed at both illegitimate "jackals" and "legitimate" armies.

In the previously cited dispatch written on his approach to Istanbul through the Balkans, Hemingway speaks of "just wars." Looking out the train window at the "rich, pleasant farming country," he defends a people's desire to go to war first by itemizing concrete images of the land and only then concluding with a reference to geo-politics.

> As you ride through it you can see how the love of the land can make men fight wars. It is a matter of land, of fields of corn and yellowing tobacco, of flocks of sheep and herds of cattle, of heaps of yellow pumpkins in the shocked corn, of beech groves and peat smoke from chimneys, as matter of mine and thine that is the cause of all just wars—and there can never be peace in the Balkans as long as one people holds the lands of another people—no matter what the political excuse may be. (Hemingway 1985, 287)

Hemingway's own intimacy with nature as a hunter and angler would influence his political ideas about the relationship of people to their environment. While the passage of the Balkans may be read as a Romantic, pastoral, and thus naïve rendering of struggles for self-determination, Hemingway would not change his position as he "grew up." Fighting would never lead to a stable peace, Hemingway argued in *Men at War,* "until all *lands* where the people are ruled, exploited and governed by any government whatsoever against their consent are given their freedom" (qtd. in Stephens 1968, 182). This was a mantra he applied to all countries, including Turkey. Hemingway makes his position on the Turkish Independence movement clear in an October 23, 1922, dispatch in which he puts the struggle in the context of foreign interests and foreign interference in the governance of Turkey.

> About two years ago Mustapha Kemal Pasha was denounced by the Earl of Balfour as a common bandit. He was, speaking in the broadest sense, for sale to the

> highest bidder. The French bought him. They supplied him with arms, ammunitions, money. In return, it is rumored they received certain oil concessions in Asia Minor.
>
> The British wanted control in Asia Minor but Kemal did not look like a good buy to them. So they backed the Greeks. The Greeks looked like an excellent bet. But, as several people have remarked in the House of Commons, Mr. Lloyd George backed the wrong horse. (Hemingway 1985, 299–300)

The language is declarative and frank and contrasts with the complexity of the political maneuvering he is glossing. Like the verbal irony that salts the narrative voice in the early fiction, particularly that of *A Farewell to Arms,* there is a gap in this dispatch that is easy to fill between what the correspondent says and what he intends to mean. Borrowing from the discourse of the auction to describe French back room negotiations with the Nationalists, and the discourse of the horse races for British negotiations with the Greeks, Hemingway suggests that while politicians bargain and gamble, people die. The result of these negotiations, which implicate Turkey and Greece in their own entanglements with outside forces, is the Greco-Turkish war.

After having established some of the economic contexts for the war, he moves on to discuss the battle on the ground. His voice changes. The short sentences, which create a glib effect, begin to latch on to each other in a rush of clauses. Urgency replaces irony.

> Kemal whipped the Greeks, as everyone knows. But when you realize he was fighting a conscript army whose soldiers hated the barren country they were fighting to gain, who had been mobilized for nine years, who had no desire as men to conquer Asia Minor, and who were thoroughly fed up and becoming conscious that they were going into battles to die doing a cat's-paw job, it was not the magnificent military achievement that it is made to be. Especially is that shown when you realize that Kemal's troops were fanatical patriots, anxious to drive the invaders out of their country.
>
> The ratio of effectiveness of well-trained, well-armed, highly fanatical patriots fighting in their own country against half-hearted, poorly officered, homesick conscript invaders is somewhere about ten to one. However, when Britain backed the Greeks she did not know the state of efficiency the Kemalists were going to reach. (Hemingway 1985, 300)

Hemingway announces the legitimacy, in his eyes, of the Nationalist movement, a position not necessarily echoed in the cables of other foreign journalists at the time. Just as he supports independence movements in the Balkans against the Ottomans or Europeans, he endorses the independence movement of the Turks against both foreign occupation and the occupation by neighbors supported by those same powers. Turkish patriotism is justifiably fanatical, he suggests: what is barren country to a "half-hearted" and "homesick" "invader" is home to the Turks. Because Hemingway never made it to central Anatolia, he could not describe it as he does the Balkans to the reader, though he may have found it as inhospitable and barren as the Greek soldiers if he did. Love of one's land transcends particular topographies, however, and just as he argues that "there can never be peace in the Balkans as long as one people holds the lands of another people—no matter what the political excuse may be," so does he suggest that the Turks, whatever their imperial past, have a right to fight for self-determination within their own already diminished borders.

But as a man and as someone familiar with soldiering, he empathizes with the actual men fighting on the ground, whichever the side. The Greeks, deceived by their own government, which in turn has allowed itself to be manipulated by foreign influences, are the victims of bad geo-political decisions both home and abroad. While he may pit political leaders against one another in the dispatches, he does not do this with national character or the lives of normal people who are caught up in struggles they cannot control. He may support the Nationalist movement, but he also supports the Greek troops as groups of men rather than as mere appendages of a body politic. He allocates more space in the dispatches to the betrayal of the Greek troops in Anatolia by their own government and their foreign backers than he does to lauding the Kemalist victory. He would rely on eyewitness accounts, or inside stories, of the fighting in Anatolia to express his solidarity with the Greeks as professional soldiers, even if he could not condone their war.

> Might-have-beens are a sad business and the end of the Greek military power is sad enough as it is, but there is no blame for it to be given to the Greek common soldier. Even in the evacuation the Greek soldiers looked like good troops. There was a sturdy doggedness about them that would have meant a hard time for the Turk if Kemal's army would have had to fight for Thrace instead of having it handed to them as a gift at Mudania.

14. Mustafa Kemal, 1920s.

> Captain Wittal of the Indian Calvary, who was attached to the Greek army in Anatolia as an observer during the Greek war with Kemal, told me the inside story of the intrigue that led to the breakdown of the Greek army in Asia Minor.
>
> "The Greek soldiers were first-class fighting men," Captain Wittal said. "They were well officered by men who had served with the British and French in Salonika and they outclassed the Kemalist army. I believe they would have captured Angora and ended the war if they had not been betrayed.
>
> "When Constantine [after Venizelos] came into power all the officers of the army were suddenly scrapped, from the commander-in-chief down to the platoon commanders. These officers had many of them been promoted from the ranks, were good soldiers and splendid leaders. They were removed and their places filled with new officers of the Trio [Constantine] party, most of whom had spent the war in Switzerland or Germany and had never heard a shot fired. That caused a complete breakdown of the army and was responsible for the Greek defeat. (November 3, 1922; Hemingway 1985, 316)

Just as he expresses pity for the suffering refugees, he feels sympathy for the Greek soldiers. Captain Wittal's account would reappear fourteen years later in the memories of the dying and hallucinating Harry in "The Snows of Kilimanjaro":

> That same night he left for Anatolia and he remembered, later on that trip, riding all day through fields of poppies that they raised for opium and how strange it made you feel, finally, and all the distances seemed wrong, to where they had made the attack with the newly arrived Constantine officers, that did not know a god-damned thing, and the artillery had fired into the troops and the British observer had cried like a child. (Hemingway 1987, 48)

Hemingway would always criticize the pride of politicians and the adverse effects of their incompetence on the lives of normal people entrusted to their care. While this is already evident in the dispatches, Hemingway would later say that discussions over brandy with a South African journalist, William Bolitho Ryall, writing for the *Manchester Guardian* at the Lausanne Conference, "were the beginning of whatever education I received in international politics" (Mellow 1992, 203). He was impressed by Ryall's views on "the malady of power," or as Mellow points out, his version of "Lord Acton's dictum that 'all power corrupts and absolute power corrupts absolutely" (Mellow 1992, 203–4). Hemingway would mock the leaders of countries participating in the Lausanne conference in an acerbic poem, "They All Made Peace," published in the *Little Review* in the spring of 1923. No one, neither Turk nor Greek, neither Britain nor Russian escapes ridicule:

> All of the Turks are gentlemen and Ismet Pasha is a little
> deaf. But the Armenians. How about the Armenians?
> Well the Armenians.
> Lord Curzon likes young boys.
> So does Chicherin.
> So does Mustapha Kemal. He is good looking too. His eyes
> are too close together but he makes war. That is the way
> he is.
> . . .
> Well what do you boys know this morning?
> Oh they're shrewd. They're shrewd.
> Who have we got in on the subcommission this morning,
> Admiral?
> M. Stamuliski walks up the hill and down the hill. Don't talk about
> M. Venizelos. He is wicked. You can see it. His beard
> shows it.
> . . .
> Then there is Mosul
> And the Greek Patriarch
> What about the Greek Patriarch?
>
> HEMINGWAY 1979, 63–64

Influenced in style by Gertrude Stein's disjointed and teasing experiments in modernism, and probably, as Mellow suggests, alcohol, the poem is as much a satire on news-speak and the business of news gathering as it is on the subjects catalogued. Hemingway mixes the high and the low, grave political and social disasters with gossip about the sexual preferences of powerful leaders. The Armenians are suing for statehood; there are secret deals going on for oil in Mosul; and the Greek Patriarch of Smyrna had been hung by the Turks (Mellow 1992, 217). Subcommissions representing men of questionable ethics—as elsewhere Hemingway associates homosexuality with moral deviance—meet behind secret doors. Nobody is innocent in the cynical eyes of the narrator, and the conference, depicted here through infantile phrasing, seems more a circus than a meeting of nations come together to determine the future of vast regions of the world.

Whatever his disillusion over the war in Asia Minor and with its leading parties, Hemingway's experiences in Istanbul would nevertheless furnish material for his future fiction. The Greco-Turkish war would provide the frame for his first collection of stories, *In Our Time,* published in 1925. "On the Quai at Smyrna," which opens the collection, is a highly abstract account of a British Navy officer who witnesses the consequences of Allied political miscalculations from the safe distance of his ship as Turkish soldiers and civilians take revenge on Greek and Armenian men, women, and children. As thousands of fleeing minorities drown in the harbor, the British fleet, ordered to remain neutral, look on and help no one. Matthew Stewart's very good reading of Hemingway's depiction of the tragedy in "It Was All a Pleasant Business; The Historical Context of 'On the Quai at Smyrna'" (2003) argues that the writer, although he never visited Smyrna as a young correspondent, was very aware of the magnitude of the human disaster. Chapter 2 of *In Our Time* begins with a description of the Thrace evacuation; chapter 5 begins with a short account of the shooting of six Greek cabinet ministers. L'Envoi, which concludes the book, features the last Greek King and Queen imprisoned in their garden by the revolutionary committee, drinking whiskey and soda and commenting politely on the usefulness of political assassination and immigration to America. The "forewards" read like snapshots and frame the life of Hemingway's recurring protagonist Nick Adams from childhood to adulthood. Besides appearing in the dying man's last thoughts in "The Snows of Kilimanjaro," his Turkish experiences are what furnish the material for the war scenes in *A Farewell to Arms,* according to Robert O. Stephens (Stephens 1968, 258). Hemingway's service in Italy was too brief and late for him to have witnessed the scenes depicted in the novel. What he learned about retreats and evacuations he had learned in Thrace. It is certainly true that Hemingway the creative writer went to school to journalism. But it is also true that Hemingway's early experiences as a journalist would furnish material for his fiction, just as his early devotion to telling the truth would impel him to transmit historical information through fictional means.

4

Orient Express

John Dos Passos, American Socialism, and the War of Independence in Turkey

> There are reasons for learning Turkish.
>
> —*Orient Express,* 16

FOR MANY, John Dos Passos still represents the better novelists of social protest in the United States. Due to the heady but dubious reputation of leftist literature as art in North America, it is understandable that writers like Dos Passos, who applied their creative energies to social progressivism in the early twentieth century and have remained central to the literary canon into the twenty-first century, should be acknowledged for their national literary achievements. And yet, like many of our celebrated national writers, Dos Passos's life and writings are more international in scope and consequence then we tend to acknowledge. And like the other canonical writers discussed in the present text, Dos Passos traveled as far as Istanbul in search of intelligence that could be applied within his own national borders. The twenty-five-year-old writer brought a youthful Harvard and Greenwich Village socialist agenda with him to Turkey in 1921. He left with a notebook full of piquant verbal sketches, stirring anecdotes, and journalistic reports perhaps more controversial now, three-quarters of a century later, than when he first recorded them at the front of one of Europe's most furious postwar conflicts.

Critics tend to describe Dos Passos's visit to the Near and Middle East as a vacation from his real life in the United States, a journey through "exotic lands," a hiatus from Western reality that had little to do with his past or future literary production (Rosen 1981, 29). This says more, of course, about the critics'

15. A 1920s poster advertising the Orient Express.

dearth of information about the region than of Dos Passos's experience there. It also suggests that critics underestimate both the writer's own comprehension, or desire for comprehension, of the liminal topographies of Western Christendom and empire and the representation of that experience in his writing. This positing of Dos Passos's Near East journey as peripheral to his project that was America is in keeping with a general glossing over of his life abroad by nearly everyone but those who discuss his time in a more familiar Spain, or by biographers who are obliged to record all his journeys outside the United States. Fellow writers and friends of the "lost generation" such as Ernest Hemingway and F. Scott Fitzgerald are often discussed in the context of foreign cultures and climates because of the continental wars, sport, and society that figure in their novels and short stories. Discussions of Dos Passos, however, tend to confine him to America because of his compulsory role as modernist spokesman of the active political left and critic of industrial capitalism in his earlier work. His later focus on the early founders of the American Republic in a number of biographies has also worked to seal his reputation in the popular consciousness as a writer concerned only with the fate of his own nation.

Born in Chicago in 1896, Dos Passos, despite his denizen American reputation, spent the first eleven years of his life mostly in Brussels and London, where his mother had moved to be near his father, a wealthy man of Portuguese decent whose business involved trust and corporate law and often took him to Europe. Though Dos Passos had been born illegitimately, his parents would be married upon the death of his father's first wife in 1911. Graduating early at the age of fifteen from a preparatory school in Connecticut, he was sent with a tutor in 1911 on a Grand Tour of Europe and Egypt. In February 1912, "Jack" and his tutor, whom he referred to in letters home as "Uncle Virgil," made an unscheduled visit to Constantinople where they stayed for four days in the Pera Palace, the hotel where the writer would again be based on his second visit to the city nine years later (Carr 1984, 42). Dos Passos would continue to travel extensively, particularly in his earlier years. He studied architecture in Spain after his graduation from Harvard in 1917, and then from 1917 to 1918 joined the Norton-Harjes Ambulance Corps in France, "the most distinguished of all the lost generation's finishing schools," and later the American Red Cross ambulance unit in wartime Italy (Kazin 1974, 105). Though he was an avowed pacifist, had spent much time protesting the war, and initially admired Woodrow Wilson, whom he believed was trying to keep the United States out of the European conflict, he followed on the heels of the first convoy of American combat troops to France. As his biographer Virginia Spencer Carr notes, had he not decided to join the ambulance service, despite his "horror of serving in the army," he would probably have been arrested and prosecuted under the Espionage Act of June 15, 1917 (Carr 1984,

120). Or worse, he might have been drafted. "To gain support for war," Dos Passos writes later in *Mr. Wilson's War* (1962), Wilson "had unleashed blind hatred, suspicions about foreigners and foreign ideas . . . used suppressive measures to weaken 'progressive movements,'" ordering, for example, "2000 prosecutions of socialists, pacifists, syndicalists" (Dos Passos 1962, 433–34). He would say of his pending journey to France: "I don't believe in the 'spiritual good' of war and I expect to have a hell of a time until I get accustomed to taking ambulance loads of pulverized people about" (Carr 1984, 122).

After the Armistice in 1919, Dos Passos applied and was accepted to the Sorbonne in a study-abroad program sponsored by the Army Overseas Educational Commission, despite his family's remonstrances that he come back to the United States and get a real job (Carr 1984, 161). While in Paris he worked on his novel *Three Soldiers,* considered later by many to be one of the most realistic representations of war by an American writer to date because, as noted by one friend, it "tweaked self-righteous America by the nose" (Frederick van den Arend, qtd. in Carr 1984, 186). Later that year he would go back to Spain as a correspondent for a British labor paper. After finishing *Three Soldiers* he decided to quit the New York literary scene before the book appeared, boarding a Portuguese steamer with his friend E. E. Cummings in the spring of 1921 to do a walking tour in Spain and work on his collection of travel essays, *Rosinante to the Road Again* (1922). It is then that Dos Passos began thinking about returning to Istanbul. The opportunity arose when he made plans to meet in Turkey a former artillery captain, Paxton Hibben, whom he had met originally in New York and again later in Paris. A diplomat, foreign correspondent, and writer, Hibben was now secretary for the Russian Committee of the Near East Relief, organized by the Red Cross in 1920, and was on his way to observe the conditions in the Russian Provinces of the Eastern Black Sea region (Carr 1984, 179). Dos Passos also hoped to get a post with the Near East Relief in order to travel into Russia and en route revisit the city he had seen briefly nineteen years before. After Turkey and Russia, he would travel on to the Middle East.

Orient Express would be the literary outcome of this trip to the Near and Middle East. It is also the product of a young man whose family history and private political convictions had nurtured in him an interest in independence movements wherever he experienced them in the world. A collection of travel narratives, *Orient Express* is also a collection of critical assessments of the social tensions and tragedies that continued in the region after the Armistice. It is the record of a journey that takes him into the heart of occupied Constantinople, into its elegant hotel lobbies, modest cafés, open-air cabarets, mosques, tennis clubs, and crowded streets. It records the conflict from a haunting distance off the coast of Trabzon on the Turkish Black Sea coast. It then takes us beyond Turkey to the Caucasus in the aftermath of the Soviet conquest, to Persia during the rise of the Reza Khan, and then to the creation of Iraq by the British. In the book's climactic ending Dos Passos joins a camel caravan of nomadic Arabs traveling from Baghdad to Damascus. These unbound men will prove the final champions in a text peopled by groups and individuals who suffer varying degrees of repressive economic and social conditions. He would conclude that the nomads are "the finest people I have ever known. I felt like kissing their feet I was so fussy and gawky beside them" (letter to Ramsey Marvin, January 10, 1922; qtd. in Carr 1984, 185).

Before leaving New York Dos Passos had acquired press credentials from *Metropolitan Magazine* and the *New York Tribune* by committing himself to write articles for each, though he would ultimately feel disingenuous in his role as roving international journalist: "I'm no more a journalist than I am a guinea pig," he says in a letter after three months in the Middle East, "and the sooner I go home and get to work writing and stop playing Richard Harding Davis the better" (Carr 1984, 180). Writing to another friend from Tehran, Dos Passos would use the image of the dervish, "the symbol of mystery errant on the face of the world," a vagrant personage he encountered in Turkey and various other Muslim countries along his route, to describe further his discomfort with journalism as a means of travel (Dos Passos 1927, 103):

> I've decided that this wandering about the world's hotels is a low form of existence . . . If one's got to travel, one should have the courage of one's convictions, take a staff and begging bowl and a jar of hashish like a proper dervish and a fig for the city-bred world . . . one comes into contact with nobody but personages, chamber maids and drummers. (Carr 1984, 183)

He nevertheless opted for more a worldly mode of existence in Turkey, Russia, and the Middle East, despite his bohemian convictions. He would also publish articles based on his travels in U.S. journals such as *The Freeman* (October 5,

1921) and *Asia* (April and June, 1922) in order to help finance his wandering. He would eventually collect these articles and the diary entries that he saved, revise them, and then publish them in 1927 under the title *Orient Express.*

Dos Passos's uneasiness with his privileged status as a press-credentialed "Eastbound American," or "EA," as he ironically refers to himself throughout the text, is not simply the result of his natural humility or bourgeois anxiety—though these were certainly character qualities of his youth—but rather a manifestation of the socialist convictions he had acquired as a student at Harvard. As the son of a wealthy capitalist whom he admired even if he disagreed with his theory of economics, Dos Passos became increasingly involved with the ideological movement against "the traditional" brewing on the Ivy League campus. Though initially less outspoken than his classmate and friend E. E. Cummings, Dos Passos, as a contributor to *Harvard Monthly,* used fictional devices to criticize surreptitiously what he considered (and would continue to believe for as long as his political principles remained on the left) were the two main American vices of his day: unregulated business and the genteel tradition, both the results of industrial capitalism. He would become convinced that the American administration's main reason for entering World War I was to repress the socialist revolution in Europe and prevent it from traveling to the United States (Lee 1987, 177). Later, as a young writer in Greenwich Village, and before going to Europe as an ambulance driver, he cultivated his college convictions, sitting around his first apartment at 15 East Thirty-third Street on Turkish carpets, arguing "socialist doctrine and talk of revolution" with friends "over wine and Turkish coffee" (qtd. in Carr 1984, 118).

Having rejected his father's estate upon the latter's death—"I hate money more than ever. I feel like taking a cockle and script, giving my goods to the poor and my body to be burned, and making a pilgrimage to Jerusalem . . . A constant stripping process is needed before one can live naked and clean—in the full blast of experience"—the American bohemian adds this political angle to his experimentation with asceticism: "Even if I did survive [the war] the Revolution would sweep away stocks and bonds, landed interests, property rights . . . 'Naked I came into the world' was my motto (qtd. in Carr 1984, 118). Exaggerated rumors abounded for years that he had rejected a million dollar estate. It was in fact much less than that, and Dos Passos would spend the rest of his life worrying about money, often in the form of debts to friends. For the moment, however, he was a staunch supporter of Emma Goldman and May Eastman, vocal conscientious objectors to America's entry into the war, which in the opinion of the left was a capitalist action (Carr 1984, 119). He read *The Masses* until it was banned by the government, its editors charged with "conspiring to obstruct the draft" (Carr 1984, 119). Mocking his youthful political idealism in a later memoir, he says of the spring of 1917 that "some people," including himself, "caught socialism the way others caught the flu" (qtd. in Carr 1984, 119).

> In Russia the Revolution had put an end to war. It was the red dawn of an era of peace, freedom and justice. The Russians were socialists. It was socialists who had taken action to stop the butchery. Suddenly I believed I was a socialist. Even then I think I marveled a little at the suddenness with which passionate convictions develop in the youthful mind. It was a contagion. (qtd. in Carr 1984, 119)

To read Dos Passos's later judgments of his early leftism is as misleading as reading his right-wing critics in the 1920s and 1930s. The argument is grounded in an ideological stance that disallows an impartial consideration of, in this case, his own motives at the time. His direct experience of socialist revolution in Europe and Russia would certainly destroy forever his trust in party socialism. As most critics seem to agree, however, his early leftist passion would be the compelling force behind his best writing, including *Manhattan Transfer* (1925), the *U.S.A.* trilogy (1938), and, as I will suggest here, his early collection of politically motivated travel texts, *Orient Express.*

Dos Passos's final disillusionment with the Communist Party would not come until a late 1930s trip to Spain where he had gone to work with Ernest Hemingway (and Archibald MacLeish and Lillian Hellman) on a film promoting the cause of the Loyalists against Franco's Fascist rebellion in the Spanish civil war. The mounting brutality of the Loyalist's methods of maintaining order, including the murder of Dos Passos's friend José Robles, ostensibly for being a "fascist spy," not only created a rift in the long friendship between Dos Passos, who believed in the loyalty of Robles, and Hemingway, who went along with the story from the Kremlin, but it also turned Dos Passos once and for all against the socialism that Stalinism had irrevocably and inevitably (as he would later believe) destroyed (Rosen 1981, 107; Carr 1984, 367). In *The Adventures of a Young Man* (1939), Dos Passos would depict a labor organizer disappointed by the party exploiting workers for propaganda. But Dos Passos's socialism was still fervent enough in the 1920s that Edmund Wilson, a fellow critic of industrial capitalism and its accompanying genteel sensibilities, could write of *Manhattan Transfer* in 1929, "Dos Passos is, one gathers from his work, a social revolutionist: he believes that, in the United States as elsewhere, the present capitalist regime is destined to be overthrown by a class-conscious proletariat" (Wilson 1952, 431). Wilson, however, does not trust Dos Passos's zeal:

> His bias against the economic system is so strong that it extends beyond its official representation to all those human beings whose only fault is to have been born where such a system prevails and to be so lacking in courage or perspicacity as not to have allied themselves with the forces that are trying to fight it . . . There are moments in reading a novel or seeing a play by Dos Passos when one finds oneself ready to rush to the defense of even the American bathroom. (Wilson 1952, 432)

Wilson can nonetheless conclude his essay on Dos Passos with the following endorsement of the writer's commitment to social and political reform.

> It is true that the lack of real leadership is felt by us today as a stone. It is Dos Passos' recognition of this—his relentless reiteration of his conviction that there is something lacking, something wrong, in America—as well as his insistence on the importance of America—that give his work its vitality and power . . . Dos Passos is now almost alone among the writers of his generation in continuing to take the social organism seriously. (Wilson 1952, 434–35)

Alfred Kazin perhaps comes closest to identifying Dos Passos's particular variety of socialism in his 1942 essay "Dos Passos, Society and the Individual." Considering Dos Passos as the literary link between the aestheticism and individualism of the postwar decade—the inward-looking "lost generation"—and the "crisis" or social novelists of the depression period, Kazin sees in Dos Passos's work a "conviction of tragedy" that is "the steady protest of a sensitive democratic conscience against the tyranny and the ugliness of society" (Kazin 1974, 102). Kazin, like other mid-twentieth-century American critics of Dos Passos, makes a move to distance the writer from Marxist ideology. This says as much about the cultural climate of the cold war in the United States as it does about the critics' weakness for taking the writer at his revised word. But despite the obvious pressures to recast the writer's past, Kazin is right to argue that Dos Passos, from the beginning of his initiation into political thinking, had mixed feelings about the role of the individual in his struggle for self-determination. Dos Passos "comes closer to socialism than most artists in his generation; yet it is significant that no novelist in America has written more somberly of the dangers to individual integrity in a centrally controlled society" (Kazin 1974, 103–4). He is "saved" from the folly of leftist party politics, because his concern is with the "primacy of the individual," the human self that is, argues Kazin, the Emersonian individual. While Dos Passos, in his early years, was more an adherent of Marxist collectivism than Emersonian individualism, it is nonetheless right to say that Dos Passos in his writing tends to posit the individual as someone who needs to be saved from his society rather than to be established "in or over it" (Kazin 1974, 104). While his primary complaint is "against the failure of a complete human development under industrial capitalism," his writing in the 1920s and 1930s narrates his opposition to all forms of "degradation" in the operations of societies or systems (Kazin 1974, 102).

IT IS THIS "sensitive democratic consciousness," developed at Harvard, tested in wartime Europe and intensified in Greenwich village, that Dos Passos brings to Turkey in 1921. Like his friend Hemingway, who would come to Istanbul the following year as a reporter for the *Toronto Star,* Dos Passos brought his American biases with him, and in his case, his sympathies would lie with those he read as the social underdogs of Turkey at that historical moment. The subjects that concern him in Istanbul in 1921 are the same that concern him in New York: on one hand economic entitlement, the culture it glorifies, and the rule of "Things"; on the other, economic insecurity and the anger, anxiety, and resentment it fosters. What is added to *Orient Express* is a severe critique of the chauvinism and economic misery that result from wars of imperialism, in this case those of the Eastern and Western Europeans.

What differentiates this "nonfictional" text from his earlier and later fiction and nonfiction is at once its maturity and its freshness. More formally sophisticated than his first collection of travel essays about Spain, *Rosinante to the Road Again,* Dos Passos does not sacrifice the distinctive contours and colors of people and places in *Orient Express* to the ideological determinism characteristic of his later fiction. There is a sense of play in the text that is absent in later work, a sense that the writer acknowledges, however irreverently, the value of aesthetics in the struggle for social and political reform. With only an informed tourist's knowledge about the historical facts of the disintegrating Ottoman Empire, Dos Passos can only offer the reader what he sees and hears, and these he inscribes with precision. What he is looking and listening for are certainly things that strike him as familiar. And what is familiar to him in Istanbul, not surprisingly, are the enormous disparities between those who have and those who have not. Yet his representative images are not emptied out in the service of this idea, but enhanced for the sake of veracity.

Calling *Orient Express* an "impressionistic record" of Dos Passos's "travels through exotic lands," Robert C. Rosen in *John Dos Passos: Politics and the Writer,* complains that the text's approach to its cultural subject is "rarely analytic, sometimes intuitive, and often simply a recording of details "(Rosen 1981, 30). He adds further that "unlike *Rosinante to the Road Again,* it draws few conclusions: there is no search for the soul of the region, no detailed analysis of political forces." It is because Dos Passos avoids drawing conclusions and does not search for the soul of the region—a Romantic understanding of travel and topography that would not appeal to the modernist—that the text is successful. Rosen does not allow the nonfictional travel text the same aesthetic flexibility as the fiction, although it is precisely its unconventional style that makes it interesting as travel literature. The chapter on Istanbul opens with the following kaleidoscopic sentence, whose images deduce less about what an onlooker might intellectually grasp of the city at first glance than how he might ready the particular kind of liberal, nonfiltering gaze the city will demand of him if he is to see anything at all.

> Under my window a dusty rutted road with here and there a solitary paving-stone over which carts jolt and jingle continually, climbing jerkily to Pera, rumbling down towards the old bridge, all day long from dawn to dusk; beyond, tall houses closer packed than New York houses even, a flat roof where a bare-legged girl hangs out laundry, and across the red tiles the dusty cypresses of a cemetery, masts, and the Golden Horn, steel coloured, with steamers at anchor; and further, against the cloudy sky, Stamboul, domes, brown-black houses, bright minarets set about everywhere like the little ivory men on a cribbage board. (Dos Passos 1927, 11–12)

Preparing his reader for the point of view the text creates in order to keep up with Istanbul, the opening lines are a postimpressionist vision of a subject: sketches from multiple, simultaneous perspectives. Using a painterly technique applied to language and narrative by many early modernists such as James Joyce, Gertrude Stein, and Ezra Pound, Dos Passos, a younger, more unambiguously socially oriented writer, adopts this modernist technique for political purposes in *Orient Express*. He replaces or displaces a centralized narrator with a chorus of narrators or perspectives in order to offer a multifarious reading that is also a democratic vision of self-representation, an ethic and aesthetic that characterizes his most important fiction. This initial surfeit of urban sounds and scenes is a taste of what will follow in the narrative: it lays out the intricate cosmopolitanism that is threatened as well as threatening, as Turkey makes the difficult transition from empire to republic.

When "two tall men with gaudy turbans round their fezzes come out of a lane leading a monkey," the tune they play on a bagpipe and tambourine is "the very soul of the monkey's listless irregular walk" (Dos Passos 1927, 12). While no intervening interpretation is offered, when the city—the "carters," "beggars," and "waiters"—stops for a moment to watch and "the two men with the monkey thump their tambourine in derision and swagger away," the reader is left with a complex of images and postures that will make some, but not complete, sense retrospectively (Dos Passos 1927, 12). The carnivalesque is made particularly grotesque by the suffering of the enchained monkey; insolent and arrogant the fanciful masters of the monkey—most likely the gypsies that have always been an integral part of Istanbul's population—are described in terms that will resurface in the context of ethnic superciliousness and military occupation further on in the chapter. Rather than a mere "impressionistic" description of an "exotic" scene, offering "no detailed analysis of political forces," Dos Passos in fact writes a subtle critique of the postwar occupation of Istanbul by European powers (Rosen 1981, 30). The text will also offer negative portrayals of certain minority groups, ethnic and economic, within Ottoman society that, in his eyes, fear the coming of Mustafa Kemal's troops to Constantinople because they, like the Czarists whom they are made to resemble in the text, regard the establishment of a populist government as a threat to their privileged mode of life.

This exterior street sketch is immediately juxtaposed with an interior hotel lobby drama at the Pera Palace where Dos Passos had stayed at sixteen on his first

16. Pera Palace Hotel, 1920s.

visit to Istanbul in 1912 and where he stayed now at twenty-five. Situated in a quarter of the city housing most foreign embassies, Pera as an international district with a large concentration of Ottoman Greeks and Armenians is, as the young writer knows, an ideal place to observe the crisis in the Ottoman Empire at its nerve center. In half a page, Dos Passos introduces many of the players implicated in the political intrigue and social uncertainty that plague postwar Constantinople.

> Downstairs in the red plush lobby of the Pera Palace there is scuttling and confusion. They are carrying out a man in a frock-coat who wears on his head a black astrakhan cap. There's blood in the red plush arm-chair; there's blood on the mosaic floor. The manager walks back and forth with sweat standing out on his brow; they can mop up the floor, but the chair is ruined. French, Greek and Italian gendarmes swagger about talking all together each in his own language. The poor bloke's dead, sir, says the British military policeman to the colonel who doesn't know whether to finish his cocktail or not. Azerbaijan. Azerbaijan. He was the envoy from Azerbaijan. An Armenian, a man with a beard, stood in the doorway and shot him. A man with glasses and a smooth chin, A Bolshevik spy, walked right up to him and shot him. The waiter who brings drinks from the bar is in despair. The drinkers have all left without paying. (*Orient Express*, 12–13)

The "Armenian" issue, a determinedly imprecise euphemism still used today to avoid placing blame for the unresolved problem of the Armenian diaspora that began during World War I, is central to Dos Passos's Turkish chapters in *Orient Express.* What is particularly interesting about his treatment of the problem, which continues to unfold while he is there, is his attempt to record the collision of peoples, who for centuries had lived together, from multiple angles, the guiding perspective of the narrative as a whole. Thus we are introduced to the political tensions between the Armenians and Azerbaijanis at Baku who had made opposing alliances during and then after the war: the Armenians with the Allied Forces and then some with the White Guard against Bolshevik rule and some with the Bolsheviks, and the Azerbaijani with the Ottoman Forces who had chosen to fight on the side of the Germans partly to prevent Russian expansion into Turkey.

The murder, depicted by its effects on the furniture and clientele, is particularly interesting because it illustrates the confusion of allegiances that characterizes the period and place. As power changed hands from Ottoman to Allied, with the Kemalist Nationalists fighting both, minority populations with histories that preceded the Ottoman Empire began to reconsider their loyalties and options. Armenians who had sided with the winning Allied forces against the Ottomans were isolated and vulnerable communities in the Eastern provinces during and after the war, where Turkish forces and civilians could carry out what they defined as reprisals for Armenian violence against Turks. Dos Passos makes no attempt to analyze the deep-seated trouble that results in the killing of thousands of people on all sides; rather, six pages and many fragmented scenes later, he includes a letter under the subtitle "Assassination" that forces the reader back to page twelve if she desires a context for the sudden intertext, and then to consider, yet again, how individual lives, whether Turkish, Armenian, or Russian, are degraded and destroyed by the operations of societies and systems. Similar to the "newsreel" technique he will push to its abstract extreme in *U.S.A.*, Dos Passos allows letter extracts written by the Russian wife of the murdered Azerbaijani—an envoy from the first Azerbaijani Republic—and published in the *Presse du Soir* to speak for themselves with no interference, save for their existence in a text that highlights the dubious nature of war in the service of suspect economic and political gains.

> I the undersigned . . . trust to your kindness for the publication of certain facts which will put an end, I hope, to the false rumors that are attainting the dead man's good name.
>
> I have never been separated from my husband and God has made me witness of all the horror of these last years.
>
> March, 1918. The wreck of the Russian army crawling back from the Turkish front. At Baku the power is in the hands of the Armenians who have adopted the Bolshevist platform. By order of no one knows who, according to a prearranged plan, there is organized a massacre of the Muslim population.
>
> Never till my last breath shall I forget those terrible days. They were tracking my husband . . .
>
> Months passed. Power changed hands, and my husband was called to the post of Minister of the Interior in the first Azerbaidjan Cabinet. Turkish detachments draw near to Baku and again, before they reach the town, the bloody happenings of September are unrolled. It was a terrible reply of the Muslims to the March massacres.
>
> My husband hastens to Baku to put an end to these riots, but by the time he arrives the wave of national hatred has subsided. National hate gives way to class hate; the Bolsheviki aspire towards power and the local population, tired of national and religious strife, see in the Reds a neutral force. (Dos Passos 1927, 19–20)

Going on to recount the arrival of her and her husband in Constantinople where he had been offered a post in the commissariat of foreign affairs, and then murdered in the lobby of the Pera Palace by a member of his own "Mousavat" party for allegedly betraying his companions, the wife is a suffering witness to the infighting that further exacerbates hostilities in the war-torn provinces. Her letter is offered as one of a number of ways to read the Armenians' troubled fight for nationhood in a text that, because of the diversity of views offered, seems to privilege none.

Itself a *tribune libre* for views on the political ruptures and changes in what is left of the Ottoman Empire, *Orient Express* regularly creates space for conflicting points of view (Dos Passos 1927, 18). The first Armenians we meet are on the Orient Express train itself as Dos Passos makes his way through the Balkans toward Constantinople. The contrast between the profiles of the two men speaks of the extreme experience of a people:

> An egg-shaped Armenian from New York who was brought up at the monastery of San Lazzaro in Venice, studied painting at Asolo, hates priests, clergymen and Balkan cooking and talks plaintively of Tiffany's and old Martin's restaurant on Twenty-eighth Street; there's another Armenian whose mother, father and three sisters were cut up into little pieces before his eyes by the Turks in Trebizond. (Dos Passos 1927, 9)

Later in the chapter "One Hundred Views of Ararat," which takes Dos Passos into the Caucasus, Christian and Muslim opinions and allegiances are contextualized. Small groups of Turks tell of the "atrocities of the Armenians and the sufferings of the Muslims" while an Armenian whom he speaks with in "ragged French and even raggeder English" tells him of the "frightful things the Turks and Tartars had done" (Dos Passos 1927, 73). When they come to the frontier of Armenia and Azerbaijan, "as usual there is no house standing in the town. The Muslims say it was destroyed by the Armenians, and the Armenians that the Turks did the job" (Dos Passos 1927, 73). In the aftermath of so much destruction, objective reality has given way to constructed opinion. Blood allegiances are drawn down lines of faith. Doing in these passages what he does best in his later fiction, Dos Passos relates individuals to their environment, and then subsumes both to the pressures and movements of history (Lee 1987, 176). The result is a dialectic that locates reality beyond the effects of history, because these effects, these reciprocal killings and then the conflicting interpretations of them, are the results of forces that are operating above and beyond local ethnic grudges.

Dos Passos follows this exchange of conflicting accounts with a scene of a woman dying of typhus; it becomes an existential commentary on the futility of ethnic rivalry:

> Then they bring her out and lay her on a little piece of red and yellow carpet beside the railroad track. She is a Russian. Her husband, a lean Mohammedan with a scrabbly beard, sits beside her, occasionally stroking her cheek with a furtive animal gesture" (Dos Passos 1927, 73)

Within twenty lines that describe in rapid and vivid succession the colors of the woman's dying face, the composition of the landscape—the sun "sinking in crimson fury behind Ararat"—the woman lies dead "on the red and yellow mat beside the track." Nature goes about its dramatic but routine business as

Muslims and Christians suffer and die together. The repeated image of what may be a prayer rug—its red and its yellow echo strangely—suggests upsurges of the imagism that animates Dos Passos's prose. It seems the metaphorical equivalent of something modest but beautiful in the couple's union; free of sentimentality, the image nevertheless captures the bitter sadness of their parting. The husband's gesture contrasts with the accusatory language that precedes it: it is a gesture of compassion and fear in the face of the death that is visiting Muslim and Christian, man and wife.

In the next section, the narrator finally breaks through the surface of the text with what strikes one as an exasperated need to name names in the Armenian crisis. Dos Passos's traveling companion, as well as his principal speaker throughout the Russian and Persian sections of the text, is "the Sayyid," a Persian. As the Sayyid here holds forth on his Pan-Islamic agenda, the Eastbound American, suffering from the heat, narrates his own thoughts in cynical, fiery, hallucinatory succession:

> Armenia. A second's glimpse of a war map with little flags, Russian, Turkish, British. What a fine game it is. The little flags move back and forth. Livelier than chess. Then the secret intelligence map. Such extraordinary cleverness. We'll exploit the religion of A to make him fight B; we'll buy up the big men of D so that they'll attack A in the rear; then when everybody's down we'll neatly carve up the map. The flies are droning: "Carve dat turkey, carve him to de heart." Call the sections Armenians, Georgians, Assyrians, Turks, Kurds. But somehow, when everybody is down, they can't find the carving knife. So everybody just stays down, and when they get tired of massacring each other they find they are starving. And death and desert encroach, encroach. Where last year was a wheat-field, this year is a patch of thistles, and next year not even thistles will grow there. And the peasants are beggars or bandits. And that's all there is of the map game in the East for the present. (Dos Passos 1927, 77)

Dos Passos names no names, but certain culprits are clear: foreign powers, as well as the Ottomans whom they now "manage," are the forces operating above and beyond the civil wars erupting in the Near East. Divide and conquer is the exported game plan and Dos Passos will agree with the Sayyid who argues in the next paragraph that the foreigners who exploit people and then hunt them as bandits must be driven out so that nations may organize themselves. While he does not agree with the Pan-Islamic component of the Sayyid's argument, he suggests, though only obliquely here, that any organizing principle that might replace foreign or imperial occupation must be one like the Bolshevik's socialist plan, which unlike the Pan-Islamic plan is pragmatic and transnational, at least in theory (Dos Passos 1927, 44–45).

Members of the Allied forces occupying Constantinople during Dos Passos's sojourn there, the representatives of the "we" in the above passage, saunter and "swagger" through the Constantinople chapter much like the men leading the monkey on a leash in the opening section. Present at the Pera Palace when the murder takes place—one superior, the British colonel, not knowing "whether to finish his cocktail or not"—the Allied gendarme is not so much a collection of individuals in the text as an amorphous extension of oppressive political bodies. When the Inter-Allied police forces are given specific features, they often mock that body:

> There are two Italian gendarmes with shiny three-cornered hats and buttons on their coat-tails, some British military policemen with hard red necks, French flics with the whiskers familiar to Paris cartoonists . . . all red faced and sweaty from their rounds. (Dos Passos 1927, 29)

But they are never given individual voices. They seem puppets, their strings manipulated from the Pera embassies whose officials in turn answer to London, Paris, or Rome.

In *Mr. Wilson's War,* Dos Passos writes of the Machiavellian role played by the British vis-à-vis the Ottomans during World War I:

> Even the humblest clerk [in the British Foreign Office] knew that the Foreign secretary was busy day and night tempting the Italians, the Greeks and the Bulgarians into the war on the Allied side with promises of hunks of Austrian, Hungarian and Turkish territory. (Dos Passos 1962, 121)

And further along the older Dos Passos notes ways in which the British were inciting the Ottoman provinces to revolt, less in support of local independence movements than in preparation for their own colonial expansion in the region:

> The Turks lacked money and munitions and the will to fight . . . Romantic British agents like Philby and Lawrence were lashing up the Bedoins to revolt . . .

> In the Aegean the Turkish rule was threatened by the Greeks whom the British were cautiously arming under Venizelos. (Dos Passos, 314)

The Ottomans would become the "monkey" of foreign masters after their defeat, and it would be the "listless . . . wheezing" of those in power that would rouse Mustafa Kemal, formerly a commander in the Ottoman army and the leader of the Turkish Nationalist Movement in Anatolia, to take up arms against his own government and those of the occupying armies. On a ship going to Russia via the Caucasus, Dos Passos meets "six Turkish army doctors in uniform" on their way to join the Nationalist movement in Ankara (Dos Passos 1927, 36). They are "worried about the Greek cruiser *Chilkis* that was sinking fishing-boats and taking potshots at villages along the [Turkish Black Sea] Coast." Once again, Dos Passos opens the text to voices that tell a version of the Turkish story, this time a populist, nationalist, if not chauvinist version that he has saved for the end of his journey through Constantinople.

> "You Europeans are all hypocrites. When Turkish soldiers get out of hand and kill a few Armenians who are spies and traitors, you roll your eyes and cry massacre; but when the Greeks burn defenseless villages and murder poor fishermen, it's making the world safe for democracy."
>
> "I'm not a European, I'm an American."
>
> "We believed your Meester Veelson . . . All we want is to be left alone and organize our country in peace. If you believed in the rights of small nations, why did you let the British set the Greeks on us? You think the Turk is an old man and sick, smoking a narghile. Perhaps we are old men and sick men, but originally we were nomads. We are sober and understand how to fight. If the Allies drive us out of Constantinople, very good. It is a city of misery and decay. We will make Angora our capital. We are not made to live in cities. Our life is in the fields and on the plains. If they drive us out of Angora we will go back to the great plains of Central Asia, here we came from. Tell that to your high commissioners and your Meester Veelson. You have been to Stamboul. Did you see many Turks there? Only old people, beggars, Armenians and Jews, riffraff. The Turks are all in Angora with Mustapha Kemal."
>
> "Are you going to Angora?"
>
> They nodded gravely. "We are going to Angora." (Dos Passos 1927, 36–37)

Dos Passos would not agree with the ethnocentric bigotry that frames the doctors' declaration of independence, just as he would never condone his father's chauvinism even when he agreed with a premise. He makes this clear here by including the callously disingenuous phrase "kill a few Armenians" when everybody, and especially doctors in the Turkish army, know the extent of the killing. Dos Passos likewise allows the Turkish doctors to articulate the fascistic potentiality of their nationalist ideology: youthful, productive, pureblood Turks rather than "old people, beggars, Armenians and Jews, riffraff," would populate an "uncontaminated" Turkish capital.

However, many of the sentiments and ideals expressed by the Turkish doctors reflect his own reading of independence movements in general, as well as the present state of affairs in Turkey. Sovereignty and self-determination, central premises in his country's own Declaration of Independence, a document he would always admire, were the undeniable rights of any people, even the remaining populace of a vast empire. Dos Passos would later extend this right to the citizens of post–World War II Germany even though he avidly opposed the Nazi regime. He supported independence movements when grassroot, and like his friend Hemingway the following year, this is how he would read the action in Anatolia. Mustafa Kemal would grasp his imagination and heart, which, as Alfred Kazin notes, "always had gone out to the men who were lonely and human in their rebellion" (Kazin 1974, 106). Even if it was only the "defeated Bolshevik whom Dos Passos ever really likes," and even if he may have been critical of the man once he had become Atatürk, in these early days of the Revolution, when Mustafa Kemal was still branded a bandit by European prime ministers and many in the Ottoman government, Dos Passos admired and supported him for realizing what the writer believed was the will of the people (Kazin 1974, 106).

The real Turkish people, ideally depicted above by the doctors, are the youthful descendants of self-sufficient nomads who do not admire what they consider the exhausted, cosmopolitan decadence of Constantinople. As a lifelong advocate of Jeffersonian agrarianism, which by the early twentieth century meant defending the small independent farmer against the urban industrial capitalist, Dos Passos would admire this heritage of the fields and plains. He lets the severe, resolute doctors speak *his* mind when they criticize American President Woodrow Wilson, "Meester Veelson," for not coming to the defense of a people, at least in the legislative courts of Europe, whose rural heritage and spirit of independence resemble in so many ways their own. Implicating the

Americans in the British-manufactured war between the Greeks and Turks—"If you believed in the rights of small nations, why did you let the British set the Greeks on us?—the Turkish doctors also give voice to Dos Passos's own fundamental distrust of ethnically driven geopolitical war. Joseph Warren Beach points out that the French soldiers in Dos Passos's World War I novel *Three Soldiers* "do not share the hatred of the Huns so assiduously cultivated by the YMCA men in the name of Jesus," but rather "take for granted that the war was made by financial pirates and feudal lords; that it was but a symptom of the ruthless greed which was the central evil of the world" (Beach 1972, 33). The Turkish doctors, like the French soldiers, understand that the war with their immediate, tangible adversary, the Greeks, is a symptom of something not only systemically larger (the result of markets and the politicians who protect and promote them) but also ontologically more vast. Though they voice no love for their immediate neighbors to the West who have been encouraged by the British, as the text will suggest in various places, to realize their "historical mission" and re-Hellenize Asia Minor, the doctors suggest that the Greeks are being used in a colonial war that promotes itself as an ethical and righteous defense of social equality in Turkey.

Orient Express will have given ample space to privileged members of the Greek community of Constantinople to incriminate themselves at this point in the text. Thus when the doctors on their way to join the Kemalists in Ankara state that Greek cruisers are firing on Turkish fishermen and coastal villages, "making the world safe for democracy," the irony rings particularly bitter. Greeks and Turks are interwoven together in the subchapters, but Dos Passos does not present them with an even hand. Greeks are presented as socially and economically advantaged, arrogant and highly intolerant of their Turkish compatriots, while Turks are presented as humble, sometimes but not always poor, noble, ruminative, enduring, and at times threatening, though justifiably so in context. The first incident of direct speech in the chapter is that of a Greek girl with whom the first-person narrator converses in the "Jardin de Taxim," a subchapter that attempts to capture the vulgar, maudlin, but flirtatious energy of the city through the pastiche images of a multicultural cabaret. "'Why do you want to learn Turkish?' a Greek girl asks me, a look of puzzled irritation on her face. You must side with the Greeks; you mustn't learn Turkish'" (Dos Passos 1927, 15). This bit of badgering, which partly introduces the primary subtext of the chapter, the Greco-Turkish war—"A party of Greeks is very gay. Their army has taken Eski Chehir"—and which concludes the cabaret scene, is followed shortly by the first detailed human sketch in the chapter:

> Flits through my head the memory of . . . a beggar, inconceivably old, yellow like frayed damask, gnarled like a dying plum tree, had asked for a light from my cigarette and then smiling had pointed to the glass of water that stood beside my little coffee-cup, and how when I had handed him the water, he had had to crouch low to the ground to drink it, his back was so bent; and the gesture full of sceptred kings with which he had put back the glass and thanked me with a wave of a skinny corded hand. There was something in that wave of the hand of the soaring of minarets and the cry of muezzins and the impassive eyes of the elderly Turkish gentlemen in white vests sitting so quiet beside rejoicing Greeks in the Jardin de Taxim. There are reasons for learning Turkish. (Dos Passos 1927, 15–16)

There is an imagistic quality to the language: Dos Passos not only captures the appearance of the old man with his initial descriptive similes, but also the nature of his living. Worn thin and physically contorted by hard labor, probably a lifetime of hiring out his back for the transport of goods throughout the city, the

17. Jardin de Taksim, Taksim Square, 1930s.

scars of poverty hinder the simplest of human gestures. But if he must stoop to drink a glass of solicited water, he can nevertheless offer his thanks with a gesture that will remain with the writer due to its improbable decorum. Dos Passos might well be cited for a momentary lapse of Orientalist embroidering, "There was something in that wave of the hand of the soaring of minarets and the cry of muezzins"—a moment whereby the human subject disappears into the Western writer's fancy, stimulated, yet again, by an exotic encounter in an exotic landscape. But this is not the case here, though there may be something of the progressive socialist's sentimental rendering of the poor. Dos Passos, writing in a Naturalist vein here, places the old man and his gesture within a contemporary social and historical context that grants his aesthetic language a political function. The old beggar's unexpected civility under hardship, like the "elderly Turkish gentlemen in white vests sitting so quiet beside rejoicing Greeks," denotes not a torpid passivity, another Orientalist motif, but rather grace in the face of privation and adversity. Change is in the air, the chapter suggests throughout; if it is change that creates better conditions for its honorable albeit afflicted citizens, then it is progressive change. This is his slant and complex answer to the Greek girl's question. These are the "reasons for learning Turkish."

Back in the "red plush salon of the Pera Palace Hotel" in the subsequent section, "Massacre" is another transnational gathering. The principle character is the Archbishop of the Greek Orthodox church (to this day still based in the Patriarchy at Istanbul) who is commenting somewhat publicly on the Kemalist threat to the "men of orthodox faith" as well as to Greek women and children in Anatolia.

> The archbishop, a tall man in flowing black with a beautiful curly chestnut-coloured beard and gimlet eyes, is pouring out an impetuous torrent of Greek. Listening to him a Greek lady elaborately dressed in rose satin, an American naval officer, a journalist, some miscellaneous frock-coated people. Chink of ice in highballs being brought to two British majors across the room. The archbishop lifts a slender Byzantine hand and orders coffee. Then he changes to French, lisping a little his long balanced phrases, in which predominate the words *horreur, atrocité, oeuvre humanitaire, civilization mondiale.* (Dos Passos 1927, 17)

The expensive interior of the salon contrasts with a haunting scene of exodus "beyond," the writer's "vision of dark crowds crawling inland over the sun-shrivelled hills" (Dos Passos 1927, 17). The distressed talk of massacre and the genteel minutiae of the tearoom are interlaced in the section, producing an atmosphere of alarm simultaneously real and feigned:

> The Archbishop's full lips are at the rim of his tiny coffee-cup. He drinks quickly and meticulously . . ."the women were crying and wailing in the streets of Samsoun," says the officer. "The news must be sent out," continues the archbishop; "the world must know the barbarity of the Turks; America must know. A telegram to the President of the United States must be sent off." (Dos Passos 1927, 17–18)

Dos Passos again contrasts the "red plush salons," "polished phrases," and "official telegrams" with ominous images from the hinterlands, the "dark attentive eyes of children," the sound of horsemen. The overall hermeneutic effect of the interwoven contrasts is that the Ottoman Greeks seem to be both sedentary spectators and living sufferers in the war, both the guilty and the innocent. Class struggle is the source of strife in the section's implicit assessment of war, not ethnicity as the archbishop would have it. The safety of privilege, of which the Pera Palace is a symbol, marks both the real and imagined boundaries of this war. While socially advantaged, urban Greeks display the reductive, divisive thinking that perpetuates the struggle, "Turks are barbarians"; their relatives, the rural Greeks, are the victims of that same war and the same kind of tribal fanaticism. Throughout the conversation a Turkish gentleman "with grizzled eyebrows, and with eyes as soft and as brown as the archbishop's beard" "sits in a big arm-chair by the window" hearing everything, looking "unmovedly at nothing" (Dos Passos 1927, 18). He seems an embodied adjustment of both the archbishop's worse fears and his worst prejudices: he can afford to sit in the same salon, but he is isolated from those around him. His silence is well mannered, unlike the archbishop's, and also threatening. Again Dos Passos invokes an Orientalist cliché, "the inscrutable" Turk, only to give the enigmatic moment a political reading. The Constantinople Turk, perhaps equally uneasy about the changes the Kemalists will bring to the country, weighs the situation, nonetheless, with a sense of stoic reserve as "one by one the oval amber beads of a conversation-chaplet drop through his inscrutably slow white fingers" (Dos Passos 1927, 18). Like other privileged Ottomans in Constantinople, many Turks have much to lose if Mustafa Kemal's troops win the war. However, in the case of the Turks, what might be won for the country as a whole may be worth the personal sacrifice.

Dos Passos stages further the Eurocentricity and cultural arrogance that he suggests is fueling social crisis in Turkey. As in Hemingway's later dispatches, French is the vehicle used to represent the kind of civilized pride that may well lead to the downfall of the speaker.

> Little Mr. Moscoupoulas threw up pudgy hands.
>
> "But the Turks have not studied the Greek Classics. They are ignorant. They do not know Aristophanes or Homer or Demosthenes, not even the deputies. *Et sans connaître le classiques grecs on ne peut être ni politicien, ni orateur, ni diplomate.* Turkey does not exist. I assure you, sir, it is a mere question of brigandage. And this city"—we peered out of the window of the Pera Palace at a passing Allied staff-car—"you know the legend. A Constantine built it, a Constantine lost it, and a Constantine shall regain it." (Dos Passos 1927, 27)

"*Sans connaître le classiques*" will function as a refrain throughout the rest of the section punctuating various "Turkish" scenes: small groups of low-talking men in a café, shepherds and their harried sheep, Inter-Allied surveillance. Removed from the particular story that *Orient Express* tells, and placed further West, Mr. Moscoupoulas's announcement might seem reasonable enough to some readers. However, placed as it is in the center of a military struggle for the soil and the soul of a city and a country famous, or infamous, for its ancient mélange of Western and Eastern ancestry and tradition, the ramifications of these Hellenocentric sentiments appear neither sound nor wise. Dos Passos underscores this point by contrasting Mr. Moscoupoulas's "pudgy hands," fleshiness a sign of excess in the text, and hysteria—there is a compulsive insistence to the repetition of his lines—with the calm composure of the café and those in it.

> In the purplish shadow of the vine arbour little tables and stools of unpainted wood, and on each table a pot of rosemary or basil or thyme, or a geranium in flower. In a group in one corner old men with grave gestures discuss some problem with quietly modulated voices. Their white turbans are almost motionless; now and then there is a flash of white when a head nods in a patch of sun, or a hand, lean and brown, is lifted to a grey beard. Beside me three young men in fezzes of new bright red are exchanging witticisms. An old gentleman with

> a puffy red face, dressed in the eternal white vest and broadtailed frock-coat, listens, looks across his narghile with eyes sparkling and occasionally throws his head back and roars with laughter. A yellow slender man with green carpet slippers beside him is looking into vacancy with large yellow-brown eyes, in his hand a long amber cigarette holder that is bright gold when the sun strikes it. (Dos Passos 1927, 28)

Dos Passos seems to offer further reasons in this section for "learning Turkish," the least of which is the opportunity to participate in the harmony this urban space seems to share with nature. The cafe is modest, the setting bucolic. But rather than inscribing the kind of mythologized, because aestheticized, space that many travel writers would be inclined to describe, Dos Passos again makes the painterly scene serve a political purpose.

The agreeable description of the Turkish men is not one that attempts to paint them into a world of ascetic freedom beyond the actual historical and political moment. As David Spurr in *The Rhetoric of Empire* suggests, this is a common quality of the imperial rhetoric found in the writing of such contemporaries as T. E. Lawrence, who is rousing Arab revolts against Turkish domination in the Ottoman provinces at the same time that Dos Passos is in the Near and Middle East (Spurr 1993, 129). Rather than serving the interests of the British, as in the case of Lawrence, or of the Americans as would perhaps be the case in another American writer, *Orient Express* as a text serves the spirit of rebellion against feudalistic forms of oppression exemplified by the peoples' revolution in Russia of which Dos Passos is becoming a spokesperson in the United States. In Constantinople hegemonic power is repeatedly represented by genteel Greeks with visions of rebuilding their empire—"A Constantine built it, a Constantine lost it, and a Constantine shall regain it"—and the Allied Powers whose forces appear in sentences and scenes with them like keystone cops and cronies. Although Turkish women tend to float through the text behind veils only, the demeanor of the Turkish men, often located in cafés in the open air, is meant to contrast with that of the Greek men and women who lounge in comfortable rooms. This contrast exemplifies an ideological argument: the average man, wherever he is found, is the righteous inheritor of the earth. A Turkish republic, "a mere question of brigandage," may not exist in the world view of Mr. Moscoupoulas, but the Greek gentleman's nostalgia for empires and the demigods who run them is obsolete in the discourse of world socialism. Thus, the Turks, *ni politicien, ni orateur, ni diplomate* in the "classical" sense of the terms—a sense that Dos Passos does not necessarily trust—seem pinnacles of Aristotelian balance rather than masters of sophisticated phrases.

Contrary to that of Mr. Moscoupoulas, the gestures of the men in the cafe are not dramatic but "grave"; hands are not "pudgy" but "lean"; and if a face is "puffy red," it is also a laughing one with animated eyes. There are quiet exchanges of intelligence between old men and lively displays of oral wit among the young. These people do not appear to be "ignorant" as Mr. Moscoupoulas would have his listener believe, though they may be discussing a cultural tradition unfamiliar to the Western reader. What counts for knowledge is a relative concept, the passage suggests, but in this city whose cosmopolitan character is frequently

18. Local café, early 1900s.

underscored, Turks and Greeks talk past each other like the nonitalicized English and italicized French on the page. When a party of Inter-Allied police arrives in a flurry of mechanical car noise and leave having aggressively "stared their fill at the people in the café," Dos Passos concludes the section with the following serene, though ultimately ominous description.

> Under the vines no one has noticed them. The voices of the old men continue, and the slow movement of a hand stroking a beard. In the upper bowl of the narghiles there is a little red glow at long intervals when the smoker pulls deeply. Above the grey towers and the wall, kites with black curved wings and hawk-beaks circle in the porcelain-blue sky. (Dos Passos 1927, 29–30)

Suggestive of the final line of W. B. Yeats's poem "The Second Coming," the image of the sinister black kite circling in a perfect sky seems a foreshadow of disaster to come. While the threat posed by the agitated Greek and the Inter-Allied police is overt in the section, the detachment of the Turkish men from the occupying forces, emphasized by the timeless, simple present tense, demonstrates its own covert menace.

If Stephen Crane in 1897 had upheld the Occidental convention of vilifying "the Turk" in his newspaper dispatches covering the Greek revolt against the Ottomans in Northern Thrace and in his last novel *Active Service,* based on his experiences there, Dos Passos seems intent in his text on presenting the Turkish side of a new imperial war, the side less familiar to the American or English speaking public. As if the previous section were not enough to solidly equate the post–World War I incursion of Greek forces into Anatolia with Pan-Hellenism, Dos Passos offers more evidence of this particular form of colonial nostalgia, this time from a tennis club in Therapia (Tarabiya) on the Bosphorus.

> People in frock-coats sat whispering round little tables. Mr. Deinos, who was starting a steamship line to run from Constantinople to New York, sat, in a lavender-grey linen suit, between two tall ladies with lurching eyes and Cupid's-bow mouths coyly puckered . . ."Greece," he began, "is going to fulfill her historic mission." (Dos Passos 1927, 30)

The section, as well as the chapter on Constantinople, concludes with this final scene and what has amounted to its formal refrain:

> Outside on the terrace Mr. Deinos and the two tall Greek ladies with Cupid's bow mouths were eating pistachio-nuts and drinking douzico in the amethyst twilight. "Greece," continued Mr. Deinos, "has always been the bulwark of civilization against the barbarians. Inspired by Marathon and Salamis, and I hope by the help and sympathy of America, Greece is once more going to take up her historic mission." (Dos Passos 1927, 33)

Similar to his rhythmic use of the phrase "*sans connaître le classiques*" Dos Passos frames section 8, entitled "Alexanders"—a sylleptic pun on the cocktail and the Macedonian colonizer—with "historic mission," a histrionic reference to Greece's ambitions in Anatolia. The repeated lines, and the ellipses that draw them to an inconclusive end, call attention to themselves. The aural effect is musical, something like a chant that echoes until it dies somewhere off the page. While there is no answering music, no voice from the other side but the low murmuring of Turks in the cafes, the hermeneutic effect is not ambiguous: the reader is directed to note the silences.

This intention is partly established by the company Mr. Deinos keeps in the section.

> I slipped away and strayed into the bar. A British major with a face like the harvest moon was shaking up Alexanders. A man in a frock-coat was trying to catch in his mouth olives that an American relief worker was tossing in the air. The talk in the bar was English, Oxford drawl, Chicago burr, Yankee twang, English and American as spoken by Greeks, Armenians, Frenchmen, Italians. Only the soberer people in the corners spoke French. (Dos Passos 1927, 30–31)

These representatives from the various occupying forces lend little credibility to Mr. Deinos's aims. Drunk and idle, the foreign community sits around the exclusive club exchanging speculative gossip about the progress of the independence movement and the future of Istanbul.

> "Kemal! He's finished . . . Like hell he is. There's a lot of legendary stuff about him going round. How at Eski Chehir the Turkish army sank into the ground and come up behind the Greek lines. That's the kind of stuff that makes a hero in the east."
>
> "They say that three divisions of Bolos [Bolsheviks] are going in through Armenia and that he's promised 'em Constantinople in return for their help."

> "Let 'em try and get it."
>
> "They will get it some day."
>
> "Nonsense, the Greeks'll have it—the British—the French—the Bulgarians . . . the League of Nations—the Turks. I suggest it be made neutral and presented to Switzerland; that's the only solution." (Dos Passos 1927, 33)

These snatches of scene and dialogue together with the many others in *Orient Express* as a whole are early illustrations of Dos Passos's signature "collectivistic" method, made well known in his novels *Manhattan Transfer* and *U.S.A.* Through isolating fragmented observations of a subject or a subject's speech, and presenting them side by side, Dos Passos attempts to present in language a synchronic cross-section of Constantinople society. While this is a common modernist technique, Dos Passos's aim is somewhat different in *Orient Express* from that of Stein in *The Making of Americans* or Pound in *The Cantos.* Like theirs, his "collectivism" is a grid used to register a social structure, offer an overview in which individual lives and dramas, "the cellular stuff, the protoplasmic basis" of human communities, merge into the general patterns of a place and a time (Beach 1972, 41). But because his Modernism is also informed by socialist ideology, Dos Passos's subjects are selectively chosen to mean something within a particular sociopolitical framework. In the case of the tennis club scene above, this framework is one of pending political and social revolution in a country that, according to Dos Passos, is in desperate need of transformation, although not necessarily of the kind Mr. Deinos or his friends propose.

It is often argued that Dos Passos's frenetic collectivist technique is mainly a formal correlative of life in Manhattan or urban America. This is the opinion of mid-century critics invested in establishing a national literature figuring America as its primary subject. Before Dos Passos applies his collectivist technique to Manhattan, however, he has already tested it on Istanbul.

> Leaning my chin on my hands and looking down at the strip of cracked and dusty pavement between the bare feet of the boys who sell cakes and pistachio-nuts and fly spotted sweets along the terrace wall, and the row of motors for hire, of which the drivers, mostly Russians in various patched uniforms, loll and sleep and chat . . . across that space shoes, feet, shambling legs, crossed arms, arms swinging vacantly, stoop shoulders, strongly moulded backs under

19. Karaköy Square, 1930s.

thin cotton, chests brown, sweat-beaded, shawls, black veils of women, yakmaks, faces . . . A stout Greek business man in a Palm Beach suit. Tommies very pink and stiff. Aggressive thick-jawed tramps playing with small maggot-like beggar children. Pale-faced Levantines with slinking eyes and hooked noses. Armenians with querulous mouths and great gold-brown eyes. In the bright sun and the violent shadows faces blur and merge as they pass. Faces are smooth and yellow like melons, steely like axes . . . They merge slowly in the cruel white sunlight, brown faces under fezzes, yellow faces under straw hats, hale northern faces under khaki caps—into one face, brows sullen and contracted, eyes black

> with suffering, skin taut over the cheek bones, hungry lines about the corners of the mouth, lips restless, envious, angry, lustful. The face of a man not quite starved out. (Dos Passos 1927, 24–25)

The discursive techniques that Dos Passos would exploit in his future novels are already operating as the narrator pans the crowded, cosmopolitan streets of Istanbul. Yet rather than identify Dos Passos's collectivism with a particular urban culture, be it 1920s Manhattan or Istanbul, it is more accurate to look to cinematography as a model for his method, whatever the cultural context. Dos Passos would later assert that rather than being influenced by particular writers or artists, he would "absorb 'certain . . . styles and methods . . . in the air'" (Townsend 1996, 44). Just as Walt Whitman was indebted to developments in photography in the mid-nineteenth century for his catalogues of freeze-frame images, the emergent new cinema equally influenced Dos Passos's prose style. The techniques of cinema direct the collection of images above, the cross-cutting from boys selling pistachio-nuts to the parallel action, or inaction, of Russians lounging near their taxis; the imagistic montage of feet and arms and other body parts; the juxtaposed close-ups of Russians, Greeks, Levantines, and children; the double and multiple projection of images, faces "like melons" and faces "steely like," and the accelerated motion of the crowd that comes to a full stop when it merges, as the "camera eye" pauses, on the face of one man.

This "substitution of the camera for the mediating, reflective narrator" would interest Jean-Paul Sartre, who in 1938 would conclude an essay on *1919* with "I regard Dos Passos as the greatest writer of our time" (Lee 1987, 182; Sartre 1955, 92). But an existential reading of *Orient Express* presents certain problems. Brian Lee, following Sartre's lead, argues that it is a mistake to read Dos Passos as a writer of social protest "inspired by democratic or even revolutionary zeal" (Lee 1987, 187). The "newsreels" and "camera eye" of *U.S.A.*, he argues, signify "a disembodied sensibility interpreting experience in a pure stream of consciousness" (Lee 1987, 186). While the "montage of unmediated and meaningless dramatic incident" in *U.S.A.* may induce the "nausea" as defined by Sartre—the subject's inability to digest the "impenetrable, unalterable" world "devoid of essential meaning" by reflecting on it—this is not necessarily the modus operandi of the "camera eye" in *Orient Express* (Lee 1987, 187). Lee, like Sartre, argues that Dos Passos wanted to express the "unrelieved stifling" of human life in capitalist society where "men do not have lives" but "only have destinies" (Sartre 1955, 91). The man above, "brows sullen and contracted, eyes black with suffering," is a historical being, however. With his "skin taut over the cheek bones, hungry lines about the corners of the mouth, lips restless, envious, angry, lustful," he is not a representation of the vague social tragedy that is "his time," but a literal embodiment of the social abuses of a world war followed by civil war. He is at once everybody and somebody; his is "the face of a man not quite starved out," and the party responsible for the starving out of the Istanbul population, the repressed agent of the passive phrase, is not among the crowd on the streets.

The modern condition of Istanbul in 1921 is not the same as that of Paris, London, or New York. Rather than an interim between world wars, in which nations took the opportunity to rebuild themselves, in the case of Europe, or recreate themselves, in the case of the United States, Turkey is simultaneously under foreign occupation, under Greek invasion, and mired in civil war. Yet the general Turkish population seems to be facing the crisis with "Oriental" forbearance in *Orient Express*. Dos Passos for the most part restricts the voice of the people who are the direct victims of the postwar land-grab to a murmuring in cafes, to the mute "face of a man not quite starved out." There is a vignette in the subchapter "The Crescent," however, in which voices are raised above the silence. Dos Passos once again employs cinematic techniques, this time to reinforce the range of socioeconomic classes that come together to listen to the politicized prayers of spiritual leaders at one midday prayer.

> The huge red-carpeted floor under the dome and the dais along the sides were full of men, beggars and porters and artisans in leather aprons and small boys with fezzes too large for their bullet heads, and stately gentlemen in frock-coats and white vests with festooned watch-chains, and grave-bearded theological students in neatly wound white cotton turbans, all squatting close together with their shoes beside them. (Dos Passos 1927, 21)

The synchronization of individual "shots" gives again a dynamic collectivist quality to the crowd in the Beyazit mosque, but this time the assembly also suggests solidarity: beggars as well as stately gentlemen are there to pray together for the past and future of the war weary country. But before recording his impressions of the dramatic monologues of the "mollahs" or priests—with no knowledge of

Turkish he can only interpret the cadences of the speech— he reinforces the visual impact of the scene with impressionistic strokes of color that revolve around the principal player in the mosque and prepare us for the fiery sensation of the language to come:

> A yellow-bright beam of sunlight striking across the pearly shimmer of the dome fell full on the bronze face and shining beard of the mollah who was reading the Koran and brought fierce magenta flame into the silk hanging that fell from the front on the pulpit platform. (Dos Passos 1927, 21–22)

Having established the diverse nature of the crowd—a coming together of classes we see only in the street scenes in *Orient Express*—and the luminous quality of the atmosphere, Dos Passos lets a "young man with the green tassel on his beads" translate the subject of the "wooden staccato voice." This voice belongs to the first speaker who is answered at the end of each verse by a "soft Ameen growled through the crowd." "'It is for the fall of Adrianople, this day every year' . . . Many of these people come from Adrianople, fled from the Greeks . . . Commemoration . . . Now we will pray for the army in Anatolia.'" The low voice then gives way to "harsh ringing consonants and brazen upward cadences," as the sorrowful memorial of the first imam and the "soft growl" of mourners swell to the fierce prophecy of the second imam and the responsive "roar" of warriors.

> His body erect, his eyes staring straight into the sunlight, his hands raised level with his beard in the attitude of prayer, the new mollah shouted a prayer full of harsh ringing consonants and brazen upward cadences. His voice was like war-horns and kettledrums. And all through the mosque under the faintly blue dome men looked beyond the palms of their raised hands at the flaming magenta silk and the priest praying in the yellow shaft of sunlight, and the Ameen at every pause rose from a growl to a roar, grew fierce and breathless till the little glass lamps tinkled in the huge flat chandeliers above the turbans and the fezzes, rolled up the stucco walls . . . (Dos Passos 1927, 22–23)

Like the conflicting adjectives used to describe the crowd merged into the face of the man, "sullen," "suffering," "hungry," "restless, envious, angry, lustful," the descriptive language used to register the words of the *imam* and the responding voice of the crowd is also unstable. It is at once militant and magnificent, violent and inspired. If it makes the writer think of a war cry, it also makes him think of the Old Testament prophets, their revolutionary arms raised in petition to a higher power. Thus into the representation of the "inscrutable," passive Turk, fingering his worry beads as others talk past him, is inserted this unambiguous depiction of political and religious activity.

Unlike most Western readings of war in the Near and Middle East—both then and now—Dos Passos does not demonize the Muslim "enemy" of Christians, even as he represents him through the rhetoric of holy war. If he gives a contemporary political context for the grievances of Turks, the current occupation and the dreams of annexation of "misguided" minority populations, he also ends the section with a passing reference to the "fall" or "conquest" or "metamorphosis" of Constantinople—one's point of view will determine the verb—that is equally sympathetic to the Turkish position. The "Ameen" that agitates "the great dome" does so, he concludes, just as it must have when Fatih Mehmet entered the city in 1453: "The domes of churches must have shaken with the shout of the fighting-men of Islam the day Constantine's city was carried by assault and the last Constantine killed in his purple boots" (Dos Passos 1927, 23). Unlike most Western or Christian writers who see the change in command at Constantinople as a disaster rather than a triumph, Dos Passos remains himself enigmatic on the subject: if the Ottomans "carried by assault" the city, and killed the last Byzantine ruler, he was, nevertheless, wearing "purple boots." Not only a symbol of royalty, the "purple boots" also tell the story of an irresponsible demagogy that had left the empire in a weakened state. It can be argued that the Byzantine Empire was taken because it could be. Cyrus Hamlin, a nineteenth-century American missionary to Istanbul and founder of Robert College, now Bosphorus University, the first American university established outside of the United States, writes in his memoir of his life in Istanbul, *Among the Turks,* that while the "fall of Constantinople" may have given a great shock to Europe and the "civilized world," "it was probably the salvation, rather than the destruction of Christianity, even in the East, which was then placed on the defensive" (Hamlin 1878, 20). Hamlin as a Protestant missionary has his own reasons for this positive reading of the collapse of the Eastern Empire: it gave the corrupt and decadent Orthodox and Catholic churches what was coming to them: "If it did not lead directly to its reform it arrested its degeneracy."

Dos Passos's own sympathetic rendering of Islam, however, comes less from any religious leaning than toward the affinity he felt some aspects of the faith had with socialist thinking. As the primary representative voice of Islam in *Orient Express*, the Sayyid is admired by the narrator for his generosity and charity to the poor and sickly. Dos Passos also admires the Muslim intellectual's position on the necessity for the self-determination of peoples in the former Ottoman provinces that were then in the process of being newly colonized by Western powers. Mostly, however, he admires the Sayyid's lucid analysis of colonialism in the Near and Middle East:

> "As for the British here in Persia . . . yes, I know they are great people. I knew then they were *braves genes*. But here it is not so, not towards us, and for that reason I shall fight against them, *avec diplomatik*, as long as I live. And among the Turks it is the same, and among the Arabs it is the same, and among the Afgans it is the same. First we liked the British because they were better than the Russians; but now there is no pressure from Russia, and the British have changed. And there is not so much resignation in Islam as there used to be. Europe is teaching us, giving us weapons." (Dos Passos 1927, 99–100)

The Sayyid is a Western-educated "man of science" who endorses neither "ignorant" and "fanatic" followers of mullahs nor the primitive economies of the Middle East in the early twentieth century (Dos Passos 1927, 92). This latter opinion leads to a "furious argument about industrialism" with the narrator over dinner, an argument in which Dos Passos exposes his own patronizing idealism as a Western socialist, even as it reveals the inconsistent allegiances of the Persian ascetic.

> I tried to tell him that the life of an industrial worker in Europe and America was not all beer and skittles, and even wondered whether those people hammering away at their copper pots, miserably underpaid as they were, might not get more out of life than, say, the steel-worker in Germany, for all his moving pictures and Bierhalle with which to amuse himself. But he snowed me under with a long list of famines and extortions of grandees and mutjahids and governors. 'No,' he said at last, 'we must have fabriks and railways. Then we shall be a great nation." (Dos Passos 1927, 94)

Dos Passos will question his Harvard-acquired collectivist ideology throughout *Orient Express*, enough to satisfy some uneasy mid-twentieth-century American critics that in 1927 (the publication year of the book) he was already convalescing from the Marxist "flu" of his youth and moving toward the more benign and acceptable Jeffersonian agrarianism that would accompany his move from the political left to the political right (Carr 1984, 19).

But to doubt is not to deny. "Watching in *Orient Express* the earliest stirrings of the Utopian infant that was to become such an enigmatic giantess, our novelist is hesitant," says Rosen (1981, 31). His "hesitation" on the question of socialism, "his lack of 'assurance,'" or, as one 1927 reviewer says, the "impotent pity" Dos Passos feels for the "appalling heritage of misery left by war and colonialism" in the Near and Middle East constitutes the particular power of this early text rather than its weakness (qtd. in Rosen 1981, 31). *Orient Express* is a literary testing ground for Dos Passos's leftist allegiances. In the international arena of the text, an arena he is familiar with but makes no claims to expertly understand, his prose does not yet suffer the ideological rigidities imposed on it by his allegiances to progressivism in his American novels. Rather than offering the foregone conclusions of socialist ideology in American capitalist society, however modernist in technique, Dos Passos still allows himself the luxury of a certain lyricism in his collectivist accounts in *Orient Express.*

What is read as hesitation in his accounts of Turkey, or Russia and Iran, is the narrative play of ideas he allows in the text, which contrast with the clearer convictions of *Manhattan Transfer* or *U.S.A.*, despite their experimental narrative structures. "*Orient Express* is perhaps the gayest of Dos Passos's works, placed as it is amidst massacres, plagues, and revolution," and the "gaiety" of the text is the result of the literary panache Dos Passos allows his empirical facts (Geismar 1961, 104). In this early text, unlike his later novels, he does not yet insist that sociology pose as literature, or offer a confident, albeit cubist, anthropological record of an itemized society in which that society, rather than the individuals in it, is the main character, as is ultimately the case in his American novels. Rather, Dos Passos offers in *Orient Express* a collection of real characters on the brink of uncertain political and social change. If this change becomes inconceivable to him in his own country where Henry Ford and the "universal suburb" have already colonized the minds of its people, the promise of another kind of change in Turkey inspires an enthusiastic prose that is aesthetic as well as political.

Mustafa Kemal would not advocate, at least initially, a highly centralized form of government when his forces took control of Anatolia in 1922 or in Istanbul in 1923 when the allied occupation of the city finally ended. The Nationalists would abolish the caliphate in a move to secularize the new Turkish state and establish a European parliamentary model of government. The Nationalist Party would later come into conflict with the Communist Party in Turkey. Dos Passos would reject his early socialism after his experiences with the Spanish Civil war and Stalin in the late 1930s and early 1940s. The political trajectory of his writing would continue to veer increasingly to the right, to the dismay of such old friends and fellow progressives as Edmund Wilson and Granville Hicks, the latter of whom would write in 1950 in *The Antioch Review:*

> Twenty years ago he was as romantic a rebel as American letters had seen since the death of John Reed, passionate in his attack on capitalism, quick to support a radical cause. Today this pioneer fellow-traveler defends the profit motive, quarrels not merely with communism but also with the New Deal, looks in dismay at the program of the British Labor Party, and finds in Senator Taft the qualities of leadership he thinks America needs. (Hicks 1974, 15)

Orient Express remains, then, a work of youthful leftist protest against the failure of human development under oppression. The corrective for oppression that he identifies in Turkey and Istanbul comes in the form of the Nationalist movement. Later he would confine himself primarily to the United States for subject matter. His writing would take the "camera eye" to its ascetic, indeterminate extreme until his modernist experiment gave way to traditional, plodding histories and biographies of great American men. In *Orient Express* Dos Passos indulges his literary fancies while he looks for ways to represent social inequity. Neither political journalism, nor fiction, nor traditional travel narrative nor abstract impressionistic description of exotic lands, *Orient Express* is a collection of experimental essays in which the young writer gives an early airing to modernist literary techniques in various politicized, historical contexts. While most famous for the American political epic, Dos Passos nonetheless did much of his study abroad. Often voicing in *Orient Express* his admiration for the dervish, "the symbol of mystery errant on the face of the world," he acknowledges that the vagrant seeker of wisdom would be considered nothing more than a bum "in civilized countries" (Dos Passos 1927, 103). So he goes back home and goes to work. But he brings Istanbul and Turkey, the Crimea, and Damascus back with him and incorporates his attentive notes on the social and political struggles of the Eastern regions of the old world into his own national literature.

5

Paul Bowles in Istanbul

The Perils of Forced Hybridization

IT WAS ALICE B. TOKLAS, the partner of Gertrude Stein, who first suggested to Paul Bowles that he go to North Africa. He went in 1931 at the age of twenty-one with his friend and mentor, the American composer Aaron Copland. Gertrude Stein, who had been in Tangier in 1901 and then again with Toklas in 1912, had this to say of the North African city: it was a place "which you cannot come into contact as it exists of itself and by itself and looks as it does when it is" (qtd. in Stewart 1973, 12–13). Tangier was a good place because it did not admit easy penetration by the foreign visitor. Such abstruseness was necessary for a young man like Bowles, who could not write poetry, according to Stein, but who was a promising composer (Vidal 1986, 6). Alienation was useful for a modern artist because it released him from, among other things, the psychological burden of identification:

> There is no possibility of mixing up the other civilization with yourself you are you and if you are you in your own civilization you are apt to mix yourself up too much with your civilization but when it is another civilization a complete other a romantic other another that stays there where it is you in it have freedom inside yourself. (qtd. in Stewart 1973, 12)

In the first half of the twentieth century, before the series of wars of independence that would free the North Africa countries from mostly French colonial domination, Tangier was simultaneously the perfect "another" as well as one of the most wildly cosmopolitan cities on the Mediterranean. European powers had come together after World War I in 1923 and "internationalized" the city in order to prevent the Straits of Gibraltar from becoming dominated by one particular nation (Mullins 2002, 4). The coalition of European powers that governed Tangier from 1923 to 1956 renamed the city "the Interzone of Tangier"; when Paul Bowles eventually settled in Tangier after World War II, it had long become a "free port with a population equally divided between Europeans and Moroccans, an economy based on smuggling and questionable financial transactions" (Mullins 2002, 4). It was a city famous for eccentric crossover, a place where East and West, and their respective languages, "mixed promiscuously," where sex, and sexual crossovers in particular, defined the free zone until independence (Mullins 2002, 4).

Bowles would not begin writing again until he was in his mid-thirties, and from 1929 to 1945 he would make a name for himself as a composer. In 1927 at the age of seventeen he had published a poem in the twelfth volume of *transition,* the Paris-based literary journal central to the Modernist movement. He would not take up writing again, however, until 1942 when he became a music critic for the *New York Herald Tribune* (Hibbard 2003). In 1945, his first short story, "The Scorpion," appeared in *View.* His literary career relaunched, his reputation as a fiction writer eventually overshadowed his career in music, at least in the popular imagination. His wife, the writer Jane Auer, whom he had married in 1938, returned to Tangier with Bowles in 1947. Back home Auer and Bowles had been popular, "on a first name basis," with everyone on the New York art scene (Mangan and Herrmann, 260). Thus, when they moved to Tangier much of New York came to visit. Their home would become a destination for the American literary establishment: Truman Capote spent time there as did Tennessee Williams, for whom Bowles wrote music. The Tangier residence of the expatriate also became a destination for the American literary antiestablishment: Timothy Leary, then at Harvard, appeared; William Burroughs visited for long periods, primarily for the hash and young men. The then-infamous band of Beats, Allen Ginsberg, Gregory Corso, Jack Kerouac, and Ira Cohen made pilgrimages to Bowles, the unofficial guru of the countermovement.

Norman Mailer in *Advertisement for Myself* (1959) says the following of Bowles's Tangier-inspired contribution to American culture: "Paul Bowles opened the world to Hip. He let in the murder, the drugs, the incest, the death of the Square, the call of the orgy, the end of civilization" (Hibbard 2003). But beyond his reputation as a *kef* (hash)-smoking writer of late-gothic tales about the clash of cultures, the destructive relations between Western travelers to North Africa and local inhabitants—often tragic, though never classically rendered—Bowles, as a spokesperson of mid-twentieth-century American "hip" harbored other, more theoretically ambitious inducements to his storytelling: he wished to save non-Western "primitive" cultures from European global expansion. He was highly critical of French colonialism in North Africa and Western cultural colonialism in the world in general. Bowles shared with his character Port in *The Sheltering Sky* "a distaste for the cosmopolitan sharing of ideas in the modern world and preference for the 'pure' traditional way of life" (Mullins 2002, 25). Like a humanist anthropologist, Bowles was more interested in illiterate than literate Moroccans because "the literate are less interesting. They have generally absorbed French ideas from their professors" (Bowles, qtd. in Mullins 2002, 25).

Bowles, who died in Tangier in 1999, still attracts a substantial posthumous following, both in popular and "underground" culture, but also among academics. But apologists, those who tend to write about the cult figure most enthusiastically, are obliged to do much selective censoring of the man and his work in order to continue to exonerate him to a contemporary audience versed in postcolonial academic discourse. Bowles, of course, at no time asks to be defended. Ethically risky, his fiction resists easy identification with a prescribed audience and instead often aims to repel even the most sophisticated and world-weary with scenes of physical, sexual, and psychological violence. While his later fiction would move away from apocalyptic scenes of physical mutilation, rape, or compromised sexual relations, early short stories such as "The Delicate Prey," "A Distant Episode," and "Pages from Cold Point" and some of the later scenes of *The Sheltering Sky* sealed his reputation early as an accomplished provocateur. But Marilyn Adler Papayanis, in her good book, *Writing in the Margins: The Ethics of Expatriation from Lawrence to Ondantje*, suggests that Bowles is among those expatriate writers whose texts are "nuanced" and of "sufficient complexity" to "throw ideological patterns into relief and raise questions about their own fictional processes" (Papayanis 2005, 3). This, she argues, is enough to warrant a revisionist consideration of his "mythologized narrative of displacement," a phrase shared by Caren Kaplan in her critique of expatriate Occidental literature. Pushing human experience to extreme limits, Bowles, like Nietzsche and Georges Bataille in particular, Papayanis argues extensively, makes a "virtue of excess," his protagonist "suspended between alienation and totality . . . the very embodiment, in fictional terms, of Bataillian 'sovereignty' or 'a state of absolute overcoming'" (Papayanis 2005, 11–14). Thus because Bowles's characters and texts are not readily consumable, because they induce a kind of conceptual queasiness, they resist the criticism of hegemony directed at much Western travel writing.

But there are classical complications with his anticolonial position, much less nuanced, perhaps, than Papayanis's defense, that manifest themselves in the writing. For a writer who claimed not necessarily to speak for, but to empathize with, the threatened subjective position of natives, Bowles, as is often noted, rarely writes from a native's point of view, whether personal or public. His fiction is primarily concerned with the incommensurate powers—psychological, emotional, and other—of Americans and Europeans faced with forces that circulate in the desert landscape and among the people who call it home. Efforts to give the reader access to an individual Arab's or Bedouin's consciousness often lead to flaws in the narration. In *The Sheltering Sky,* for example, we note a wavering between full omniscience and partial omniscience in the novel. After experiencing only the foreigners' points of view (primarily Kit's or Port's) for most of the novel, we are asked to suddenly enter the thoughts of the Arab boy who helps Kit at the onset of Port's illness (a question pleases the boy), and later the thoughts of Belqassim, Kit's nomad "lover" (he is angry because Kit's sores from the thorns have marred the whiteness of her body) (Bowles 1949, 192, 276). While these may seem insignificant lapses in the text, they nevertheless point to a struggle to represent the minds of people who played an ambiguous role in the life of the expatriate writer. Furthermore, the confusion within the narrative point of view suggests that behind Bowles's anticolonial position lie certain attitudes about North Africans that undermine them as viable players in the postcolonial period emerging, and violently, in much of the mid-twentieth-century Muslim world.

Problems in the North African fiction can be partially accounted for by examining other texts where Paul Bowles writes about "alien" and specifically Muslim cultures. Bowles was respected for his knowledge of Moroccan culture, particularly its music. He is particularly well known for his research and recording of Moroccan folk music, for which he received a six-month Rockefeller Foundation Grant in 1959 and traveled "some twenty-five thousand miles around Morocco" recording the music of various regions (Bowles 1957, 173). The collection was given to the Library of Congress in Washington and is still considered the most extensive collection of Moroccan folk music ever recorded by a Westerner. "The most important single element in Morocco's folk culture is its music," Bowles writes in the opening of his essay about his music travels, "The Rif, To Music" (Bowles 1957, 97).

> In a land like this, where almost total illiteracy has been the rule, the production of written literature is of course negligible. On the other hand, like the Negroes of West Africa the Moroccans have a magnificent and highly evolved sense of rhythm which manifests itself in the twin arts of song and dance. Islam, however, does not look with favor upon any sort of dancing, and thus the art of dance, while being a natural mode of religious expression of the native population, has not been encouraged here since the arrival of the Moslem conquerors. At the same time, the very illiteracy which through the centuries has precluded the possibility of literature has abetted the development of music; the entire history and mythology of the people is clothed in song. (Bowles 1957, 97)

Bowles's arch, objective voice suggests that of a cultural anthropologist here and throughout his collection of travel essays, *Their Heads Are Green and Their Hands Are Blue*. His fiction, as is often noted, also maintains a similar clinical distance between action and locution. And like cultural anthropology, the fiction often concerns itself with the interface of indigenous and colonial cultures. While here he identifies Muslims as early "conquerors" and colonists of the African continent whose religious strictures stifled or altered "natural modes" of native culture, his treatment of Islam varies depending on which colonial condition, Eastern or Western, Muslim or Christian, he wishes to hold responsible for a country's spurious transformations. In his essay on Istanbul titled "A Man Must Not Be Too Muslim," he will lament that due to westernization, Turkish people are not Muslim enough.

IN 1953, Bowles booked passage with the *Denizyolları*, Turkish Maritime Lines, and in September of that year "sailed to Istanbul" (Bowles 1972, 321–22). He had agreed to write an article on the city for the magazine *Holiday*, and the travel piece initially titled "Their Heads Are Green and Their Hands Are Blue" would become part of a collection by the same name published in 1963 in London by Peter Owen and simultaneously in New York by Random House. The title was taken from "The Jumblies," a poem by the Victorian "absurdist" Edward Lear, four lines of which Bowles included in the introductory pages of the published text.

> Far and few, far and few,
> Are the lands where the Jumblies live;
> Their heads are green, and their hands are blue,
> And they went to sea in a Sieve.

He concludes the foreword that immediately follows with an explanation of the antic lines' significance in the context of foreign travel.

> Since human behavior is becoming everywhere less differentiated, the Jumblie hunters are having to increase the radius of their searches and lower their standards . . . It may be, says W. H. Auden, "that in a not so remote future, it will be impossible to distinguish human beings living on one area of the earth's surface from those living on any other." It is comforting to imagine that when that day arrives we may be in a position to have the inhabitants of a nearby planet as our Jumblies. There is always the possibility, too, that they may have us as theirs. (Bowles 1957, ix)

While Bowles wryly signs off with an acknowledgement of the relative disposition of the word "Jumblies" or "aliens," he nonetheless underscores what he considers the problem of travel writing in an increasingly accessible world: there is no comfort in identification for those in quest of difference, even for its own sake.

Bowles's essays on such varied destinations as Ceylon, India, Mexico, and, of course, North Africa, seem to have been less the result of assignments than of the spontaneous by-products of his itinerant life. His trip to Istanbul seems to have been considered work rather than play, however. He offers no commentary on his voyage in his autobiography *Without Stopping,* and reference to the trip in other places is cursory. While Bowles did not consider himself a travel writer and referred to these essays somewhat dismissively as "reportage" or "travel sketches," his chapter on Istanbul is the most striking of the collection and the most frequently anthologized in collections of travel narratives (Caponi 1998, 104). Despite his lack of mention of the city in other writing, the essay shines an enabling light when and where Islam and colonialism are concerned in his oeuvre, which means nearly everywhere.

Bowles opens the travel sketch by describing the travel companion he has chosen to take with him to another "Muslim" culture.

> When I announced my intention of bringing Abdeslam along to Istanbul, the general opinion of my friends was that there were a good many more intelligent things to do in the world than to carry a Moroccan Moslem along with one to Turkey. I don't know. He may end up a dead weight, but my hope is that he will turn out instead to be a kind of passkey to the place. He knows how to deal with Moslems, and he has the Moslem sense of seemliness and protocol. He has also an intuitive gift for immediate understanding of a situation and at the same time is completely lacking in reticence or inhibitions. He can lie so well that he convinces himself straightway, and he is master at bargaining . . . He never knows what is printed on a sign because he is totally illiterate; besides, even if he did know he would pay no attention, for he is wholly deficient in respect for law . . . Obviously he is far better equipped than I to squeeze the last drop of adventure out of any occasion. (Bowles 1957, 74–75)

Many of the qualities listed as useful for travel in the Muslim world— familiarity with "Oriental" public formalities, interpersonal and social intuition, boldness, dishonesty, illiteracy, lawlessness—could be lifted directly out of an eighteenth- or nineteenth-century European armchair travel guide. While Bowles admits that there may be some differences between Moroccan and Turkish Muslims, he seems to assume, nonetheless, that Turks will have more in common with a North African than will an "Occidental." Though the term "adventure," may be used ironically (adventure in a Bowles text is mostly extrasensorial), the speaker anticipates a certain psychological thrill. The adventures will in fact take the form of Abdeslam's frequent and animated invectives against Turkish religious practices, or the lack thereof, and the political history that has destroyed, according to the faithful Muslim, the country's now secularized soul.

The personage behind the pseudonym Abdeslam was Bowles's intimate friend Ahmed Yacoubi, a young Moroccan painter with whom Bowles transcribed oral Maghrebi stories and traveled frequently, and whose friendship had a great influence on his conceptions of Muslim life (Stewart 1973, 101). A "Cherif on both his father's and mother's side; that is to say a descendant of the Prophet Mohammed," Yacoubi was also the object of much romantic fixation on the part of the older artist (Stewart 1973, 160). Rather than proving a "dead weight," Yacoubi, or Abdeslam, becomes the principal character in nearly all the dramas that ensue in the chapter on Istanbul. He also becomes a mask through which Bowles tests and weighs his own arguments with Westernization and "passionate" Islam, the

20. Rumeli Castle on the Bosphorus, 1950s.

adjective he prefers in contrast to "fundamentalist" or "radical," the qualifiers most popular in Western discourse (Bowles 1957, 34). Ultimately, it is the former, the Westernization of the "developing" republic, that Bowles will consider the worst of the two options for Turkey.

Bowles has many positive things to say about Istanbul, though most compliments come with caveats.

> Istanbul is a jolly place; it's hard to find a sinister element in it, notwithstanding all the spy novels for which it provides a handsome setting . . . The cupolas and minarets rise above the disorder of the city like huge gray fungi growing out of a vast pile of ashes. For disorder is the visual keynote of Istanbul. It is not slovenly—only untidy; not dirty—merely dingy and drab. And just as you cannot claim it to be a beautiful city, neither can you accuse it of being uninteresting . . . It is a city whose esthetic is that of the unlikely and incongruous, a photographer's paradise. (Bowles 1957, 83)

Like many an Occidental writer-cum-traveler to Istanbul before, Bowles is both drawn to and repulsed by the aesthetic disorder of the city. Like Melville, he recommends wandering as the optimum way to experience its complicated topography. His eye is keen enough to allow him to note that "the mass is not an ethnically homogeneous one. The types of faces range from Levantine through Slavic to Mongoloid, the last belonging principally to the soldiers from eastern Anatolia" (Bowles 1957, 84). Often in Bowles's fiction, the "native quarters" of North African cities and towns are the sites of dislocation or the undoing of foreigners. These labyrinthine, fictionally exoticized neighborhoods contrast with the European hotels, restaurants, and bars where the French and other Occidentals rendezvous in familiar surroundings away from the native crowds that, like the weather, tend to oppress them. When Bowles notes that in Istanbul "there is no native quarter, or if you like, it is all native quarter," the observation offers an unintended commentary on the demographics of independent nations: unlike colonized North Africa, Istanbul does not display, at least to the casual observer, the kind of distinct communities of foreigners and locals that are seen in Bowles's Moroccan fiction (Bowles 1957, 83). It is a city that may have housed large foreign communities, but as it was never conquered by a foreign power after the end of the fifteenth century, an integrated confusion of nationalities and classes mingle in the streets, a fact often noted by writers.

While Bowles appears at moments to appreciate the liminality and excitement of another "interzone"—the cosmopolitanism of Istanbul certainly rivaled that of Tangier in the 1950s—the bulk of the essay nevertheless is dedicated largely to criticism of the perils of the "hybridization" he sees everywhere around him. He breaches this topic by way of language. On the boat he happens to look at a cookie he is about to put in his mouth: "It was an ordinary little arrowroot tea-biscuit, and on it were embossed the words HAYD PARK. Contemplating this edible tidbit, I recalled what friends had told me of the amusing havoc that results when the Turks phoneticize words borrowed from other languages" (Bowles 1957, 75). A "funny" discussion follows in which Bowles mocks the "parroting" of English words in Turkish: "SKOÇ TUID looks like nothing; suddenly it becomes Scotch Tweed. TUVALET, TRENÇKOT, OTOTEKNIK, and SEKSOLOJI likewise reveal their messages as one stares at them" (Bowles 1957, 75). The humor and havoc, however, quickly give way to the cultural critique that concludes the subchapter.

> Synthetic orthography is a constantly visible reminder of Turkey's determination to be "modern." The country has turned its back on the East and Eastern

> concepts, not with the simple yearning of other Islamic countries to be European or to acquire American techniques, but with a conscious will to transform itself from the core outward—even to destroy itself culturally, if need be. (Bowles 1957, 75–76)

"Synthetic orthography" refers to the language reforms introduced in the nineteenth century by modernist intellectuals who argued for an official language closer to that of common people. The educated used Ottoman Turkish, a sophisticated mixture of Arabic, Persian, and Turkish, which belonged to three different language families, Ural-Altaic, Indo-European, and Semitic. After the War of Independence, the "language revolution" (*Dil Devrimi*), officially begun in 1928, became central to the nationalist program of Kemal Atatürk. Aiming to steer the new Republic toward democratic forms of government and away from its Ottoman and thus theocratic past (the Sultan was both the civil and religious leader); Atatürk made language a central concern. Replacing the Ottoman alphabet with Latin letters plus a few variants, each sound in Turkish was given a symbol. And because vowel sounds have not had the time to change as they have in English, Turkish in 1957, as well as today, remains perfectly phonetical. Language reform was one of many reforms actualized by Atatürk and his ministers, along with the abolishment of the Sultanate in 1922 and the adoption of a constitution in 1924; the annulment of the Caliphate in 1923, and thus the replacement of the *Shariat* with European legal codes and the shutting of the *Medresses* or religious schools; the interdiction of the fez for men (due to the social status and factionalism connected to them) and the discouragement of the veil for women. Atatürk saw the future political and social alliances of Turkey as Western rather than Eastern oriented.

Paul Bowles may or may not have been aware of the complicated historical and political conditions that led eventually to the "synthetic orthography" of modern Turkish, a language spoken and written today by over sixty million people. While it may be correct to say that the language reforms had, and still have, the unfortunate effect of cutting Turkish people off from much of their Ottoman past, a subject of debate today among Turkish intellectuals and scholars, it is difficult to conclude that Atatürk's reforms have led only to the destruction of culture. Bowles, like many Occidentals who critique the independence movements of "developing" nations, is not, in any case, as concerned with Turkey per se in his essay as he is with the anticolonial polemic he applies to all Muslim countries. Neither is his ambivalence toward Turkish reforms singular. Countries who appear too eager to adopt "Western" forms in a national attempt to forge a "better life" out of the ruins of exhausted monarchies have often been criticized by Western sources. Westernization is seen as a weakness by those whose own wars of independence based on distant Enlightenment theories of self-determination now seem the stuff of legend.

Antipathy toward modernization in "third world" countries is seen throughout Bowles's fiction. In "A Time of Friendship," his short story about an older woman's relationship with a young boy in the Sahara, the protagonist, Fraulein Windling, expresses hatred for the African ports: "This place would be a convenient model for Hell," she writes a friend, "a full-blown example of the social degeneracy achieved by forced cultural hybridization" (Bowles 1986, 344). Hybridization, a catchword in Bowles's lexicon for elements that are mixed and impure in "native" cultures, is often synonymous with "degeneracy" in the texts. Characters such as Fraulein Windling who seek the recovery of an organic community or unmediated connection with nature and "natural" people are often frustrated in their quests. Fraulein Windling holds Western powers responsible for the bad conditions, the "populace debased and made hostile by generations of merciless exploitation" (Bowles 1986, 344). Yet she is ambivalent about the War of Independence brewing in the North of the country:

> There in the south the fighting was far away, and the long hours of empty desert that lay between made it seem much farther, almost as though it had been across the sea. If the men of her oasis should ever be infected by the virus of discontent from the far-off north—and this seemed to her almost inconceivable—then in spite of the fact that she was certain that the war could bring them nothing but unhappiness, she would have no recourse but to hope for their victory. (Bowles 1986, 337)

Bowles consciously examines the inconsistencies in the foreign woman's allegiances. The story is about, among other things, the end of her access to the beloved oasis where she has passed three-quarters of each year for an indeterminate number of years. Her departure—foreigners at the end of the story are ordered to leave because of the war—signals an end of innocence, both hers and the country's. It is an innocence grounded, however, in Fraulein Windling's kind-hearted but ultimately narrow vision of a country's political future. Her utopia, Bowles shows us, has been another person's segregation, for better or for worse, in the twentieth century.

The following commentary on *The Sheltering Sky,* and on the attitude therein toward hybridization in the Arab world in Bowles's fiction, is revealing if only because the writer ignores the pains Bowles takes to treat the subject with subtlety.

> The Arab world . . . with its filth, disease, and poverty is an innately destructive world dominated by an ancient spirit of evil. Because of its mixture of races, creeds, and castes, it has no fixed center of moral or religious law. It becomes, therefore, the perfect external equivalent of the spiritual emptiness and moral anarchy of the Moresby's and, through them, of all modern civilization. (Aldridge 1971, 186)

Antedating postcolonial theories of the later twentieth century, at least in English, (the publication date of the American text above is 1971), the statement nevertheless identifies a dominant strain in Bowles's treatment of the Arab or Muslim world: the lack of a "fixed center" due to the "mixture" of races is the site of tension in the stories. In the essay on Istanbul, that mixture is also identified as a source of "spiritual emptiness and moral anarchy," at least according to Abdeslam:

> Abdeslam asked for the check, and objected when he saw that it was written with Roman characters. "Arabic!" he demanded. "You Moslem? Then bring the check in Arabic." Apologetically the manager explained that writing in Arabic was "dangerous," and had been known on occasion to put the man who did it into jail. To this he added, just to make things quite clear, that any man who veiled his wife also went to jail. "A man must not be *very* Moslem," he said. But Abdeslam had had enough. "I *very very* Moslem," he announced. We left the room. (Bowles 1957, 80)

As in the fiction, Bowles avoids making secure pronouncements. Screened by a dramatic monologue, as it were, Bowles allows Abdeslam to tease out the injustice

21. Karaköy Square and the no longer existent Karaköy Mosque.

both the American and the Moroccan locate in the State's continued suppression of Islam influenced Ottoman practices. Each has his own reasons for disapproval: Abdeslam because he honors *Shariat,* not secular democracy; Bowles because he honors democracy, but not necessarily secularism, at least in Eastern countries.

> Sometime after we had gone to bed, following a long silence during which I thought he had fallen asleep, Abdeslam called over to me: "That Mustapha Kemal was carrion! He ruined his country. The son of a dog!" Because I was writing, and also because I am not sure exactly where I stand in this philosophical dispute, I said. "You're right. *Allah imsik bekhir.*" (Bowles 1957, 80)

Bowles avoids taking a stand at the end of the subchapter. His abstention, however, suggests that he is willing to entertain the idea that Turkey would be better served by turning the clock back to the days of Ottoman rule (which in 1953 would be only a question of thirty-odd years). Westernization has led to the repression of "passionate" Islam as well as certain civil rights. Turkey, as far as Bowles can see, has chosen the wrong path of atonement. The rejection of the East and all Eastern concepts has meant the rejection of the country's pure unmixed native roots. Next to the devout Abdeslam, the Turks in the subchapter are made to appear rootless, thus spineless, and, in consequence, often apologetic.

In an earlier chapter of the collection, "Mustapha and his Friends," Bowles offers another cynical sketch of modern, urban Muslims, this time Moroccans of Fez. He applies the name "Mustapha" allegorically to signify the "illiterate city-dweller," the main character of the lengthy animated invective. Mustapha of Fez, like Mustapha of Istanbul, he suggests by association, is also incapable of participating in modern democratic processes.

> Mustapha does not believe in the same good or evil as we do. Such personal concepts as continence and honesty, such social virtues as taste for "the democratic way of life" and a sense of civic responsibility, mean very little to him. He thinks of peace as that boring and meaningless interlude between wars, of democracy as a weak and corrupt substitute for autocracy. The best ruler is a benevolent tyrant. (Bowles 1957, 60)

This is not conventional racist rhetoric. The urban Moroccan, like the urban Turk, has reached this acute state of degeneration because he is not Moroccan enough—Moroccan in the pure, premodern sense. The confusion of ancient tradition and modern urban culture has reduced Mustapha of Fez to a bad "Easterner": he is generally ignorant and thus dangerous; an outdated fatalism keeps him unproductive; an incapacity for conducting himself honestly makes him unpredictable. Whatever the historical reasons for the respective devolution of the species, both Moroccans and Turks are not, at present, and in the context of the nonfiction collection, suitable candidates for European forms of civil government.

> That which is all-powerful goes far beyond the realm of moral considerations. The supreme law of the universe is that what is inexorable is thereby right, and he wants to feel that there is something of this quality in the character of his earthly ruler. As long as he remains the way he is, he will align himself with the faction which has the greatest number of visible attributes of ruthless power. This is something which the statesman, both Moslem and otherwise, seem inclined to overlook when they speak of imposing upon him the onus of universal suffrage and make their perilous plans for initiating him into the mysteries of the democratic way of life. (Bowles 1957, 73)

This conclusion to "Mustapha and his Friends" serves as a harbinger for the kind of social and cultural wasteland he identifies in the following chapter on Istanbul. The statesmen he refers to in the case of Morocco are those behind the independence movement. Just as Mustafa Kemal erred in imposing democracy on the Turkish population from without, present agitators for civil democracy in Morocco, according to Bowles, are naïve in their expectations of the average "illiterate city-dweller's" capacity for self-rule.

APOLOGISTS FOR BOWLES insist that he is different from other twentieth-century Orientalists. Greg Mullins in *Colonial Affairs*, a study of desire and discourse in the "Interzone," argues that because Bowles is continually struggling with his colonial position, his writing answers "the rigid, stereotyped roles structured by colonial discourse" with "multiplicity" and "indeterminacy" (Mullins 2002, 8). He "forges new forms of affect, desire, and deterritorialized subjectivity," and finally "critiques the nostalgic fantasy for a lost colonial era" (Mullins 2002, 5, 18). Similarly, Marilyn Adler Papayanis argues that while some of Bowles's fiction is "radically isolationist and dehumanist" (though she argues that if considered in terms of, for example, a postmodern discourse of eroticism à la Foucault or Bataille, and not merely in terms of classical Orientalist hedonism, much of the violence is productive rather than gratuitous), other stories "explore, however provisionally, the possibility of intersubjective recognition between the expatriate and the native" (Papayanis 2005, 141). In such stories, "an ethics of constructive engagement with the other" produces tensions that "animate" the literature (Papayanis 2005, 141). Papayanis also notes that due to their contact with the industrial West and the colonial powers, Moroccan figures are usually "hybrid products of colonial occupation" in the fiction (Papayanis 2005, 144). Those "drawn to zones of dis-integration," the "intercises of cultural, religious and political systems" are drawn to Morocco also because they are in search of the other side of the cultural equation that hybridity creates: a way "to recuperate some sense of the premodern" (Papayanis 2005, 144).

Nostalgia is certainly not a sentiment or atmosphere one associates with Bowles's stories of disintegrating identities. His preoccupation with the premodern, however, lends his fiction and nonfiction an air of restless ennui, wrestling as it always is with the ascendancy of the modern. In the preface to *Their Heads Are Green and and Their Hands Are Blue* Bowles quotes from *Tristes Tropiques* in the context of a discussion on the "charm" of the cultural "backwardness" at risk worldwide from irresponsible Western industry:

> M. Claude Lévi-Strauss, the anthropologist, claims that in order for the Western world to continue to function properly it must constantly get rid of vast quantities of waste matter, which it dumps on less fortunate peoples. "What travel discloses to us first of all is our garbage, flung in the face of humanity." (Bowles 1957, viii)

Bowles's interest in the premodern is influenced by his reading of Lévi-Strauss and other French cultural anthropologists such as Lucien Lévy-Bruhl who worked on "primitive" cultures (Papayanis 2005, 151). Like that of Lévi-Strauss, Bowles's conception of "the savage mind" resembles that of Montaigne's cannibal: untainted by a corrupting modern civilization the savage, as natural man, is superior to his cultivated, thus unnatural cousin who dumps the excesses of his overproductive, superfluous culture in the former's port and at his front door. Of particular significance to Bowles's representation of the primitive throughout his oeuvre are Lévi-Strauss's ideas on the function of the imaginative or instinctive faculties under modernization. Hayden White in *Tropics of Discourse* discusses this idea at length in the work of Lévi-Strauss and others:

> [Lévi-Strauss] suggests that what civilized men conventionally call "the savage mind" is a repository of a particularly powerful imaginative faculty that has all but disappeared from its "civilized" counterpart under the impact of modernization. The savage mind, he maintains, is the product of a unique kind of relation to the cosmos that we exterminate at the peril of our own humanity. (White 1978, 177)

This "unique relation to the cosmos" is what Bowles regularly laments the loss of in the countries he visits and writes about. Like Freud, Jung, and Lévi-Strauss, Bowles mourns the external triumph of technology, and in his fiction in particular he directs the quest for the "noble savage" into the human psyche (White 1978, 154). Occidentals in the fiction experience mysterious crises in the native quarters of North African towns and villages, and more often in the vast silence of the desert. What ensues is enlightenment, but not enlightenment in a humanist sense. Characters—Kit in *The Sheltering Sky*, Frauline Windling in "A Time of

Friendship"—learn things that broaden their understanding of their place in the universe, but the universe is not one the reader recognizes, nor is understanding a cognitive act. Each character is drawn into a "savage" space where something they do not recognize in themselves is released. Kit, modern and high strung yet intellectually and emotionally dependent on her abstracted husband, disappears into the role of concubine and then fifth wife of the Bedouin Belqassim. When Frauline Windling's enthusiasm reveals itself as a mission to teach the native boy and results in his destruction and consumption of a crèche she painstakingly constructs for his religious edification, she is shocked into the recognition that after so many years she has no real idea where she is and who these "natural" people are. When she leaves, she takes her interrupted development back with her to Switzerland. Bowles never suggests that foreigners are improved by their "savage" experiences in Morocco. He shows only that something in each character's psyche is released, allowing them to lose or forget themselves and enter into previously inconceivable relations with others. For better or for worse, the subjective positions of each shift in the case of Frauline Windling, or dissolve in the case of Kit.

Hayden White argues that in times of "universal rejection of the conventional image of 'normal' humanity . . . radicalism lay in the adoption" of antitypes (White 1978, 172). Primitives become idealized as reformers capable of throwing off the restraints of civilization; releasing us from normal social contexts, primitivism "insists that this lost world is still latently present in modern, corrupt and civilized man . . ."(White 1978, 171). Past Romantic primitives like Montaigne and Rousseau, he says, were not necessarily concerned about the conditions of the natives they reference in their texts in support of primitivism. Rather they are interested in criticizing the values and lifestyles of the nobility in their respective societies. Montaigne's primitive, like Lévi-Strauss's and Bowles's, function as "repositories of all we have lost through civilization," most importantly our organic relationship to the universe (White 1978, 176–77). White traces the roots of modernity's preoccupation with the primitive back to Greek and Hebraic myths of the Wild Man, a figure existing beyond the realms of social control. For many Greek thinkers the barbarian (the *barbaros*) was anyone who did not speak Greek, one who babbled, and thus "lacked the one power by which the political life could be achieved and true humanity realized" (White 1978, 165). Similarly, in Hebraic myth, the Wild Man is unable to speak; "in a morally ordered world, to be wild is to be incoherent or mute, deceptive, oppressive and destructive, sinful, accursed and exiled": Cain, Ham, and Ishmael (White 1978, 162). In both cases, Greek or Hebraic, the Wild Man is incapable of establishing culture.

Paul Bowles harnesses the role of language, or lack of language, depicted in both traditions in his own representation of the primitive. In "A Distant Episode," a short story written in 1945 and published in *Partisan Review* in 1947, he writes of a professor of linguistics who has his tongue brutally cut out by members of a desert tribe in Morocco. Through the action Bowles allegorizes the words of St. Augustine, "As the tongue is the instrument of domination, in its pride was punished" (from *City of God,* 2:112, qtd. in White 1978, 162). The protagonist mutates from self-contained Western academic to "holy maniac" running in the streets of a southern Saharien village (Bowles 1986, 48). Punished for his pride, or rather, released from it, the professor is banished forever from language, and thus from culture and political life. The Reguiba tribe functions as an instrument of God's vengeance in the story—a common function of the "heathen" in Christian texts (see, for example, Martin Luther). Bowles, however, adapts the idea not only for the orthodox message it contains, but also for the unorthodox story it helps foster.

Bowles's idealization of the premodern in his fiction carries within it these allegiances to the transgressive, primitive antitype. We note, however, that these myths also inform his nonfiction, and most particularly his essay on Istanbul. The city, like the professor, is guilty of pride. In this case, however, it has forged an unnatural relationship with an inorganic concept of existence. Consequently, it too has had its native tongue removed, its original language replaced with a kind of barbaric mimicry. Initiating his discussion of the corrupting effects of Western civilization on Turkey through a discussion of language, Bowles summons classical Greek and Hebraic mythic associations of language with culture and political life. Modern Turkey, intent on destroying itself "from the core outward," has turned its back on its "natural" allies in the East first by rejecting their language (Bowles 1957, 75–76). In its incoherent state, Turkey, continues Bowles's primitive logic, is now incapable of establishing or maintaining a meaningful culture.

Everywhere he looks in Istanbul he sees other signs of the corruption of an original, premodern culture. Like Mark Twain, Bowles notes the hybrid dress of the crowds on Galata Bridge:

> By Western standards it is not a well-dressed crowd. The chaotic sartorial effect achieved by the populace in Istanbul is not necessarily due to poverty, but rather to a divergent conception of the uses to which European garments should be put . . . Apart from language there seems to be no one common element, not even shabbiness, since there are usually a few men and women who do understand how to wear their clothing. (Bowles 1957, 84)

Just as Turks are confused by the clothing imposed on them by their government in league with the West, neither can they defend their eating establishments against the intrusion of the modern technology that corrupts the native atmosphere.

> Pandeli's is the only native restaurant I have seen that doesn't sport a huge refrigerated showcase packed with food. You are usually led to this and told to choose what you want to eat. In the glare of the fluorescent lighting the food looks pallid and untempting, particularly the meat, which has been hacked into unfamiliar-looking cuts. During your meal there is usually a radio playing ancient jazz; occasionally a Turkish or Syrian number comes up. Although the tea is good, it is not good enough to warrant its being served as though it were nectar, in infinitesimal glasses that can be drained at one gulp. (Bowles 1957, 87)

Not recognizing the native traditions he claims to covet when he stumbles upon them, Bowles unwittingly lists small tea glasses (a way of drinking tea that dates to before the landing at Plymouth) in what amounts to a list of primitivist complaints. If modern technology and Western tastes are not grafting themselves onto the developing economy with enough grace for Bowles's taste; it is not merely a question of incompetence on the part of Turks. Corrupt as the desire to modernize is from the onset, there is no graceful way to yoke two civilizations so fundamentally distinct from one another.

As figures who tend to challenge systems—threatening cosmic order, in the case of Prometheus, or civil order, in the cases of Ishmael and Cain—the archetypal primitive also poses a biological threat, that of "species corruption" (White 1978, 160).

> Natural disorder . . . has its extreme form in species corruption, the mixing of kinds . . . , the joining together of what God in his wisdom had, at the beginning,

22. Park Hotel near Taksim, 1950s.

> decreed should remain asunder . . . mixing is unnatural and destructive of a condition of species isolation that is a moral as well as natural necessity. The mix of kinds is taboo. (White 1978, 160)

Bowles holds the perils of hybridization responsible for the disorder that is Istanbul. The unnatural mixing of language, material culture, and political philosophy has led to the devolution of the country. According to Bowles, Turkey is a Muslim country rather than a secular republic whose constitution, like those of other modern nations including the United States, mandates a separation of church and state; Turkey is an Oriental or Eastern culture, rather than a cosmopolitan metropolis geopolitically poised at the crossroads of many civilizations, past and present. Thus, behind Bowles's anticolonial argument for Turkey lie other more compromised notions of what is natural and right for it.

Because Islam is consistently the site of danger for Occidental characters in his stories, a danger albeit sought out, Islamic culture is never an unnuanced signifier in his work. Thus, when he speaks out in support of Islamic law, one may be inclined to charge him with contradicting himself. But there is no contradiction. In Istanbul, a city where East and West come "dangerously" close together, Bowles makes a reactionary move to reestablish borders. The mixing of kinds, though he represents these phenomena as the negative fallout of Turkey's postcolonial condition and not as racist theory, is nevertheless demonized. Bowles does not say this directly: he lets Abdeslam curse the country for him in terms he distances himself from, but nowhere contradicts. The Moroccan Muslim has been berating Turkish worshippers in a mosque for wearing Western clothes, berets, and caps "with the visors at the back":

> [Abdeslam] knows that the wearing of the *tarboosh* is forbidden by law, but his hatred of Kemal Atatürk, which is growing hourly ever since his arrival, had become too intense, I suppose, for him to be able to repress it any longer. His big moment came when the imam entered. He approached the venerable gentlemen with elaborate selaams which were enthusiastically reciprocated. Then the two retired into a private room for ten minutes of so. When Abdeslam came out there were tears in his eyes and he wore an expression of triumph. "Ah, you see?" he cried, as we emerged into the street. "That poor man is very, *very* unhappy. They have only one day of Ramadan in the year." Even I was a little shocked to hear that the traditional month had been whittled down to a day. "This is an accursed land," he went on. "When we get power we'll soak it in petrol and set it afire and burn everyone in it. May it forever be damned! And all these dogs living in it, I pray Allah they may be thrown into the fires of Gehenem. Ah, if we only had our power back for one day, we Moslems! May Allah speed that day when we ride onto Turkey and smash their government and all their works of Satan!" The imam, it seems, had been delighted beyond measure to see a young man who still had the proper respect for religion; he had complained bitterly that the youth of Turkey was spiritually lost. (Bowles 1957, 90–91)

While the qualifier "proper" for the noun "respect" is used ironically (Bowles might not condone Abdeslam's murderous sentiments, but nevertheless enjoys his "fiery," histrionic, "Eastern" rhetoric), Bowles will agree with Abdeslam that Turks are spiritually lost. The language he assigns himself is not theological but it corroborates Abdeslam's reactionary assessment of Turkey's misguided secularism.

> Material benefits may be accrued in this worldwide game of refusing to be oneself. Are these benefits worth the inevitable void produced by such destruction? The question is apposite in every case where the traditional beliefs of a people have been systematically modified by its government. Rationalizing words like "progress," "modernization," or "democracy" mean nothing because, even if they are used sincerely, the imposition of such concepts by force from above cancels whatever value they might otherwise have. There is little doubt that by having been made indifferent Moslems the younger generation in Turkey has become more like our idea of what people living in the twentieth century should be. The old helplessness in the face of *mektoub* (it is written) is gone, and in its place is a passionate belief in man's ability to alter his destiny. That is the greatest step of all; once it has been made, anything, unfortunately, can happen. (Bowles 1957, 95–96)

While Bowles is just in his claims concerning the wholesale abuse of words like "progress" and "democracy" in the twentieth century, what he seems to propose for the void created by modernization in Turkey is an Islamic, or Islam-influenced form of governance. And certainly an indifferent, or moderate Islam is as good for the West as indifferent or moderate Christianity is for the East—particularly when both religions, as well as many of their derivatives, share geography, as is the case in Turkey. But Bowles is speaking ironically. His statement implicates the Christian West in the spiritual crisis of the Muslim East.

His lamentation over the collapse of fate as a governing existential principle in modern Turkish lives and his disappointment over the ascendancy of such Enlightenment virtues as the exercise of free will is one more illustration of his primitivism. His assumptions of what is spiritually particular to or appropriate for the East, of what in Turkey constitutes a "unique" relation to the cosmos, are classically Orientalist in scope. Opposing technology and its attendant secularism to spirituality and its attendant Islam in Turkey, Bowles argues that the extermination of the latter by the former has put the country's humanity in peril. In an earlier essay in the same collection, "Notes Mailed at Nagercoil," Bowles makes a similar argument concerning the threat of modern technology in India.

> Today's paper announced an outbreak of bubonic plague in Bellary. I keep thinking about it, and I wonder if the almost certain eventual victory over such

> diseases will prove to have been worth its price: the extinction of the beliefs and rituals which gave a satisfactory meaning to the period of consciousness that goes between birth and death. I doubt it. Security is a false god; begin making sacrifices to it and you are lost. (Bowles 1957, 58)

The final sylleptic pun puts the stability of his claims in question here ("sacrifice" is associated with "ritual" and "real" gods in the Western imaginary), making this conclusive remark an example of the sleight of hand at which Bowles is deft, and that invites claims to his provisionality. But the semiotic given at the center of this text is, in fact, "better their bodies die than their spirituality." "Such diseases" are the same that devastated populations in the Middle Ages, destroyed most of London in the eighteenth century, and have since been eradicated in the plague-weary West. But in order to "be oneself" in India, or Turkey, according to Bowles's logic above, one must reject the kinds of knowledge that compromise mysticism, even if this means death by rejection of technology.

Bowles falls into the Occidental primitivist misunderstanding that knowledge, as opposed to sorcery or religion, is not universal but Western. Forgetting or ignoring the transfer of knowledge from East to West during the Middle Ages, the kinds of discoveries in math and science that gave rise to the Renaissance in Europe, the idea that knowledge is something the East receives, either willfully or by force, from the West is, in the big picture, anachronistic at best. Highly conscious of the double bind endemic to the primitivism in his own cultural anthropology, Lévi-Strauss concludes as follows the critique of Western hegemony in the "third world" that Bowles refers to in his own preface.

> And so I am caught within a circle from which there is no escape: the less human societies were able to communicate with each other and therefore to correct each other through contact, the less their respective emissaries were able to perceive the wealth and significance of their diversity. (Lévi-Strauss 1955, 51)

Unlike Bowles's nervous treatment of cross-fertilization, primarily from West to East in his nonfiction, and from East to West in his fiction, Lévi-Strauss does not register the loss of innocence of one culture through its contact with another without reminding himself and the reader that such binary ways of thinking are reductive and thus potentially dishonest. "I am subject to a double infirmity," he continues, "all that I perceive offends me, and I constantly reproach myself for not seeing as much as I should (Lévi-Strauss 1955, 51). Bowles carries with him the heavy weight of self-loathing common to expatriates from imperialist nations. Unlike his mentor, Bowles remains offended by any signs of home he sees, and rarely, at least in the writing, reproaches himself for not seeing more. In a 1933 letter to Aaron Copland, Bowles explains why for him America feels "haunted."

> I hate America because I feel attached to it, and I don't want to feel that way. In Africa for instance, I can sit and feel unlocated; I can look at the landscape and turn the page and look at another, and it means nothing. But here I look at the landscape and it looks back at me, and I am frightened of it, and I want to get out as fast as possible. (qtd. in Papayanis 2005, 145)

While twenty-odd years separate this youthful statement from things written in *Their Heads Are Green and Their Hands Are Blue,* we nevertheless see the early traces of what will blossom into full-fledged Oriental primitivism in the nonfiction.

Bowles concludes the essay on Istanbul with a sentimental tribute to Abdeslam's "archaic" convictions:

> Abdeslam is not a happy person. He sees the world, which he knows is a good world, being assailed from all sides, slowly crumbling before his eyes. He has no means of understanding me should I try to explain to him that in this age what he considers to be religion is called superstition, and that religion today has come to be a desperate attempt to integrate metaphysics with science. Something will have to be found to replace the basic wisdom which has been destroyed, but the discovery will not be soon; neither Abdeslam nor I will ever know of it. (Bowles 1957, 96)

Abdeslam's lack of "means" for understanding "alternative" ontologies is not treated as a deficiency but as evidence of his purity. Ignorance, however, is not necessarily bliss in Abdeslam's case; he is, we are told, unhappy. But this Muslim's apocalyptic brand of Islam is preferable to a Western Humanism, fraught as it is with contending realms of belief that leave no room for older, purer forms of "basic wisdom." A primitivist essentialism informs Bowles's construct of modern Turkey: primitivist desire rather than a considered assessment of the country's place in history motivates his critique of the young republic.

In 1953 Bowles would still prefer an Istanbul more like the Oriental cities one finds in *Thousand and One Nights,* the collection of ancient Indian, Persian, and Arabic folk tales popular in the West where landscapes, unlike those in "serious" works of classical Arabic literature, are haunted by sorcerers and jinns (Dawood 1954, 7). In the 1970s, Bowles gives the following reasons for his continued residence in Tangier:

> So far it has been touched by fewer of the negative aspects of contemporary civilization than most cities of it size. More important than that, I relish the idea that in the night, all around me in my sleep, sorcery is burrowing its invisible tunnels in every direction, from thousands of senders to thousands of unsuspecting recipients. Spells are being cast, poison is running its course, souls are being depossessed of parasitic pseudo-consciousnesses that lurk in the unguarded recesses of the mind. (Bowles 1972, 369)

Bowles primitivism, like his conception of the picturesque, is darker, thus more interesting, than that of the average tourist. More dangerous than sorcerers and jinns is the willful disregard of primitive forms of spiritualism in the East, or the disregard of that corollary in the West, the unconscious that has left the night air and migrated to the intangible seat of the primitive (Stewart 1973, 78). Apparently unaware of pre-Islamic forms of shamanism in Turkic cultures, Bowles chooses for Turks an orthodox spiritualism that satisfies his demands for the unconscious of the "Moslem world."

Primitivism for Bowles has existential ramifications which he often couches in the apocalyptic rhetoric of Old Testament prophets: "The seeker of the picturesque sees the spread of technology as an unalloyed abomination" (Bowles 1957, viii). Technology in the East as abomination is "unnatural," a portent of disaster to come. Imploding the divisions of labor as delineated by a binary construct of West as industrial and East as preindustrial or primitive, Western technology in the picturesque East threatens the souls of natural men who like children have "no means of understanding" the monster in their midst.

And what they do not understand will not cure them; it will kill them. Bowles wants nothing to do with the mysteries of the industrial world and travels in search of refuge from it, insisting that "alien cultures" remain innocent, unravaged brides of time. And if and when the "Third World" gains access to Western forms of knowledge then it is necessary to locate and isolate initiates who threaten native culture from within.

Bowles blames internal abomination on educated native minorities in Muslim countries who, due to their "irrational longing . . . to cease being themselves and become Westerners," are enthralled by the "various gadget-forms of our "garbage" which "make convenient fetishes to assist in achieving the magic transformation (Bowles 1957, viii-ix). Focusing on material culture alone in his preface (or "beatnik," thus Westernized arts culture among Moroccan youth in his chapter "Africa Minor"), he avoids a critical discussion of Western ideology in terms of the independence movements that are being instigated by "educated minorities" in Morocco and Algeria in the mid-twentieth century, and that were instigated by similar groups in Turkey at the turn of the century. An essentialist "barbarism" in the Moslem world, a lack of understanding, and an inability to speak the languages of modern geopolitics may be positive things in the light of the expatriate's antimodernism. And while he may have the "developing world's" best interests and aesthetics at heart, he is also worried, according to a 1952 interview, about the effects the modernization of Moslem cultures will have on world stability:

> I don't think we're likely to get to know the Moslems well . . . their culture is essentially barbarous, their mentality that of a purely predatory people . . . These political aspirations . . . are absurd, and any realization of them will have a disastrous effect on the rest of the world. (qtd. in Stewart 1973, 99)

Barbarians and predators are not bad characters in Bowles's fictional world; they are, as we have seen, instruments of regenerative destruction. But when these same characters step into the world of nonfiction by developing political aspirations, they become less aesthetically contained, less agreeable, and finally dangerous to the civilized world. Bowles thus asks Moslem countries not to struggle for what Christian countries have fought numerous wars for: universal suffrage and the pursuit of modern forms of happiness, like world travel or voluntary expatriation.

Bowles often appears to be quite conscious of his historical position as a privileged American in Tangier in the 1950s. In retrospect, he says the following of the beach parties and champagne in Tangier with his wife Jane, Truman Capote, and other New Yorkers: "The summer proved to be the apogee of postwar prosperity in the international zone. Immediately afterward the cracks in the façade grew wider, until the entire edifice collapsed in the riots of 1952" (Bowles 1972, 291–92). But Bowles's radicalism is ultimately reactionary. As Freud, Marx, and Nietzsche all agreed, when one group of men in society purchases its peace of mind or security at the cost of the suffering of another, we often witness a "return of the repressed" (White 1978, 179–80). The "return" takes the form of the independence movements of developing democracies in the twentieth century, phenomena Bowles may support somewhere in principle but which offend his aesthetics nonetheless. Though he maintains a certain ambiguity in his fiction concerning reform in the Muslim world, his essay on Istanbul clarifies his position. In Turkey, the Nationalist Movement has come and gone, its battle scars still evident in the asymmetric textures of the city. He sees the future of North Africa in Istanbul and he realizes the end of his Eastern relief is near.

> Each time I go to a place I have not seen before, I hope it will be as different as possible from the places I already know. I assume it is natural for a traveler to seek diversity, and that it is the human element which makes him most aware of difference. If people and their manner of living were alike everywhere, there would not be much point in moving from one place to another. (Bowles 1957, vii)

Read today, these opening lines in the preface to *Their Heads Are Green and Their Hands Are Blue* sound like a wry parody of postcolonial rhetoric, because the Bowles we know would locate the catchwords "diversity" and "difference," find them banal and altruistic and in need of deflating. And he does purposefully solicit the ire of "strong minded" liberals in 1963 (he mentions a "French lady") with self-consciously reactionary lines: "But the visitor to a place whose charm is a result of its backwardness is inclined to hope it will remain that way, regardless of how its inhabitants may feel" (Bowles 1957, viii). Jokes aside, however, Bowles, like Kit at the end of *The Sheltering Sky,* turns away from the West and looks toward the desert for personal fulfillment: "No other place is quite strong enough for you, no other surroundings can provide the supremely satisfying sensation of existing in the midst of something that is absolute" (qtd. in Stewart 1973, 72). And it has no answering language. The desert, at least, is silent.

6

"Dearest Flower of Istanbul"

Nelson Algren, Simone de Beauvoir, and Who Lost an American?

> Dearest flower of Istanbul . . .
>
> —SIMONE DE BEAUVOIR to Nelson Algren, March 5, 1961

NELSON ALGREN may no longer be a household name except in Chicago. Many American men over fifty, however, nod their heads at his mention as if to suggest that Nelson Algren, like minor league baseball, still holds a distinct though distant place in their collective psyche. Algren is most famous for his novel *The Man with the Golden Arm* (1949) made into a Hollywood movie in 1956 starring Frank Sinatra (though Marlon Brando had initially been chosen for the part). The novel received the National Book Award in 1949, but as the Beat writer Edward Sanders tells us, Algren remained "neglected by the poohbahs of literary officialdom," while Sanders, "like hundreds of thousands" of other high school kids across the country in the 1950s, read what amounted to a cult novel (qtd. in Horvath 2005, 153). He would also become known for his 1956 novel, *A Walk on the Wild Side.*

"I was going to write a war novel," says Algren in a 1955 *Paris Review* interview, "but it turned out to be this *Golden Arm* thing. I mean, the war kind of slipped away and those people with the hypos came along and that was it" (qtd. in Simon 1998, 81). *The Man with the Golden Arm* is a transitional novel. Conceptually and stylistically grounded in the social realism of the 1930s, the novel sustains the tradition on through the end of World War II and applies its hard-edged palpability to the lives of the postwar urban poor. The protagonist, Frankie Machine, a hard-luck war vet, is now a junkie, and his life and the lives of those around him on the South Side of Chicago contradict and darken the popular conception of postwar prosperity and contentment. Algren, like Frankie Machine, had served unenthusiastically in the war, though his early allegiances to the political Left had initially caused him to be aggressively opposed to it. Like many progressives in the 1940s, he conceded only after Pearl Harbor and after his horror of European forms of Fascism outweighed his distrust of U.S. foreign policy. But to locate Algren's ethos, the one that both made and then unmade his place in American letters, one has to look to his background as well as to the literary community he joined as he was coming of age as a writer.

Born in Detroit in 1909 to working-class parents of Swedish and Jewish origin, Algren grew up on the South Side of Chicago. Educated in the public school system, he played on the streets but was bookish and later managed to enter the University of Illinois. He was studying journalism when the market crashed on October 29, 1929, and thus became one of the many unfortunate Americans who entered the job market just as it was disappearing. Unable to find work as a journalist in Chicago and without a family able to support him, he began to travel the roads of America looking for a livelihood. And like tens of thousands of other poor Americans, his means of transport and support were precarious. He traveled by foot, hitchhiked cars and boxcars, was a door-to-door salesman in New Orleans, a grapefruit picker, and carnival worker in Texas. He had started to send stories to papers while on the road and would return to Chicago in 1932 to concentrate on his writing. By the age of twenty-two, he had already experienced enough of the "great underworld" to furnish him with material for the rest of his writing life.

Despite the federal relief and the efforts of Roosevelt, there were breadlines and demonstrations at home. The American Communist Party was leading the efforts of the Left to challenge the systems that they felt had brought on the crash. The party had established a national network of John Reed Clubs to encourage young working-class writers and artists, and Algren began stopping by the South Michigan Avenue branch on his return to the city (Drew 1989, 50). It was here that Algren would make his first contact with the writers whose work would later be associated with his own. Richard Wright was a regular member of the club and the success of his book *Native Son,* whose title Algren lent him, would later inspire Algren to maintain faith in his subject, the great underworld of Chicago. "To my old friend Nelson," Wright would inscribe in Algren's copy of *Native Son* when it came out in 1940, "Who I believe is still the best writer of good prose in the U.S.A.—Dick" (qtd. in Drew 1989, 121).

It had not only been personal experience and the influence of literary social realism that had directed his early aesthetic. A college interest in sociology had contributed to his habit of recording the lives of the people around him. When he received a commission from the Vanguard Press to write a novel in 1933 at the age of twenty-four, he set off for a second time to travel the United States, but this time as a commissioned "sociological observer, not a destitute, unemployed vagabond" (Drew 1989, 55). Again, he moved "almost entirely by boxcar, openly friendly with hobos, asking questions as he went getting thrown in jail with them, recording their stories and expressions with an observation sharpened by political perspective" (Drew 1989, 55). Later as a field worker for the Venereal Disease Control Project in Chicago, a wartime government project, Algren gathered the colloquial Chicago expressions of the poor who were most often infected due to the cost of medical care (Drew 1989, 148). It would be Algren who "encouraged Studs Terkel in compiling the kind of oral-history interviews for which he would eventually win the Pulitzer Prize" (Drew 1989, 311).

Algren, like many Leftist writers, would not necessarily become a card-carrying party member. Like Dos Passos, he was not inclined to join political parties. But his sympathies and activism would always be with the Left, though he would pay the price for his early affiliation with the John Reed Club during the anti-Red hysteria of the 1950s. By October 1940 the FBI had classified him an internal security risk, and he would later be denied a passport (Donohue 1964, 86; Drew 1989, 146). But his politics were less ideologically motivated than grounded in the immediate economic and thus social problems of people whose lives he did not study from a distance, but understood through shared experience. Less an advocate for the working class, he considered himself a witness for the classless, a voice for Americans with no legitimate place in the culture—hobos and petty criminals, drunks and junkies, prostitutes and misguided immigrants, the underworld creatures he had grown up with or met on the road. Influenced by the precepts of naturalism and social realism, his stories and descriptions focused on the malfunctioning of society as a social organism. The "degenerates," "monsters," "maniacs," and other social infections he gave voices to were meant to be demonstrations of a cause and effect relationship between the diseases of society and the destruction of people. But if these "nonconformists" were the symptoms of the ills of poverty and injustice, they were also proof that such conditions could be diagnosed and cured. This final prospect, rather than a crippling deterministic pessimism, created the progressive energy that animated Algren's best writing, whether fiction or nonfiction.

The American literary predecessors he claimed, or are claimed for him, were writers such as Whitman, Melville, Steinbeck, Crane, Anderson, Dreiser, Sandburg, and Wright. "It would seem there is no way of becoming a serious writer without keeping shabby company," he would say of this list of socially conscious American writers whose own lives were not always joyful (Algren 1998, 18–19). Including Poe and particularly Fitzgerald in this list, writers who were so close to their subjects that they were finally devoured by them, Algren felt an affinity to writers who had taken up the cause of the nonconformist, the outsider, even at the risk of their own well being or sanity. "It would seem there is no way of becoming such a writer without becoming a victim" (Algren 1998, 19). The Chicago writers, or the Chicago literary tradition he would keep company with, included Frank Norris, Upton Sinclair, James T. Farrell, Carl Sandburg, Edna St. Vincent Millay, and, again, Richard Wright. Except for the nonfiction that would record his travels throughout the world, Chicago would remain his primary subject throughout his life," the same city where a literature bred by hard times on the river, hard times on the range, and hard times in town became a world literature" (Algren 1963, 270).

THE FEMALE CHARACTERS that Algren creates in his best writing are no less developed or rounded than his male characters, despite his reputation for misogyny in his actual life. Thus, it is interesting, perhaps apt, that Algren would also become famous, or infamous, for his seventeen-year relationship, four years of it romantic, with one of the most prominent feminist theorists of his day, Simone de Beauvoir. Algren describes their unlikely meeting in Chicago in 1947: "Somebody had told her that there were people called "Partisan Review" and she called them because she wanted to see New York . . . But chiefly she got to meet Mary McCarthy, who is still after all these years trying to figure that one out" (qtd. in Donohue 1964, 179). She had wanted to see an "Automat," and "Miss McCarthy and friends," nervous about giving "the impression that they were slumming, which would be an artificial move," would not oblige her so she went alone: "She knew the intellectual life of Paris," explains Algren, "and this sort of washed-out New York intellectual life which depended so much on Paris became uninteresting to her in no time" (qtd. in Donohue 1964, 180). In New York she met Mary

Guggenheim, who gave her Algren's number in Chicago. Algren had not caught her name on the telephone and did not know whom he was meeting. Nervous about meeting any friend of Mary McCarthy—"I don't want a date with Mary McCarthy even by surrogate"—he waited until she had gone in and out of the door four times before "deciding in her favor."

According to both Algren and de Beauvoir their attraction had been mutual, their affinity immediate. She would stay with Algren for three days, going on daily and nightly tours around his version of America, Chicago's South Side.

> I showed her the electric chair, the psychiatric wards, neighborhood bars where I told her everyone sitting around was a sinister character. She looked around awhile and then told me, "I think you are the only sinister thing around here." Then I took her to a midnight mission. I thought it was time to SAVE HER SOUL. I took her to cheap burlesques, Maxwell street, a police line-up and the zoo. I explained American literature, how the police operate, the Loeb-Leopold case, the Heirens case, the Haymarket riots, and why I was the only serious writer in Chicago since Dick Wright left in the 1930s. Later she told me she hadn't understood a single word I'd said in three days of self-perpetuating conversation. (Donohue 1964, 182)

Simone de Beauvoir's own account of her first arrival in the United States in her autobiography, *Force of Circumstance,* corroborates Algren's discussion of her antibourgeois sentiments and her reaction to American intellectualism.

> I was prepared to love America. It was the homeland of capitalism, yes, but it had helped save Europe from Fascism . . . The reality was a great shock to me. There flourished among almost all the intellectuals, even those who claimed to be of the Left, an Americanism worthy of the chauvinism of my father. They approved all of Truman's speeches. Their anti-Communism verged on neurosis; their attitude toward Europe, toward France, was one of arrogant condescension . . .
>
> All the same, I met a few writers, more or less intimate friends of Richard Wright, with whom I got on very well; they were sincerely pacifist and progressive, and though they were mistrustful of Russia and Stalin, they were free with their criticisms of their own country. And yet they loved so many things about it and taught me to become so attached to it myself . . . America became still

> closer to me when I became attached to Nelson Algren toward the end of my stay. (de Beauvoir 1992, 1:123–24)

The recording of her first tour of Chicago in her travel narrative, *America Day by Day,* tells us more specifically what she saw with Algren and why it impressed her.

> He took me to West Madison Avenue, which is also called the Bowery of Chicago; here are the lodging-houses for men only, flop-houses, squalid bars. It was very cold, the street was almost deserted, and yet there were a few men with shipwrecked faces who hid themselves in the shadows of the doorways . . . We entered a bar that reminded me of Sammy's Follies: but there was neither show nor spectators, and no tourist other than myself. N.A. [Nelson Algren] was not a tourist, for he often came here and knew all the people, hoboes, drunks and faded beauties: no one would turn around even if the Mad Woman of Chaillot came in. At the end of the room there was a little negro band, one read on a placard: "*It is forbidden to dance*"; but people were dancing. There was a lame man who waddled about like a duck: suddenly he started to dance and his legs obeyed him: he spun around, jumped and capered about with a maniacal smile . . . A drunk asleep at a table woke up and seized a fat floozy in his arms, they capered around and danced deliriously. There was something of madness and ecstasy; so old, so ugly, so miserable, they were lost for a moment and were happy. I felt bewildered, stared and said: "It's beautiful." N.A. was astounded; it seemed to him very French. "With us," he said, "ugliness and beauty, the grotesque and the tragic, and even good and evil, go their separate ways: Americans do not like to think that such extremes can mingle." (qtd. in Donohue 1964, 52–53)

In the Paris section of his collection of travel narratives, *Who Lost an American?* (1963), Algren highlights the discerning, if not uncanny, quality of de Beauvoir's intelligence: "Simone de Beauvoir's eyes were lit by a light blue intelligence: she was possessed by something like total apprehension. Her judgments seemed a fraction sooner than immediate and her decisiveness shook the *arrondissement*" (Algren 1963, 96). He also admired, at least initially, the way she actively lived her existentialist-based feminism:

> She herself was not waiting for death. To have a house, a faithful mate, no passions and no cares, to take no risks and never to play the fool was not the way

> Castor [de Beauvoir] ran her life. Existentialism, to her, was not a philosophical complex of Hegel, Kierkegaard, Kafka, and Kant, but a means of living in the world with freedom and joy. (Algren 1963, 98)

She would become one of the most important intellectual relationships of his life. Algren, in turn, "forced Simone de Beauvoir to re-examine all that usually 'went without saying': the obvious, the assumptions, the things taken for granted, the realities of the world she shared with her old friends" in Paris (Sylvie de Beauvoir 1997, 6). According to Barbara Klaw in "Simone de Beauvoir and Nelson Algren: Self-Creation, Self-Contradiction, and the Exotic, Erotic Feminist Other," Algren would function, at least in her texts, as "an exotic": not only not French, he was not a normal American either because, in de Beauvoir's eyes, he chose to "live simply" and not "conform to the status quo and care foremost about money" (Klaw, 121–22). According to two of her biographers, Deirdre Bair and Bettina Drew, de Beauvoir always maintained that Algren was the only "truly passionate love" in her life: "Algren totally bowled me over, turned my life upside down" (Moi 1964, xii; de Beauvoir, qtd. in Drew 1989, 183).

When Algren visited de Beauvoir in Paris for the first time in May of 1949, he entered the center of the French art world. He met Sartre with whom he "gets on well" despite neither knowing the other's language and de Beauvoir's admitted lack of patience as an interpreter (de Beauvoir 1992, 1:179). Considering Algren *un ecrivant engagé,* a writer actively engaged in an art engaged in the world, Sartre with de Beauvoir would translate Algren's novel *Never Come Morning* (1942) into French (Drew 1989, 204). Algren's discussion of Sartre in the Paris section of *Who Lost an American?* reveals a great respect for the integrity of the philosopher as well as a certain intimate knowledge of the man's problems with women:

> Had I passed Sartre on the street as a stranger, I would have taken him for a cheerful tradesman, cheerfully failing in the trade in men's pants. Unprepossessing in both appearance and dress, he was ugly as well. One eye out of focus and with a dryly amused air, he appeared to be more a waiter not above snatching of another waiter's tip than France's most dangerous thinker.
>
> Most dangerous because of his total commitment to the nature of man and his opposition to formal assaults, from left or right, upon the nature of man . . .

> His emotional life was, apparently, conducted upon the cheerful premise that it is better to say yes to a woman than disturb her by saying no: with the result that his work was much infringed upon by women's demands.
>
> And since these demands were made upon him at the same time he exposed himself to arrest by encouraging French youth to refuse to bear arms in Algeria, he discovered, as he always discovered, that both matters would be happily solved for everybody if the De Gaulle government would imprison him. Then he would be able to have the peace essential to completing an anthropological essay; and at the same time that it would keep the demands of women away, he would be serving a political purpose to the best interest of his country. (Algren 1963, 95–96)

The amity between Sartre and Algren was nonetheless complicated by de Beauvoir's disinclination to leave Sartre, move to Chicago, and marry Algren. Though she had not been romantically involved with Sartre for years, she remained bound to him. In a discussion of "contingent loves"—ideas of liberty and contingency on which both she and Sartre had written their exams while students at the Sorbonne—de Beauvoir offers Sartre's and her own "enlightened" alternative to marriage:

> Often preached, rarely practiced, complete fidelity is usually experienced by those who impose it on themselves as a mutilation . . . There are many couples who conclude more or less the same pact as Sartre and myself: to maintain throughout all deviations from the main path a "certain fidelity" . . . it has been our wish to experience "contingent loves"; but there is one question we have deliberately avoided: How would the third person feel about our arrangement. (de Beauvoir 1992, 1:124–25)

Used to playing by his own rules in his relations with women, Algren did not like the arrangement. And it was his refusal to be merely a "contingent love" as well as the distances that separated them that eventually eroded their romantic relation though they continued to write and visit each other for years.

But in 1949, de Beauvoir and Algren were in love and at the peak of their careers. During their time together, each wrote the text that would define them: Algren *The Man with the Golden Arm,* which received the National Book Award in 1949, de Beauvoir *The Second Sex*. In his discussion of the publication in of *The*

Second Sex in the Paris chapter of *Who Lost an American?* Algren characteristically begins by ridiculing de Beauvoir's feminist text, only to turn the table on himself and the culture that dared mock it:

> But I worried how the human race was going to perpetuate itself once Castor took over. She struck me as a bit preposterous.
>
> And, indeed, in 1949 her one-woman opposition to the single standard *was* preposterous. It was preposterized in every newspaper and magazine edited by the French bourgeoisie. She was cartooned, ridiculed, sometimes made gentle fun of and, at other times, reviled with no restraint. (Algren 1963, 97)

Algren would be with her through the initial birth pangs of the text's entry into the culture. On his second trip to Paris, he would be impressed by her fortitude and clearly pleased by the accumulating success of her achievement.

> When I came back to Paris, in 1960, there was no more laughter: she was feared. She had broken through the defenses of the bourgeoisie, of the church, the businessmen, the right-wing defenders of Napoleonic glory, and the hired press. She was, at once, the most hated and the most loved woman in France. (Algren 1963, 97)

If *The Man with the Golden Arm* represents the pinnacle of his literary career, the years after its publication, which were his years with de Beauvoir, represent the period of Algren's most fervent political activity. Since the end of World War II, as liberalism of any kind came to be associated with Communism, and Harry Truman, afraid to appear soft on Communism, joined the Republican effort to hunt down Leftists, American civil rights began to erode dramatically. As the Red scare gained momentum, "in the fall and winter of 1947–48 Algren spoke often at Chicago forums, on literary, cultural, and political affairs" always with a decided liberal bias (Drew 1989, 187). In January of 1951, Algren and fifteen other writers including Arthur Miller printed a letter in the *New York Times* exhorting people to "Speak up for Freedom!" (Donohue 1964, 86). The jailing of the Hollywood Ten in 1950; the passing of the Internal Security Act, which approved concentration camp detention for "radical" thinkers; and U.S. military action in Korea had ushered in an increased climate of paranoia and fear in the American public (Donohue 1964, 86). "In part inspired by the example of European intellectuals like Sartre and de Beauvoir, Algren's sense of his civic duties became more acute" (Donohue 1964, 86). Already considered an internal security risk by the FBI, Algren found himself high on J. Edgar Hoover's list after he became the honorary chairman of the Chicago Committee to Secure Justice in the Rosenberg Case in 1952 (Donohue 1964, 86). Between 1950 and 1953, Algren would write a collection of social and political essays which he interweaved with text from "radical" writers he admired. Despite the writer's fame, Doubleday refused to publish it due to its content and Algren's public association with the Left.

BY 1960, the relationship between Algren and de Beauvoir had long been strained beyond romantic repair. They had not written to one another for two years. Neither had been willing to give up their respective cities so essential to their work, and both had suffered terribly the loss of the other. They each brought middle-aged problems with them to a reunion in Paris in 1960: de Beauvoir her increasing obsession with aging (a fact that seems to contradict her feminist convictions, adding to a revisionist project to disparage her legacy) and Algren a new bitterness that had entered his life and writing, menacing the reputation of both. Each had long since found various other "contingent loves." They had decided, however, to travel together to Spain, Greece, and Istanbul, having concluded by post that they needed to see each other once more before they died (Drew 1989, 302). Algren had also begun a travel book and had finally been granted a passport after the FBI gave up a two-year attempt to prosecute him for fraud for answering "no" to the application question "Have you ever been a Communist" (Drew 1989, 302). They would arrive in Istanbul in the summer of 1960 and stay for only three days. De Beauvoir would make a passing reference to the visit in her autobiography, but Algren would dedicate a twenty-page travel essay to the city, which he initially published in *Nugget Magazine* in 1962 under the title, "When a Muslim Makes His Violin Cry, Head for the Door." He would include the essay in the collection *Who Lost an American?* While de Beauvoir's text offers some insight into her own bourgeois attitudes toward poverty, attitudes often masked in her political discussions of European forms of class struggle and inequity, the cursory nature of her discussion does not invite much comment. Algren's text, however, offers a symptomatic example of the troubled role of social realism in a cold war context.

De Beauvoir's narration of their arrival by plane to Istanbul establishes the sense of loss that will permeate her discussion of the city. Initially, however, it is a personal loss she describes that includes the loss of better days with another Algren:

> As we surged on toward Istanbul through the purple and sulphur sky, my heart ached with the memory of how alive I had once been, and how new the world. Yet at that moment I felt happy: but on the other side of a line that I could never turn and recross ever again. (de Beauvoir 1992, 2:229)

Upon arrival, her melancholy is aggravated into irritation by what she perceives as the cacophony and chaos of the city:

> Istanbul at night looked deserted. Next morning it was teeming with life. Buses, automobiles, handcarts, horse-drawn carriages, bicycles, porters, people walking, the traffic so thick on the Eminonu bridge that one could scarcely cross the road without risking certain death. . . . overloaded taxis rushed up, skidded, screaming, to a stop, then drove away again in a series of minor explosions; there was the clanging of metal, yells, whistles, a vast discordant uproar reverberating inside our heads already battered by the violent bombardment of the sun. (de Beauvoir 1992, 2:229–30)

Like many travel commentaries written by foreigners visiting Istanbul for the first time, the initial language reenacts what amounts to an assault on the visitor's senses. She marks a "state of collapse" of things and notes hostility in the gaze of the people toward them: "was it Americans they hated, or just tourists" (de Beauvoir 1992, 2:230). She had been to North Africa with Sartre and disparages Istanbul's attempts at Orientalist "display":

> These jostling crowds, entirely male, were a sign of the East, of Islam; but the color of Africa and the picturesqueness of China were missing. It felt as though we were on the fringe of a disinherited country, and of some dismal Middle Ages. (de Beauvoir 1992, 2:230)

All in all de Beauvoir is disappointed by the city's performance. Just as something in her is less alive than before, so has the mythic city died into the present, remaining equally unreal for de Beauvoir, but bereft of any romance:

> There was almost nothing left . . . of the long-extinguished past. Byzantium, Constantinople, Istanbul: the town did not live up to the promises of these names, except at that hour when its domes and their slender, pointed minarets were silhouetted along the hilltop against the glowing sky at dusk; then all its sumptuous, bloodstained past appeared through its beauty. (de Beauvoir 1992, 2:230)

The two short pages dedicated to the visit span from dusk to dusk. Momentarily content only when modern Turks disappear from the tableau so that clichés concerning bloodstains and sunsets can be applied, de Beauvoir projects her own loss onto a city devoid of its historicity. Instead of the promised names, she is faced with a modernism project that displaces and disappoints her expectations of an exotic primitivism.

This highly stereotypical complaint of Istanbul's post-Republic demeanor appears to be written by someone unaware of the country's trying westernization process. Yet as if responding to a compulsory, rather than sincerely felt, concern for the country's present political troubles, de Beauvoir makes passing reference to the military coup of May 1960.

> We wanted to get to know some Turks. A few weeks earlier, a military *coup d'état* had ousted Menderes; there had been riots in the city with the students joining in: what were they thinking now, what were they doing? Organized tourism has its disadvantages, but our isolation had even more. Annoyed at not being able to get beneath the décor of the place, we left after three days. (de Beauvoir 1992, 2:230)

Concluding her discussion of Turkey with a term lifted from the rhetoric of design, "décor," de Beauvoir's interest in the country's contemporary domestic political struggles appears all the more skin-deep by her use of the word "annoyed" to describe her reaction to the couple's lack of inside information. This hollow effect is aggravated further by the implicit confession that she and Algren ultimately made very little effort to "get to know some Turks" and thereby gain access to unknown territory.

The 1950s were years of severe repression of leftist intellectual activity in Turkey. Adnan Menderes, Turkish prime minister since 1950, had steered the

23. Istiklal Avenue, Beyoğlu, 1960s.

country into an increasingly close relationship with the United States, a tendency begun at the close of World War II. In doing so, he had taken an increasingly hostile stand against Russia, the "Great Bear" to the north, and anything associated with Russian political culture. Publishing in Turkey was severely repressed and grass roots progressive efforts to extend welfare and education to Anatolian villages, projects such as the village community centers and schools, or "Village Institutes," were terminated by Menderes's government over fears of the project's socialist roots and affiliations. Thus foreigners, particularly those thought to be Americans, were as popular in Turkey in the late 1950s and early 1960s as they were in the rest of Europe after nearly fifteen years of what people perceived to be a form of postwar American occupation. While de Beauvoir held these sentiments vis-à-vis the United States in the context of France, she seems to have had trouble extending this European-wide predicament in the case of Turkey. As one of the newest members of NATO (Turkey and Greece signed the North Atlantic Treaty on February 18, 1952), as well as its eastern-most flank, Turkey enjoyed the discomforts of bordering "the enemy" and little of the benefits of the security, or sense of security, its position afforded the Western members of the alliance. Some financial compensation entered the country, but little trickled down to the Turkish people.

The Turkish military establishment, the "safe keepers" of Atatürk's legacy, and other Kemalists elements in the society, became increasingly alarmed by Menderes's moves to relax laws that restricted Islam and the role of minorities. Strong Kemalist opposition to this coupled with violent social unrest that had led to large student demonstrations in April and martial law on May 1 threatened full-scale civil war. The result was the military coup d'état on May 27, 1960. Menderes and his cabinet were removed from power and parliament was dissolved. Several members of the Menderes government were tried before a criminal court and charged with various crimes including high treason. While some were sentenced to prison, Menderes himself was executed by public hanging, an act that troubles the conscience of citizens who, years later, still support the coup. This, therefore, is the social and political "tableau" that Algren and de Beauvoir walked into the thick of the summer of 1960. Some effort, due to the reticence of traumatized people, would have been necessary to learn the attitudes of intellectuals and students toward the coup. But for two writers whose fame lay in their incisive criticism of repressive regimes, one imagines they would have been versed in this kind of inquiry, at least in French and English. And neither Algren nor de Beauvoir will mention the severe financial crisis that accompanied the sociopolitical unrest in Istanbul during the period of their visit, although both will criticize the "disinherited" aspect of the city.

Algren does not ask direct, albeit disingenuous, questions about the country's internal crises as de Beauvoir does. He will, however, in the course of the essay, comment on Turkey's external position in the geopolitical tensions resulting from the cold war. He will also use the essay as an occasion to give form to thoughts concerning U.S. government policies both at home and abroad. As is most often the case with the American writer abroad, as with most writers abroad, the subject of Algren's travel narrative is primarily home.

THE ISTANBUL CHAPTER is symptomatic of what becomes of Algren's postwar aesthetic. Although his writing had always been characterized by its tragicomic approach to its subject, there is a delirium that dominates his later writing, particularly his nonfiction. The Istanbul chapter opens with just such a tendency. Algren begins the chapter, much like his predecessor Mark Twain, with a derisive examination of a guide book, this one entitled *Encyclopedia Istanbul, Including a Dictionary of Prominent Persons,* by "one Monim Eser" (Algren 1963, 201).

> "Turks are members of the White Race," Monim lost no time in cheering me up, for that's how I got my own start and I'm not going to turn on society now by asking Under What Circumstances Did You Leave Your Last Employer, Kemal? If someone wants to wait till the last possible minute to join a losing organization, that's nobody's business but some other Turk's. The moment for a fresh extension of the White Western world had come and, speaking personally, I was pleased to look upon these simple folk with new eyes; this being the color that bears closest watching. (Algren 1963, 201–2)

Ignorant of the scope of his subject here, the history of the modernization project in Turkey, Algren simply mocks Mustafa Kemal's ambitions to democratize the country along "White Western" lines after the dissolution of the Sultanate (the "Last Employer"). This opening "gag" makes unintentional reference to Turkey's modernization project, which included the reorganization of the state authority through the reformation of the army, the state bureaucracy, and the educational and legal systems. Though these reforms are still often associated with Turkish Republicanism and represented as a revolutionary ideological break from the Ottoman Empire, the reforms can be traced back to the Ottoman reformation period launched with the proclamation of *Tanzimat Fermanı* (the imperial edict of reorganization) in 1839, and *Islahat Fermanı* (the edict of improvement) in 1856.

The joke here has less to do with Turkey, however, and more to do with the failure, in Algren's eyes, of that project in the United States. Eser's insistence on a race-based national identity creates an opportunity for Algren to criticize, albeit underhandedly, the present dearth of politically progressive white people in the United States. According to Algren, the "whole American radical movement" was by the 1960s "the young Negroes in the South. This is the only thing that goes against the trend towards the right. This is the only movement that sustains

24. Galata Bridge and Karaköy Square, 1960s.

the old American radical tradition, sustains the original ideal of the country" (qtd. in Donohue 1964, 234). Speaking of the impotence of mid-century white American intellectualism in the chapter on Barcelona, Algren refers nostalgically to the heyday of literary social realism and its strongest practitioner, an African American:

> Through Richard Wright we had become aware that those who ran the white world had lost the will to act honestly. We had learned from Wright that it is those who have nothing to lose by speaking out who become the ones to speak the truth. And to these, all the horrors of poverty—schizophrenia, homosexuality, drug addiction, prostitution, disease, and sudden death on the gambler's stairs—were no more remarkable than the sight of a man with a fresh haircut.

> In the midst of life, where there are nothing but horrors, there is no horror. (Algren 1963, 141)

Algren felt the Black Muslims were "extremely right wing," and though his prose style here and elsewhere echoes the pulpit rhetoric of James Baldwin, Algren accused his contemporary of being "a perfectly joyless kind of puritanical Negro," "a very strange combination of a Negro evangelist merged with a professional Parisienne," and a bourgeois Black (qtd. in Donohue 1964, 334, 235, 240). Despite his antichauvinism, Algren is homophobic throughout his oeuvre: Baldwin is "vindictive" because he is "put out" about being a homosexual (qtd. in Donohue 1964, 239). Read against this background of Algren's critique of white America, however, the tragic component of Eser's text is better felt. Atatürk's mandate to continue the westernization process in Turkey and the further push of this program after World War II in Turkey's decision to join the ranks of NATO, strike Algren, as it did Paul Bowles, as absurd.

Even as Algren engages in self-directed or Western-directed criticism, he conflates the absurdity of Eser's claims to such an extent that the joke is as much on the Turks as it is on the Americans:

> "Turks are fine looking people, something like North Italians of medium size," Monim filled me in, "with light-blond or dark-colored hair and brown to dark-colored eyes, many having green and blue eyes and small feet. . . . "Turks are members of the Celtic race," Monim resumed his interminable nagging, "which through inter-marriage with Circassian, European, and Greek women have lost their Asiatic features" . . . Monim having just read Greek women out of Europe, I couldn't help wondering where they would go now. After awhile I discovered I didn't care. Assuming they would take their husbands with them, the idea had its appeal. (Algren 1963, 203–4)

Algren gives the impression that Eser's insistence on the Occidental origins of many contemporary Turks is not only fatuous, but also undesirable. This representation of the "New Member," as Algren refers to Turks throughout the chapter, is a mid-twentieth-century expression of many twenty-first century attitudes toward Turkey's European Union membership bid. Algren expresses a kind of incredulity over the idea that Turks could be Europeans, or equal members of the same alliance, and not just left-flank members of NATO. As is often the case, Algren does not favor one "stooge" over another, and the final insult ultimately includes all parties concerned:

> And what makes the Turk think he will be better off looking at the world through a Caucasoid eye instead of an epicanthic one is just one of those things people get to believing after they've tried everything else. (Algren 1963, 213)

Algren's goal in the text is to be taken seriously by no party, but the political satire is nonetheless there. Improvising on the theme of Greek Turkish "kinship"—"'What do you think those Greek heroes were doing while you were horsing around on the wrong side of the Bosphorus, Izmet?' I'd put the issue straight to our New Member—'playing unnatural games?'"—Algren stretches the reference to include, once again, his own country's questionable "games" in its power relations with European nations (Algren 1963, 204).

> You have to let these people know you have the upper hand or they'll take advantage every time. It once took me an hour and a half to get ham and eggs in the Alhambra, and for a Turkish waiter to hold himself the equal of a Spanish one is sheer nonsense, Spanish waiters having belonged to us so much longer. (Algren 1963, 204)

Reweaving topics from previous chapters in the text (Amerocentric food demands of tourists, waiters in Spain), Algren introduces one of the chapter's principal leitmotifs, a criticism of the Marshall Plan, the suspect nature of its pan-democratic claims, and the further political and ideological polarization of Europe.

> Not to deny Turkey's just claim to civil treatment, both countries being great democracies because if they know what's good for them they'd better be. Otherwise they can't belong to *us*. (Algren 1963, 204)

Like many American leftists, Algren was critical of the latent American imperialism couched in the Marshall Plan. Officially known as the European Recovery Program, this plan for rebuilding the allied countries of Western and Eastern Europe (Turkey included), and repelling communism after World War II, was also seen by its critics as a U.S. move toward world domination. De Beauvoir shared Algren's suspicions as early as 1947:

> Now, carried away by its own generosity, the United States was planning to make satellites out of all the countries of Europe, including those in the East. Molotov counteracted this by rejecting the Marshall Plan. The Cold War had begun. (de Beauvoir 1992, 1:130)

Aid was granted to countries willing to make certain political reforms and accept outside monitoring by the United States. Within a four-year period some $13 billion of economic and technical assistance (equivalent to around $130 billion in 2006), was offered. However, in Algren's sketches in the Istanbul chapter he defines the relationship between the United States and Turkey as one of master and slave. Turkey "belongs" to the United States in the sense that if it does not adopt and implement the State Department's definition of democracy, which includes the interdiction of Communism, the "New Member," as befits its subordinate status, will be excommunicated from the Western alliance.

In the early 1960s, Algren would use even less ambiguous language to express his opinion of U.S. machinations in other "satellite" countries, this time South Vietnam, Guatemala, Panama, and Cuba. The United States is

> an imperialist son-of-a bitch. We still own Guatemala. When I say we own it, I mean we backed the fruit company that owns it, and when things go against us, when an attempt is made to take the country back, we perform our revolutions the same as Theodore Roosevelt did in Panama—we take it back, we put our own man in. The other guy becomes a Communist. He was no Communist. He was a man for land reform, which means taking land from the United Fruit Company. We take it by force—that is, we send soldiers, we take the country back by force for the United Fruit Company exactly as more recently we attempted to get back Cuba for people who have money invested in it. (qtd. in Donohue 1964, 212)

An early critic of cold war hysteria, particularly of the deeper economic motives behind it, he would point out the ethical consequences of U.S. superiority in the arms race in a contribution to a small book entitled *The Race for Space!* "When the innocent man must prove his innocence or stand convicted on the word of an unseen accuser, though we own the moon, we are lost" (qtd. in Horvath 2005, 117).

Algren fashions a mock bestiary, a subtext within the larger chapter, which illustrates his understanding of the contemporary position of Turkey, geopolitically sandwiched between Russia and the United States during the cold war and unable to dictate unilaterally the stipulations of the Western Alliance to its own people.

> The one who gained my attention by meowing, "Take this *thing* off me, Dad," from under half a grapefruit, wasn't even thankful when I obliged her. She was a cat caught in the worldwide struggle between Democracy and Communism, so it was my duty as an American to liberate her because we had invented milk. Now we have a surplus we want to donate to undernourished peoples unconditionally in return for airbases and affection. If you don't love *us* more than you love *them*, you can't have *our* nice milk. But this was a Commie cat; she told me Keep Your Goddamned Milk, I'm a cheese-eating left-wing Radical Red and I subsist on blood and yogurt. Even her howl was curdled. (Algren 1963, 215)

This vignette outlines, however tongue in cheek, Algren's critique of the disingenuous application of America's pan-democratic program.

> Like Faust, We have two souls within a single breast. We profess to believe that a people may guarantee its happiness by military might, and in the same breath disclaim authoritarianism. We say the great word Democracy, and in the same breath align ourselves with Spanish, Greek, Chinese and Korean Fascism. (Algren 1998, 67)

In his Barcelona chapter, Algren qualifies the capitalist nature of the U.S. alignment with Spain under Franco.

> The corruption of the legalized tyranny at present holding the Spanish people under its control begins with the big-business brass. The generalship of any fascism does not begin with generals, but with men in business clothes who never handled a gun and never will. Generals can be found.
>
> This is not the work of Franco, but of France, that cut off the guns. The waste of women like Loren Domingués [a subject of the essay] is not the work of

> the generals who gave the orders, but of England; that preferred a fascist state to a democracy. It is the work of the United States' distrust of the idea of a people governing itself. (Algren 1963, 156–57)

In his second travel collection, *Notes from a Sea Diary: Hemingway All the Way* (1965), Algren will see an account of his Far East and Indian travels on board the *Malaysia Mail* as an allegory for "what is wrong with the United States" (qtd. in Donohue 1964, 177). The ship represents, "very closely" what the United States "is like" in its relation with weaker economies since its postwar economic rise. On board, he notes "isolation,"

> I mean, among the men, the confidence that these other people were inferior to them—the people of these countries, the Japanese, the Koreans, the Indians, and Filipinos. They only looked at them with a contempt . . . the docks were always crowded with people waiting for an American ship to come in . . . I mean a total dependence. . . . Their lives depend on the crew, so the crew is too used to having their own way. They can't say no to a member of the crew because he's got money. I think this is why I say the ship represents in a way what is wrong with the United States because in our dealings with a lot of the smaller countries they can't say no. Underneath that is a lot of resentment toward Americans. (qtd. in Donohue 1964, 177)

Many comical moments in the Istanbul chapter of *Who Lost an American?* thus prove to wield the double-edged sword of political satire. The critique of America's foreign policy tactics in Turkey after World War II and during the Cold War serve also as a critique of U.S. economic ascendancy in the world at large. His visit to St. Sophia incites another Swiftian treatment of the reciprocal barbarism of Christians and Muslims throughout history:

> So they [Muslims] pulled the Christians apart with wild horses and put up minarets. This is why you can scarcely blame us Christians, when we took the place back, for plastering our Muslim brothers up into the walls in the name of the Holy Trinity and to save cement. (Algren 1963, 214)

This relatively objective satire of religious factionalism, like the moments lampooning the "New Member" and the "White Western world," are the better moments in the chapter. One notes, however, that for the most part while in Istanbul Algren ridicules his subject for no apparent purpose other than a solipsistic exercise in the absurd. If the Istanbul chapter is symptomatic of what becomes of Algren's postwar aesthetic, it can also be argued that the symptoms evident in the chapter exemplify the end of an American literary tradition. Despite Algren's early and then mid-life commitment to social and political reform, his writing, grounded as it was in the ethos of the 1930s, began to lose its audience in the late 1950s. When Algren arrives in Paris in 1960, he is angry, complaining of betrayal to de Beauvoir. "'Once I used to live in America,' he said to me, 'now I live in occupied territory'" (de Beauvoir 1992, 2:216). The occupation he speaks of, however, refers as much to the new literary climate as it does to McCarthyism. In 1947 de Beauvoir could say of Algren that he was a "striking example of the intellectual solitude in which writers of America live today"; by 1960 his isolation, in his opinion, was due to the cultural despotism of the New Critics whom Algren considered academic representatives of the bourgeoisie, "men who did not know how to live their lives" (Drew 1989, 188; Horvath 2005, 128). Algren couched most of his criticism of the New York literary scene in his many defenses of his favorite antihero, Ernest Hemingway, another writer often taken to task for the naturalistic elements in his writing that no longer interested many in the academic establishment.

Algren in his Barcelona chapter satirizes what he considers the dubious political convictions of the literary left after World War II:

> I myself was one of the happy number of Americans who had once hoped somebody would defeat the Italians and Germans. I knew I was thinking along those lines because I joined the local chapter of Rear-Echelon Radicals Against Fascism. There were at that time many American writers, mostly in New York City, whose politics were left wing because of a shortage of business opportunities in the right wing. None of these could go to Spain to do any actual fighting themselves because they had a magazine called *Partisan Review* which the editors decided was indispensable to culture, the thing the Spanish people were then fighting to preserve. I didn't go to Spain to fight either, but this was only because I didn't want to die young. A flimsy excuse. (Algren 1963, 133–34)

Characteristically targeting himself also in this satire, he will represent Hemingway as an affront to the literary and academic establishment who share the position, in the 1950s, of purveyors of taste in American "high" culture. Hemingway, by contrast, actually goes to Spain to fight against Franco's army. As the title suggests, Algren dedicates much of his second travel book, *Notes from a Sea Diary: Hemingway All the Way,* to the defense and lionization of Hemingway's accomplishments, not only at the front, but also on the page.

Algren explains the hostility shown toward Hemingway's writing by a new generation of critics in terms of their own sense of inadequacy as men:

> It wasn't Hemingway's prose, but his life, which demanded "total and considered rejection." It wasn't his economy of language which made them feel small—it was his free-handedness. To men whose self-doubt put them in need of formal respect from others, the ease with which Hemingway earned the informal respect of workaday men and women felt like an accusation. (Algren 1965, 88)

In the course of defending Hemingway's appeal to the working classes, Algren simultaneously defends himself as another "man of action," an *ecrivan engagé,* who, unlike academic writers, earns his aesthetic though direct experience. "The present imbalance of books about writing, to those written from direct experience," is sufficient evidence of a culture enthralled to the "footnote," hypnotized by the new cult of sophistication that values "annotated man" over the dream of perfect mimesis that the social realists sought to realize (Algren 1965, 105). Young people, on whom this trend has the worst effects, are

> duped by a presumption: that the truths which can sustain them can be handed down by educators, critics, analysts, anthropologists and professional distributors of safe precepts: all those who . . . lose [their identity] in a world where terminology embalms alike the living and the dead. The man whose passion attained its peak in a course in cost accounting now emerges as a shaper of American letters. (Algren 1965, 103)

Hemingway would remain Algren's most enduring literary and life role model. He, along with Carl Sandburg, had sponsored Algren for a Guggenheim in 1947 for writers serving in the military, so that he could write the war novel that became *Golden Arm* (though he would never win this or any other literary grant) (Drew 1989, 181; Donohue 1964, 189). Algren would make a trip to Havana in 1955 and spend Christmas day with the Hemingways, a "pilgrimage" he recounts in his chapter "June 27th: Lions, Lionesses, Deadbone Crunchers," in *Notes from a Sea Diary.* After the publication of *The Man with the Golden Arm,* Hemingway would tell Max Perkins that he thought Algren was "'probably the best writer under 50, and name your own figure, writing today'" (qtd. in Drew 1989, 210). However, in defending the famous writer who had praised his own work, Algren was defending a literary tradition that was under siege. Throughout the 1950s he wrote articles and reviews defending the literature of social protest; "over and over he would remark that no one wanted serious fiction, that to write it was a loser's game" (Drew 1989, 298). His own criticism of the New Criticism in 1960, much like his rendering of Istanbul, will move beyond irony to cynical banter:

> They arrived directly from their respective campuses armed with blueprints to which the novel and the short story would have to conform . . .
>
> Prewar mottos still hung on the walls, ancestral homilies offering obsolescent mysteries: "No Man is an Island." "I Have Always Depended Upon the Kindness of Strangers." "While There is a Soul in Prison I Am Not Free." Their names were something like "Leslie Fleacure," "Elvis Zircon," "Lionel Thrillingly," "and "Justin Poodlespitz"—it was plain the old mottoes would have to come down. (qtd. in Drew 1989, 294)

Algren was particularly acidic toward Alfred Kazin, "Elvis Zircon," whom he also referred to as "the Footnote King" and Leslie Fiedler, "Lionell Lardass," who in 1956 in a *Partisan Review* article on *A Walk on the Wild Side* had called Algren a "museum piece—the last of the Proletarian Writers" (qtd. in Drew 1989, 293, 265).

While apologists for Algren are quick to blame the New Critic's conservative ideology and apolitical ascetism for the marginalization of Algren in the 1950s, it is more accurate to see the attack on Algren as an attack on literary social realism in general. Charles Walcott, a critic defending literary naturalism "from the trenches" in 1956, points to advances in technology as a primary culprit of the demise of the tradition after World War II:

> The drive for security began to supplant the old Dream of equality, justice, and a richer life for all . . . We are told every day that the radio and the airplane have reduced the size of the world, and the implication is that now that we can travel rapidly over the earth we should be able to see all man's problems in global

> perspectives and solve them with master plans. But the thoughtful observer knows that the world of experience, the world of problems, the world which impinges upon the individual's mind and conditions its attitudes is immeasurably more vast and complex than it was only fifty years ago. Its vastness daunts the zeal and idealism of all but the boldest spirits. (Walcott 1956, 294)

Mid-century prosperity is also another reason for the loss of public interest in Algren and his fellow social realists: "The voice of protest has faded to a whisper—or a neurotic whine" (Walcott 1956, 295). Like Algren, Walcott argues that the new cult of the individual prefers the therapist's couch to active social engagement: "The emphasis is on helping the individual to get along happily with his fellows, his limitations, and his half-buried fears. Adjustment and self-expression are now prime values, having displaced the old moral absolutes that gave early naturalism its fire" (Walcott 1956, 295). The idea that individual lives were the product of social forces that, in turn, were inextricable from the movements of history, was going out of fashion. This was being pushed aside by a literary mode whose focus on losers, wanderers, and social outcasts resembled the subjects of Algren's American social realism, but that now offered protagonists who lacked clear or concrete sociohistorical reasons for their troubles. The expanding influence of existentialism took the losing battles of Algren's back-alley bums and applied them to middle-class America.

In America, the Beats were a second wave of socially conscious writers who rejected the realism of their literary fathers by reaching back to the early abstractions of the modernists. But Algren was unimpressed by their output when compared to that of "radical" writers earlier in the century:

> There was a great radical literary movement in the twenties which you don't have now. The literary movement is conformist now, unless you want to consider Norman Mailer's challenge to the traffic department of the Provincetown police. Or Allen, what's his name, Howlberg's—you know—all his posturing is just plain crap. I mean it's just typing . . . To see the difference in the literary scene and how much more unreal it is now than it was in the twenties look at what they are writing. Compare, for example, Allen Ginsberg, Jack Kerouac, and Ferlinghetti and Corso and all the beats with Edna St. Vincent Millay and Theodore Dreiser . . . These were creative people. What we've got now is a bunch of performers . . . The only aspect of the literary scene in which we are

> much more skilled than we were in twenties is in criticism. (qtd. in Donohue 1964, 228–29)

Not only the Beats but also beatnik culture did not live up to the radical 1920s and 1930s of Algren's youth:

> The jazz was all right, but the poetry was just typing.
>
> It became plain that they were neither holy nor barbaric. They were nihilism's organization men giving demonstrations of how to be a nonconformist without risking one's personal security . . . surely no investigating committee is ever going to ask anybody, "Were you ever, or are you now, a Beatnik?" (Algren 1963, 283)

By the 1960s, America, according to Algren, no longer respected the writer as cultural critic but considered the social realist a transgressor, preferring instead the writer as entertainer:

> If you point out that the reason Americans are restless is because their lives are empty—that what we have isn't a kind of 4-H picnic going—that this is a country where there's a great deal of psychological and spiritual anguish, that we live in a nightmare, that the people in Sherwood Anderson's short stories or the plays of Tennessee Williams are closer to actuality than are the pictures we get from Herman Wouk or James Michener, or name whomever you want—the professional approvers . . . then you realize that you are a kind of criminal. You are against society and you have to be against it, it being what it is. (qtd. in Donohue 1964, 214–15)

Algren's "self-appointed function," to remind America that "society's bottom dogs" were still there, "to react," was losing credibility, at least in the form Algren offered (qtd. in Donohue 1964, 116). And even if he claimed that his "only purpose was to express my horror of what I see around me, whether it's the murderous treatment of drug addicts as though they were criminals, which they are not, [or] of prostitutes as criminals, which they are not," his causes no longer grasped the imagination of a public whose cold war reality differed greatly from the Depression and post-Depression culture of Algren. The problem lay not in the fact that the social problems of the underclasses had changed, which, according to Algren, they had not, but rather in a lack of vitality and direction in the young: "It isn't that young Americans don't wish to do great things," he quotes Simone de Beauvoir in his collection of social and political essays, *Nonconformity,* "but that they don't know there are great things do be done" (Algren 1998, 47).

By 1960, a sardonic edge dominated Algren's rhetoric, and his bitter attacks on the "establishment" critics were as much defensive gestures as offensive ones. Considered, in print, by many critics as an "anachronistic leftist, an ideological relic of the 1930s with an embarrassing attachment to America's losers," his novel, *A Walk on the Wild Side,* had been panned by the literary press (Horvath 2005, 9). His glib comments on the discursive logic of this novel, which he had recuperated from an old manuscript and revised, reveal the increasingly casual direction he had taken his writing by the mid-1950s. He describes it as a "reader's book," something not to be taken seriously: "You're more inclined to clown in a reader's book . . . You've got one ear to the audience for yaks. It's just an obligation you have to fulfill" (qtd. in Drew 1989, 267). Algren's new comedic style, which would pervade nearly all his writing after this point, and most particularly his Istanbul chapter in *Who Lost an American?* is best described as burlesque. The humor is exaggerated, often grotesque, as are the "imitations" of characters. He often employs elements of theatrical burlesque: comic skits, songs, "striptease acts," or bawdy references intermixed with "earthly" character sketches. Theatrical burlesque is mentioned often in his texts. When de Beauvoir visits him for the first time in Chicago he takes her to a burlesque show as an example of local entertainment. Familiar to him from his Chicago childhood, theatrical burlesque is a mode of dramatic representation that Algren cynically falls back on when he loses faith in the serious possibilities left to his art from the 1950s onward.

One of the more sustained burlesque skits in the Istanbul chapter is one that concerns a dancing bear and some children. The narration opens with an attention to detail that suggests Algren could still apply his imaginative efforts to the social reality of a place, in this case the ways in which the habit of poverty turns daily survival techniques into traditions for the lowest beings in the social hierarchy—children and animals.

> For a sight of pure dumb suffering there's nothing so great as a muzzled bear up on his hind legs seven foot high; a frothing brute lifting one leg then the other to the beat of a drum. In hope he's earning his dinner.

> The only spectator beside myself is a ten-year-old Mongol waif, a boy in charge of a shine-box the size of himself. The bottles lining the box's sides lend it a resemblance to a crude portable operating table. He has decorated it with Elvis Presley's face—clipped from an American magazine—under the caption *Will This Yearning Never Cease?* (Algren 1963, 206)

The caption brings into play several things: the seeming incongruity of contemporary Western pop culture in this scene that touches on Algren's critique of American globalization; the subtle suggestion that American teen yearning and the yearning of the bear and the boy are, in fact, worlds apart. Because of these allusions, the humor that results is earned. The scene quickly abandons, however, any attempt at rendering Istanbul real, sidetracks into gags about American politicians, and then descends into the ridiculous. Algren gives the begging girl attending the bear and the drummer a dollar:

> She toted that buck like a flag to the drummer, who put down the happiest rat-a-tat-tat to send the message straight through to the bear—"*We eat!*" The bear began lifting his knees to his chin, trying to show me what it felt like to have a yearning really cease. He was so happy he didn't really care if it hurt . . . I had never had my shoes shined to a drum roll before. It was my first time. And to a dancing bear at that! Talk about your happy times! But when the bear put his paws on his hips I felt he was going too far. (Algren 1963, 208)

Finally, Algren ducks behind a gag rather than tackle, in any meaningful sense, the socioeconomic complexity of the scene as he would have in his earlier nonfiction.

Algren claims in a later chapter on Chicago that this not necessarily new, but newly dominate element of burlesque in his writing is another form of witness: "The artist's usefulness has always been to stand in an ironic affiliation to his society, and every society needs him standing so" (Algren 1963, 257). The writer's ironic distance performed a civic duty:

> Poets, philosophers, scientists, men of cloth and court jesters are the people upon whom society must depend for its survival. For these, if true to themselves, lend the perspective that the business and military mind, in its eagerness for profit and war, loses. (Algren 1963, 258)

But as Algren's early self-styled role as insider witness changes to that of ironically affiliated court jester, it can be argued that rather than remaining "true to himself" he opted to remain true to what he believed the market demanded when it no longer ascribed to his brand of realism or "truth." The move is cynical and the writing suffers. The remaining pages of the Istanbul chapter contain similar moments of disingenuous writing whose sole aim seems to be "yaks" rather than perspective. His references to the difficult problems of Armenian Turks, for example, are cursory and flip. In a mock response to Eser, the writer of the encyclopedia whom he will "historically objectify," he throws out, "Slaughtered any Armenian Babies this morning, Fireball?"; later, describing some boys playing with slingshots around trolley cars, he "jokes," "This ammunition was easy to find, and I contributed a handful only on the condition it would be used against Armenians" (Algren 1963, 205, 209). The "humor" here, like that in much of the chapter, is irresponsible at best. Gone is the double-edged sword. In its place a gratuitous snare drum whose only function is to signal the audience when and where to laugh.

When an American journalist suggests that Algren is "sick" because for him "nothing is sacred," Algren counters that he is being censored for speaking the truth: "This dour demand to stop spoofing, in a country that never needed spoofing more, is accompanied by the urge to punish" (Algren 1963, 258). Spoofing in the case of Istanbul, however, serves no civic purpose for the most part because the representation of truth, if there is any, is left consistently underdeveloped. For example, unlike the aesthetically superior architecture of the Moors, "The Turks simply brought down everything that looked like Allah might not care to have it standing"; unlike the liveliness of Chicago, "There is no joy, there is no juice, there is no jazz in Istangump. A city without Negroes doesn't jump, and smiles in Turkey are not for free" (Algren 1963, 212–13). Much of the chapter descends into Eurocentric defamation:

> The Turkish claim to civilizations that once flowered between Europe and Asia, when the Golden Gate was the center of the world, is simply no good. Turkish soldiery brought down the ancestral temples of Greece pillar by pillar and marble by marble, then sold the rubble shard by shard. Had an Englishman not come along to do some salvaging, the Turk would have disposed of the lot in the nearest bazaar. (Algren 1963, 212)

A concluding discussion of Pierre Loti, the French writer and exoticist who lived in Eyüp on the Golden Horn, also becomes an occasion for Algren to gambol on the subject of homosexuality: "He had gotten his start by dwelling at great length on 'the mysterious heart of the Turkish woman.' The question thereafter arising that, if Turkish women were *that* mysterious how was it that Piyer was more interested in the mysterious heart of the Turkish boy?" (Algren 1963, 221). The remainder of the chapter relegates information to the rhetorical hustle of the pun. Once he arrives in Eyüp, he is "glad."

> It offered a view of the Dardanelles truly startling. Who was more startled, me or the Dardanelles, is a question only posterity will answer. Yet there below me lay The Golden Gate, Galata Bridge, Ataturk Bridge, Ataboy Bay, The Sea of Marmara, The Vale of Tralee, and my old buddy, Bosphorus.
>
> I could see Beşiktaş, Dolmabahçe [,] Beyoğlu, and somebody cooking shish kebab in Kabatas Iskelesi. I could even make out the umlauts in Üsküdar standing up like tiny minarets. (Algren 1963, 222)

Exploiting the slippage of reference that punning relies on—a word game he plays to excess throughout the chapter—Algren here steers the clichéd language of travel writing back to earlier personifications of the waters around Istanbul in the chapter: the Dardanelles, like the Bosphorus, take on human qualities; they can be "startled," due to the hallucinations brought on by drinking raki. The place names become exercises in phonetic slippage, which make sense only in an American dialect: "Ataboy bridge"; and finally textuality replaces the things themselves, for example, the umlauts of Üsküdar.

Who Lost an American? has been described as a "postmodern tall tale" (Horvath 2005, 124). And it is true that Algren's writing in the 1950s and thereafter displays certain characteristics of literary postmodernism. As Brooke Horvath in *Understanding Nelson Algren* notes, the text "rejects realism . . . is self-referential, playful, and nonlinear . . . replaces psychological depth with a sometimes cartoonish surface . . . collapses genre distinctions . . . erases the line between fiction and nonfiction, juxtaposes fragments, and mixes seemingly antithetical voices . . . prefers collage and performance to selectivity and polished artifacts" (Horvath 2005, 117–18). But while these postmodern catch phrases can be applied to Algren's Istanbul chapter, the final effect is perhaps less postmodern than specifically postrealist. Algren's textual play, his obsession with the self-referentiality of the pun, his collapsing of theatrical burlesque with political narrative, his general performance as an embittered court jester assaults rather than stumps the reader's expectations. We read writing that is alinear not due to epistemological or ontological experimentation, but due to its reactionary point of view. In his efforts to write a "readerly" text, as Charles Walcott notes, he "seems to have given up even the pretense that society could be improved or purified" (Walcott 1956, 299). While postmodern writing is generally discussed as if social commitment, like referentiality, ceases to determine the orientation or trajectory of the text, this is more often the claim of theorists than of writers. The best "postmodern" American fiction of the 1950s, for example Nabokov's *Lolita* or Carson McCullers's *The Ballad of the Sad Café*, offers the reader engaged critiques of American cold war culture, even if the social scrutiny is less readily apparent then that of "old school" social realism. In Algren's Istanbul chapter, the death of culture is a foregone conclusion.

The Istanbul chapter in *Who Lost an American?* is the literary consequence of a writer who has lost his subject. Though he comes face to face in Istanbul with the results of social upheaval, the poverty, and general cultural anxiety he had experienced himself in the United States, he no longer packs the literary commitment necessary to do the country's historical moment justice. Cold war Istanbul is as confusing and as inaccessible to him as cold war America. Unable to differentiate between heroes and villains, causes and effects, Algren is nostalgic for the 1930s and what he believes were the binary categories of the age, at least where art was concerned:

> Comparing this decade with the thirties, you could say that things are much better or that things are much worse. Both answers are true. For the creative writer things are much worse in the sense that while he had economic problems in the thirties—there were almost no writers I knew of who had economic security—all the writers who wrote anything in the thirties wrote accidentally—but the creative writer of the thirties had belief. They saw the world and they divided the world according to the way that decade divided it, that is, between human rights and property rights. That was concentrated in the Spanish Civil War, and they took sides. It was an easy choice. Anybody who was anybody believed in the Spanish Civil War—they were against Franco and in that way it

> was simpler then. It was easier to be right then. Injustice was black and justice was white. It was easier to be creative then. (qtd. in Donohue 1964, 240)

Sides are harder to choose during the cold war because much of the action is played out behind closed door and the players and their causes are harder to discern. If the writer's sense of conviction suffers because of this lack of clarity, it also suffers from the loss of an audience who now looks for a literary correlative to its own experience of social isolation and sociopolitical uncertainty: "The literary spirit of 'I belong to these convicts and prostitutes myself,' from which these novels derived, were written for a reader who was no longer there" (Algren 1963, 273). Algren, having lost his historical and creative bearings, admits to the end of a literary era though this acknowledgment also ultimately marks a rupture in his own identity: "Sandburg's Chicago, Dreiser's Chicago, Farrell's and Wright's and my own Chicago, that was somebody else's Chicago" (Algren 1963, 278).

Though Algren claimed to be unfamiliar with existential writing before meeting de Beauvoir, he would have become familiar with Sartre's text *Qu'est-ce que la littérature?* (1948). In the chapter "Pourqoui écrire," Sartre defines the dilemma of the writer who wishes to recreate mimetically the injustices of the world:

> The error of realism has been to believe that the real world reveals itself to contemplation, and that consequently one could draw an impartial picture of it. How could that be possible, since the very perception is partial, since by itself the naming is already a modification of the object? And how could the writer who wants himself to be essential to the universe, want to be essential to the injustice which this universe comprehends? Yet he must be if he accepts being a creator of injustices, it is in a movement which goes beyond them towards their abolition. (Sartre 1971, 1066)

Algren's difficulties as a writer from the 1950s on can be roughly summed up by this passage. Social realism's project, the revelation of things as they really are, is put into question when paradigms concerning the instability of truth begin to circulate more aggressively in the culture at large after World War II. While French existentialists Sartre and de Beauvoir lauded Algren as an American *ecrivant engagé,* it is the rejection of ontological and epistemological certainty central to their postwar existentialism that, in many ways, signals the end of

Algren's literary mode. Algren understands that his work can no longer actively participate in the abolition of injustice under these new conditions. In bed with the enemy, Algren comes to the hard realization that he is no longer essential to the universe.

Both Algren and de Beauvoir single out the Turkish poet Nâzim Hikmet as an example of an *ecrivant engagé*. De Beauvoir meets him in Paris in the early 1960s and records his account of his refusal to do military service at the age of fifty, and his subsequent escape to Europe via a Romanian cargo ship, all after a seventeen-year prison sentence (de Beauvoir 1992, 2:112–13). Algren mentions Nâzim Hikmet twice in the Istanbul chapter, both times with reference to the Irish writer Brendan Behan, whom Algren meets and writes of in his chapter on Ireland. "The first duty of a writer," says Algren in the spirit of Behan, "is to let his country down. He knows his own people best. He has a special responsibility to let them down" (Algren 1963, 65). References to the Turkish poet and the Irish poet are in the context of Turkish militarism:

> [Turkey] has only one martyr today in the best sense of the word: the poet Nâzim Hikmet. Understandably, he is in hiding for having committed what Brendan Behan has observed is the writer's first responsibility—to bring his country down.
>
> Turks are less tolerant of this sort of carryings-on than the Irish. To the Irishmen a uniform indicated subservience; to the Turk it signifies righteousness. Therefore the Turks, a righteous people, respect only action conducted in a military fashion, even though it may consist of no more than dominoes in a coffeehouse. Spectators to the contest don't just sit around; they observe in a military manner. (Algren 1963, 209–10)

And later, "What Turkey needs today isn't heroes but good old rogues, sporty-O poets and down right cowards" (Algren 1963, 212).

Thus while Algren seems to have a sense of Turkey's problems, both international and domestic—the United States shared its "red-scare" hysteria with all its friends and allies, and Nâzim Hikmet had socialist convictions—he does not attempt to engage his account in anything beyond passing generalities and jokes. By the time Algren comes to Istanbul in 1960, he does not feel essential to the injustice he perceives at home or abroad. His best resource as a writer, his capacity to locate and live among the disenfranchised, and moreover to make the reader care about them through realistic depictions, is no longer marketable. In Istanbul, therefore, he feels no responsibility to record what he sees genuinely. His chapter on Istanbul lacks the generosity he can still muster for his beloved Chicago to which he dedicates his best writing, and a third of *Who Lost an American?* "However bad and hopeless the humanity which it paints may be," Sartre continues in *Pourquoi écrire?*

> the work must have an air of generosity. Not, of course, that this generosity is to be expressed by means of edifying discourses and virtuous characters; it must not even be premeditated, and it is quite true that fine sentiments do not make fine books. But it must be the very warp and woof of the book, the stuff out of which the people and things are cut; whatever the subject, a sort of essential lightness must appear everywhere and remind us that the work is never a natural datum, but an *exigence* and a *gift*. And if I am given this world with its injustices, it is not so that I may contemplate them coldly, but that I may animate them with my indignation, that I may disclose them and create them with their nature as injustices, that is, as abuses to be suppressed. Thus, the writer's universe will only reveal itself in all its depth to the examination, the admiration, and the indignation of the reader; and the generous love is a promise to maintain, and the generous indignation is a promise to change, and the admiration a promise to imitate; although literature is one thing and morality a quite different one, at the heart of the aesthetic imperative we discern the moral imperative. (Sartre 1971, 1066–67)

Although Algren may live up to Sartre's profile of the engaged writer in much of his work, his Istanbul chapter does not invite the reader to participate in the injustices he records. Any moral imperative, in Sartre's sense of the phrase, drowns for the most part in laughter, and Algren's aesthetic imperative is left, in the end, with little heart.

7

James Baldwin on the Nation of Islam

A Letter from Istanbul

WHEN ENOUGH LEAVES FALL sometime around the end of November, one can look across Rumeli Hisarı, a quiet green neighborhood of Istanbul, and see James Baldwin's backyard. One cannot see much of the ochre villa itself, Vefik Pasha's library, but one can admire the tall evergreens that hold sentinel over the Bosphorus Straits much like the towers of the fifteenth-century fortress next door that lends its name to the quarter. It was from Rumeli Castle that the Ottoman Turks took Constantinople from the Byzantines in 1453. Vefik Pasha, a nineteenth-century governor of Bursa, was known for bringing Western theater to Turkey. He also helped broker the land deal between the Divine Porte and the founders of Robert College just up the hill. Established by American missionaries in 1863, Robert College was the first American university founded in a foreign country. It would be passed to the Turkish State in 1971, becoming Boğaziçi University, or Bosphorus University, to this day one of the most esteemed English-language universities in Turkey.

James Baldwin moved to Pasha's library in the fall of 1966 and stayed until the summer of 1967 with his brother David and a young Robert College English professor, David Leeming, his secretary and assistant and future biographer. For eight years or so beginning in 1961, Baldwin maintained semi-residency in Istanbul, first staying with his friends the theater actors Engin Cezzar, whom he had met at the Actors Studio in New York, and his wife Gulriz Sururi. He stayed in various places throughout the city: Taksim, Bebek, and eventually Rumeli Hisarı. Charles Adelsen in a 1970 *Ebony* magazine article and interview entitled, "A Love Affair: James Baldwin and Istanbul," describes the environs of the elegant stucco and wood Ottoman villa in terms of natural refuge: "A place for work, where there was earth smell and water smell and, from green hillsides, Asia to look at across the wide blue flow of the Bosphorus" (Adelsen 1970, 42). David Leeming in his 1994 biography of Baldwin described a typical day at the villa:

> Jimmy got up at noon and ate a substantial meal. He then worked until six or so, when visitors began to arrive. Drinks and dinner followed and then long nights of talking, which usually included Jimmy's reading aloud segments of *Tell Me How Long the Train's Been Gone* or parts of other projects temporarily abandoned or planned . . . More than anything else, we discussed events in America, the state of the movement, the riots in the cities. The discussions were frequently heated and there was shouting and sometimes there were tears. (Leeming 1994, 275)

James Baldwin described himself as a "transatlantic commuter," making his journeys "by radar" (Adelsen 1970, 42). No matter what foreign country it was, whether Paris, Istanbul, or in his last years in St. Paul de Vence in the South of France, Baldwin was never politically or emotionally distant from the United States.

While many readers can imagine Baldwin composing away in the lively urban isolation of Paris (we've been there, therefore, it exists), few Occidental readers travel, especially in their minds, with Baldwin further east to the frontier of modern Western Christendom. If the informed reader can think about Baldwin in Turkey, we tend to do so vaguely, dreamily, on the winds of Oriental rumor. But James Baldwin lived for extended periods of time in Istanbul throughout the 1960s. And it is also true that while a sojourner in one of the world's most fictionalized slices of geography, he wrote some of his best nonfiction. If Baldwin sailed to Byzantium to contemplate the golden messages in Aya (St.) Sophia, messages concerning the ephemeral nature of human bodies and human systems, he also flew to Istanbul to engage these bodies and systems from an enabling distance. In order to keep working, that is, continue to talk to his homeland about the trouble he felt it was bringing down on itself and the world, Baldwin had had to leave that country behind. Not only did he desire the psychological distance necessary for keen subjective contemplation, but he also required the physical detachment. His fame by the 1960s was such that he could no longer maintain the privacy indispensable to public discourse. The public stage had come to count too much on his ubiquitous grimace. When his picture appeared on the cover of *Time* magazine in May of 1963, one issue after Abraham Lincoln, he was in frequent motion above the Atlantic ocean. When he landed, it was as often in Istanbul as New York (Campbell 1991, 161).

Another Baldwin biographer, James Campbell, refers to Istanbul as Baldwin's "eastern hideaway," a "little enigma" in the American writer's life that nobody back home could fathom. While in these epithets we note a typical, enduring Occidental enthrallment to Orientalist archetypes (the attractive/repulsive, secretive, enigmatic East), Campbell does note that it was in Istanbul at the height of the writer's fame that Baldwin found a place where he could work. Yet though much has been written of Baldwin's life abroad in Paris in the 1940s and 1950s, and of his latter years in southern France where he died in 1987 at the age of sixty-three, much less is mentioned of Turkey; until recently few attempts have been made to locate the work of one of North America's more famous literary personalities within the foreign culture he often chose to work in during his most public and political years. And no efforts have been made to do the contrary: to locate Istanbul in the heart of North American literature or in the heart of its mid-century civil rights literature.

Baldwin did not make Turkey a subject of his writing, though in the 1980s he was attempting to formulate a novel about the first wave of Turkish immigrant workers in Germany and Switzerland that he had tentatively entitled "No Papers for Mohammed." He saw parallels between the lives of African Americans, Turkish "guest" workers in Germany, and Algerians in France and their prescribed social roles as the street sweepers of these respective nations. But unlike his experience of Paris, Baldwin chose to live Istanbul rather than write it. His carried with him his taste for celebrating, giving tremendous parties in his garden at Vefik Pasha's Library still remembered by those living today who were present then. Loving to cook, he barbequed chicken and spare ribs for an infamously eclectic collection of people—Turks, Greeks, Armenians, Americans, English; academics, musicians, sailors, missionaries, actors, wanderers, friends, and strangers (Cezzar 2004). He served champagne cocktails to people he had never seen before, would never see again, and who sometimes stole from him (Garwood 2004). He mixed and matched social classes, frustrating the conservative with his insistence on the inclusion of questionable personalities whom he happened upon in his wanderings about the city. "He felt free and warm in a country that never questioned him," says Mini Garwood, a third-generation Rumeli Hisarı Armenian Turk whose father was the college librarian at Robert

25. James Baldwin in Eminönü, Yeni Mosque, 1960s. Photograph by Sedat Pakay.

College, now Bosphorus University, for thirty-five years and whose husband was an American professor there. Like David Leeming, Garwood also remembers lively literary evenings at "Pasha's library." She recalls sitting on the floor and drinking cocktails while Baldwin read to his friends from the novel he was finishing, *Another Country.* Baldwin responded to Turkey, she says, a country that is "one of the most non-biased, non-judgmental unless you're a charlatan. Here one must talk from the heart and say things you believe" (Garwood 2004).

He would become a serious connoisseur of *raki* (the Turkish form of the Mediterranean absinthe alcohol), meaning, according to the journalist Zeynep Oral, that while by day he could be as pleasant as any self-satisfied cultural icon, at night he could become an insupportably "frenzied, black militant" (qtd. in Campbell 1991, 212). Asked "Istanbul, why?" by Adelsen in the *Ebony* interview, he responded:

> A place where I can find out again—where I am—and what I must do. A place where I can stop and do nothing in order to start again . . . To begin again demands a certain silence, a certain privacy that is not, at least for me, to be found elsewhere. (Adelsen 1970, 44)

When asked his thoughts on his adoptive city in a 1965 interview in the Turkish arts magazine *Varlik,* Baldwin speaks of refuge: "Istanbul is a kind of shelter for me. I can be alone here" (Baldwin 1965, 10). Hiatus, privacy, and silence did not necessarily connote inactivity or isolation. If Baldwin could rest and "breath" in Istanbul he did so within the security of trusted fellowship. His mental and physical health responded to the "great unpretentious hospitality" of the city that was still far enough away from the daily influences and pressures of American culture, but close enough to Europe to allow him the privacy he needed to work, without the geographical isolation that could impair his efficacy in the Western Civil Rights movement. He was not romantic about the perils of self-exile: "The expatriate," he says in a 1967 interview in the Turkish arts magazine *Cep Dergisi,* "may find that he has no real or relevant concerns, and no grasp of reality. He is living, really, on the hazards and energies of other people" (qtd. in Campbell 1991, 214). Yet his own semi-exile in Istanbul would nourish something in him that felt threatened in the 1960s. And while as recently as November of 2002, the critic Shelby Steele could argue in *Harper's* magazine that Baldwin lost his head and art to politics in the 1960s, it was in Istanbul and Europe that Baldwin found the "hazards and energies" he needed to remain a central player in the Civil Rights movement without being destroyed, or incapacitated by his own fame. In Istanbul, he claimed, he could "concentrate on being a writer" because he found, at least for a decade or so, the love and support of which he was in constant search.

As the great revolving door between the ambiguous frontiers of the East and the West, Istanbul proved rich not only as a symbol of the cross-cultural but also as a city that allowed him access to the broader international relevancy of America's mid-century culture wars. Within the safety of a non-Christian cosmopolitanism, he could discuss over cocktails with his friends, the poet Yaşar Kemal and Engin Cezzar, the possibilities of new world orders that would include not only America's poor minorities but also the world's disinherited. His 1960s writing was nurtured and fueled by these conversations and the experience of living in an old-world city at once European and Near Eastern. From the distance Turkey afforded, Baldwin wrote to Americans of the dangers of isolation and arrogance. If the social complexities of the city stimulated Baldwin's existent international or transnational consciousness, it further nourished one of America's great mid-twentieth-century political humanists during one of that country's most turbulent decades. Istanbul was also a place where he finished work begun elsewhere. He signs off his bestselling novel *Another Country* "Istanbul, Dec 10, 1961," and in 1962, while in Istanbul, he completed his famous long essay originally entitled "Down at the Cross." This famous jeremiad concerning the surge in popularity of the Nation of Islam in Northern U.S. cities would be published by the *New Yorker* magazine as "Letter from a Region in My Mind."

This title is in keeping with the magazine's tradition of classifying essays written about foreign places as letters. The letter in the November 18, 2002, issue written by David Remnick entitled "Letter From Istanbul: The Experiment" asks the question: "Will Turkey be the model for Islamic Democracy?" While this epistolary model is a pretense for bringing current world events, cultural and political, closer to home, the form—the letter that travels from afar—has about it an exotic unreality, if only because of the precarious journey it attests to, even in the age of overnight and electronic mail. In the case of Baldwin's letter, the title has this distancing effect. Yet like all of Baldwin's work, the potential for the overturning of expectations is carefully exploited. An inevitable, inherent paradox is exposed in all its severe absurdity. The foreign place Baldwin's letter is concerned with is the South Side of Chicago, a place certainly unfamiliar to much of white middle America in 1962; the address is the headquarters of the Nation of Islam movement, the home of Elijah Muhammad. It is a strange and frightening country to many liberals or Christians, white and black alike. And the letter, a real letter signed off in Turkey, a predominantly Muslim but secular republic, takes America to task not only for its present political failures but also for the negligence of its Christian institutions.

Baldwin tells us that he had had no intention of going to visit Elijah Muhammad that summer. He explains, however, that it was "the incredible, abysmal, and really cowardly obtuseness of white liberals" that encouraged him to go.

> Whether in private debate or public, any attempt I made to explain how the Black Muslim movement came about, and how it has achieved such force, was met with a blankness that revealed the little connection that the liberals' attitudes have with their perceptions or their lives, or even their knowledge—revealed, in fact that they could deal with the Negro as a symbol or a victim but had no sense of him as a man. (Baldwin 1985a, 357)

The essay ultimately addresses this disconnection between the political and the private, the inability of white America to comprehend the nature of black America's discontent and thereby put that comprehension to practical use. Foreigners in their own country, black Americans in pre-civil rights America are the most recent generation to suffer the humiliation of being punished not for things they have done but for who they are, and Baldwin's ultimate answer to this is that the problems white America has with black America is really a problem it has with its own soul.

The humanist notion of understanding oneself in order to understand others is a constant leitmotif in Baldwin's writing. And this Renaissance drive toward creating heaven on earth is rooted simultaneously in his early days as a young minister and in his early taste for Western classics. Yet it is this humanism at the heart of his political project that creates confusion. The elder Langston Hughes and Ralph Ellison criticize him for becoming too political in the 1960s. After Baldwin writes of Hughes's *Selected Poems,* "I am amazed all over again by his genuine gift," even as he qualifies this praise with the observation that the book contains "a great deal which a more disciplined poet would have thrown into the waste-basket," (qtd. in Campbell 1991, 130) Hughes's responds in a postcard:

> Hey Jimmy:
> Ain't you heard?
> RACE and ART
> Are far apart.
> qtd. in CAMPBELL 1991, 130

And a younger generation of black artists and activists will criticize him severely for not being political enough. His elegant prose and his self-consciously literary style prove his sycophantic adoration for Henry James and thus the white establishment. He will also be criticized, even distanced, by Martin Luther King himself, for being too overtly homosexual. Baldwin was referred to as Martin Luther Queen by some; the writer and activist Eldridge Cleaver identified a racial death wish in Baldwin's homosexuality, even though years later Cleaver would solicit Baldwin for money when he was in trouble with French authorities (Leeming 1994, 319). Thus, it is not difficult to understand why Baldwin would choose to wield his political pen from a distance, and particularly from the safety afforded by a culture with a history of political art. Besides not being made to feel like a "Negro" in Turkey (though his friends called him "*Arap*" [Arab], a derogatory term by contemporary standards), his friend and fellow literary activist Yaşar Kemal suggests that Baldwin felt at ease in Istanbul because of the general Mediterranean attitude toward homosexuality: the relative lack of fear that allows, for example, a transgender Turkish singer like Bülent Ersoy to pursue a lucrative career rather than a prison sentence or eternal obscurity. Thus, while some Americans may not have fathomed Baldwin's semi-expatriation to Istanbul, it is in keeping with the writer's penchant for overturning expectations that he, one of the most potent and effectual voices coming out of America's civil rights decade, found in a secular Muslim city the freedom necessary to speak openly to America about the pride leading to its Christian prejudices.

What precisely did America not understand about itself in 1962, according to the argument in "Letter from a Region in my Mind"? The list is long, but there are points that function in the letter like changes in a jazz tune. Baldwin, a modern Romantic who aspired in his prose to the state of music—his models were Charlie Parker and Thelonious Monk as well as Vivaldi and Schönberg—structures his essay upon the Nation of Islam's critical assessments of white Western culture and his own variation of their tune. He moves loosely back and forth between the reported speech of his dinner conversation with the religious leader and his followers, and his own interpretation, or justification, for their discontent, even if he may ultimately disagree with their conclusions. First, there is the problem of the historical role of Christianity. "In the realm of power," Baldwin argues, "Christianity has operated with an unmitigated arrogance and cruelty—necessarily, since a religion ordinarily imposes on those who have discovered the true faith the spiritual duty of liberating the infidels" (Baldwin 1985a, 351). White Christians continue to assume their moral authority even in the wake of the Third Reich, though blacks, Baldwin suggests, were less shocked by the Holocaust than whites because they sensed it could happen to them (Baldwin 1985a, 355).

The movement's condemnation of the sins of white Christian America is nothing new, argues Baldwin. In fact, Elijah Muhammad, hardly an overnight sensation, had been preaching the same sermon for over thirty years. The white man was the devil, the prophet flatly argued; an experiment had gone bad some 6,300 years ago on the island of Patmos during the days when all humans were the Original Black. And because God was black, and all black men belonged to Islam, Islam was to rule the world. Baldwin, like many civil rights intellectuals responding to Elijah Muhammad, focuses our attention on the symbolic significance and concrete repercussions of this origination myth as it concerns the genesis of whites. The story of the white devil must be considered seriously if only because it seems to offer "divine corroboration" for what people in the streets, on the South Side of Chicago and in Harlem, experience on a daily basis. Interested in the social conditions that have galvanized Elijah Muhammad's message for a growing number of Americans—conditions created by an increased impatience with the indifference of average white Americans and a new fearlessness on the part of a younger generation of activists—Baldwin acknowledges the inevitability of the movement's extremism, even as he will underscore the futility of inversed racism. It was the violence toward white Christian power structures that worried people most in the message, people who, as Malcolm X had pointed out, tended to consider violence and heroics as synonymous with glory only in their own freedom movements. The "abysmal obtuseness" that Baldwin had met with when he had attempted to enlighten liberal whites on how the Black Muslim movement had come to gain such force, the blankness over the question of racial violence, simply reinforced Elijah Muhammad's message that Christian America was out of touch with its own reality.

Another thing America did not understand about itself in 1962 was that it was imperative it take profound account of its national assumptions concerning not only people of color but also people whose definitions of freedom did not correspond with their own. Black people did not necessarily desire to be white or be integrated into white culture, Baldwin points out; they simply wished, at this point in history, not to be told who they were and what purpose they served the democratic process as it was defined by Cold War power politics. If the 1954 Supreme Court decision to outlaw segregation in the schools had come about more to serve the United States' interests in Africa—to woo the descendants of former slaves, as Baldwin, rather tentatively, argues—America would be wise to stop congratulating itself on its big-heartedness (Baldwin 1985a, 371). Ethics, rather than "the sloppy and fatuous nature of American good will," would have to reemerge as the heart of an American domestic renaissance if the country wished to have any say in a new world order not invested in a hierarchy of race and religion. Because if and when the flood gates were forced open there was going to be hell to pay. It was imperative that the country "deal with the untapped and dormant force of the previously subjugated" (Baldwin 1985a, 351). In other words, he says,

> in order to survive as a human, moving, moral weight in the world, America and the Western nations will be forced to reexamine themselves and release themselves from many things that are now taken to be sacred, and to discard nearly all the assumptions that have been used to justify their lives and their anguish and their crimes so long. (Baldwin 1985a, 351)

An important source of Elijah Muhammad's popularity was grounded in the fact that he was helping the poor in concrete ways: rather than a trickle-down social welfare system based on the charity and good will of a wealthy few, his was a system that case by case helped junkies and drunks dispel their demons and stay out of prison. The community was watching. Worldly success under the present system of rewards and punishments was less a sign of grace then greed, and unless the nation considered honestly the problems of its poorest citizens, it would never survive.

Honesty, however, was precisely what the country lacked, particularly when it came to assessing its own fears, and thus a further thing that America did not understand about itself in 1962 was that life was tragic. Just as Baldwin moves back and forth between the personal and the political, playing each off the other like musical phrases, he also plays the spiritual against the political in ways maddening to academics invested in maintaining distinctions between the intellectual and the ethical. If Baldwin is accused of being an incompetent political theorist, he is also brought to task for his humanistic, and thus for many obsolete, approach to ethics. He speaks, for example, of the soul or the heart as if they played judicial roles in postwar geopolitics. "There are too many things we do not wish to know about ourselves," he insists:

> Privately, we cannot stand our lives and dare not examine them; domestically, we take no responsibility for (and no pride in) what goes on in our country; and, internationally, for many millions of people, we are an unmitigated disaster. Whoever doubts this last statement has only to open his ears, his heart, his mind, to the testimony of—for example—any Cuban peasant or any Spanish poet. (Baldwin 1985a, 371)

Needless to say, J. Edgar Hoover directed the FBI to keep a close eye on "the well-known pervert" and listed him as a Communist (Campbell 1991, 172). When his file was closed in 1974, it contained 1,750 pages next to William Faulkner's eighteen (Campbell 1991, 158). But what this last observation also makes clear is that Baldwin, in 1962, is more determined than ever to force the personal and the domestic onto the international stage. White exceptionalism on the domestic front is directly connected, he argues, to a fear of change, and ultimately to a fear of death and the death of belief systems we cling to while assuming they are sustaining us. Black America, more and more, was gaining the force to change the system and thus put to death a reality America had clung to since the seventeenth century. And this social revolution was not confined to America's domestic borders. The world was already too small for that.

Baldwin, writing from Europe and Turkey, already had in mind the global effects of his homeland's hegemonic pride vis-à-vis the powerless. And because he loved his country, as he insisted repeatedly, he reserved the right to criticize it with passion and with an impunity that his fame in the 1960s allowed him. If he argues in "Letter from a Region in My Mind," as he does in his play *Blues for Mr. Charlie* (and nearly everywhere else), that hate springs from the projection of fears and longings onto an "other," he proposes that the powerful face this historical fact in their personal and political lives and take the enormous risk of sharing in the suffering of others. But to share is to endanger the self as we know it. And this is a good thing, according to Baldwin: "The white man is in sore need of new standards, which will release him from his confusion and place him once again in fruitful communion with the depths of his own being" (Baldwin 1985a, 375). People who cannot suffer remain forever children. They never discover who they are in any complex, or tragic, sense of the simple infinitive "to be" (Baldwin 1985a, 376).

Baldwin believed in endless conversation, the ceaseless negotiation that was man's destiny as a social animal. Though he understood the Nation of Islam's demands for the formation of a separatist black nation within the United States—the six or seven southern states that would constitute back pay and interest owed to men and women who never profited from their labors— Baldwin did not agree with exclusivity: "We, the black and white, deeply need each other here if we are really to become a nation—if we are really, that is, to achieve our identity, out maturity, as men and women" (Baldwin 1985a, 375). In addition, it would not serve the moral interests of blacks to wish harm on their oppressors: "I am very much concerned that American Negroes achieve their freedom here in the United States. But I am also concerned for their dignity, for the health of their souls, and must oppose any attempt that Negroes may make to do to others what has been done to them" (Baldwin 1985a, 369). He encouraged white liberal Americans to listen carefully to their Muslim brothers, to connect to them as men and women rather than as abstractions. He encouraged negotiation, humility, and foremost love.

The primary subject of Baldwin's civil rights nonfiction is America's self-hate and the ensuing fear that makes the nation dangerous to itself and to others. In his essay "Nothing Personal," written with Richard Avedon and published in 1964, Baldwin examines what seems now to be an all too familiar pattern: America's penchant for targeting enemies without when that which ails us most can be located within. With the attack of the World Trade Center in 2001, many Americans were able to externalize and consolidate their longing for revenge, a longing endemic to a political system that counted on a real or imagined threat for its very posturing. It is only through external threat that action heroes come into existence, and action heroes, the stuff of adolescent fantasy, are what too often pass for men and women in a culture at war with its own conscience. "It is, of course, in the very nature of a myth," argues Baldwin, "that those who are its victims and, at the same time, its perpetrators, should, by virtue of these two facts, be rendered unable to examine the myth or even to suspect, much less recognize, that it is a myth which controls and blasts their lives" (Baldwin 1985a, 383). While Baldwin will focus on the myth of white superiority, his argument translates immediately to early twenty-first-century events on the world stage concerning the relation between the Eastern hemisphere and the Western hemisphere, the Muslim and the Christian.

As the 1960s progressed and his sojourns in Istanbul extended to the point where he maintained permanent residences in the city, Baldwin's concerns over what he felt to be the national ravages of an increasingly apathetic Christian church widened to include a more international polemic. If American citizens had suffered from a church concerned primarily with maintaining the status quo, the world community had fared no better. Baldwin would combine Martin Luther King Jr.'s call for revolution within the American church with the socialist's call for international accountability. By 1968 in an *Ecumenical Review* article entitled "White Racism or World Community," Baldwin would associate racism and American colonial expansionism with the church he felt facilitated both.

> The Christian Church still rules the world, it still has the power, to change the structure of South Africa. It has the power if it will, to prevent the death of another Martin Luther King, Jr. It has the power, if it will, to force my government to cease dropping bombs on Southeast Asia. These are crimes committed in the name of the Christian Church, and no more than we have absolved the Germans for saying, "I didn't know it," "I didn't know what it was about," "I knew of people having been taken away in the night, but it has nothing to do with me." We are very hard on the Germans about that . . . When a structure, a state, a church, or a country, becomes too expensive for the world to afford, when it no longer responds to the needs of the world, that structure is doomed. (Baldwin 1985b, 441–42)

Shelby Steele argues that when Baldwin returned to the United States in 1957 he "gave up the psychological remove" of Europe that Steele believes helped sustain his individuality. This, Steele argues, partially accounts for Baldwin's losing his art to politics in the 1960s, a criticism of Baldwin's aesthetic not confined only to Hughes during these years. Steele suggests that Europe gave Baldwin distance from the American civil rights "herd" and its prescribed ethical positioning that began to "control culture" when its "moral glamour" began to achieve "the invisibility of propriety" (Steele 2002, 37, 39). There are a number of problems with this assessment beyond the simple fact that Baldwin never returned to the United States in any permanent sense. More importantly, Steele's observations offer a restricted assessment of the nature of self-imposed exile. Once one has studied one's native land from the outside for an extended amount of time, such self-conscious, self-critical examination does not cease even as one crosses back over physical, geographical borders. If anything, the sense of being an alien becomes more acute upon return. Customs no longer naturalized to the point of silence or invisibility become evident to one like crosswalk signals for the deaf and blind. And when a person comes back to social crisis, it is one's heightened objectivity that often helps one to see the ideological enormity of the problem at hand; for whatever the pressing, empirical struggle may be for or against, it is generally one piece in a larger sociopolitical puzzle. Outsiders often see that things are worse than those who endure it daily even imagine.

In Baldwin's case his color did not fully define him, nor was the struggle for civil rights his sole focus. This latter fact earned him both the indignation and the respect of his fellows. Living beyond the borders of the United States and of modern Christendom, Baldwin was intimately conscious of historical, political, and cultural factors that perhaps did not transcend race but allowed him to see American racism not as the cause of America's ills but as the culminating effect of other Western hypocrisies, hypocrisies that continue to influence U.S. foreign policy at the turn of the twenty-first century. Geographical and an attendant ideological distance lent a depth and breadth to Baldwin's analyses of American social crises in the 1960s that few others writers of his generation could muster. In a letter to Engin Cezzar, Baldwin writes and underlines the phrase "I am the only *mobile black man* left in America" (Cezzar 2004). The occasion of the letter is the murder of Martin Luther King Jr. He excuses himself to his friend for his silence since the tragedy. He is trying to get back to Istanbul, get away from the pressures of his elevated status with publishers as a token black writer. Thus if Baldwin was not continually "in the trenches" in the United States in a physical sense, he never left the field of battle. Moreover, contrary to what Steele seems to suggest, Baldwin did not suddenly become politically engaged when he quit fiction and returned to the United States, nor did he quit Europe and return to protest writing, in "blatant contradiction" to any former resolve never to do so.

The power of Baldwin's fiction, when it is powerful, lies in Baldwin's uncanny talent for transcribing pressing, contemporary social and political problems in plot and character. In "Sonny's Blues," perhaps one of the most elegant short stories to come out of twentieth-century America, each character matters to us precisely because we all have a social stake in the outcome of his or her sociopsychological struggle. Baldwin never returned to protest writing because he never left it, just as he never left America; nor did he leave Turkey, nor did he return definitively to either. Political function and aesthetic form, the West and the East, do not exist in an outmoded oppositional relationship in Baldwin's work or life. Neither do they coexist in a vague, fluid state of indeterminacy. Each necessarily contains the other: art is political, politics artful; individuals exist within groups, groups exist within individuals. The model is dialectical.

In his 1960s essays Baldwin returned again and again to the problem of America's failure or inability to assess and therefore to question its own authority, at the personal, and thus, he will suggest, the political level. This is the primary subject of his essay "Nothing Personal." Americans, he argued, are difficult to talk to. Because we not only avoid saying what we think, but avoid searching in any profound way for what we think, we live a constant crisis of identity. And this leads to a people sustained by myths that supersede historical knowledge: myths of enemies, "strangers," "barbarians," or others, "responsible for our confusion and our pain" (Baldwin and Avedon 1985, 386). At hand in "Nothing Personal" is the recent hysteria over "leftist lunatics" and the "limp" national acquiescence to Washington's official position that held these "enemies" responsible for the death of President Kennedy in 1968. Baldwin wonders why leftist lunatics would be necessary "to blow off the President's head" when in the city of Dallas a great number of people with far stronger reasons would very much have wished the Democratic president dead. He concludes with the consolatory idea that time will reveal the truth of the case, which, of course, is not yet the case.

It is "easier to murder than to change" (Baldwin and Avedon 1985, 387). It is more "reassuring" to believe in an evil without than one within. Rather than predicting, as he seems to, the widening concentric circles of violence and economic interests leading to, say, the Iraqi war, Baldwin argues that the historical America "worships" and "nurtures" violence in defense of its opulence; this has always led people to persuade themselves that lies are true. Writing from the vantage of a culture peopled with the descendants of the proverbial "barbarian horde"—the Turk mythologized beyond recognition by eight hundred years of Christian theology—Baldwin exhorts America to look within before it aims its guns without. The lie that leads most directly to war is the one that tells us an enemy, a stranger, the barbarian, threatens our wealth.

In the 1968 introduction to his play "The Amen Corner," written in 1952 but not published in book form until sixteen years later, Baldwin says the following about his early failure to become a writer in America.

> I myself once described my exile as a self-exile, but it was really far more complex and bitter than that. No one really wishes to leave his homeland. I left because I was driven out, because my homeland would not allow me to grow in the only direction in which I could grow. (Baldwin 1968, xiii)

That direction proved to be transnational even as it meant struggling to maintain a sense of local accountability. From Istanbul in the 1960s, Baldwin was telling his public that rather than fearing the evil without, middle-class Christian America must respond to the needs of the outside world. From the cultural distance of Istanbul, a city with an eye equally fastened on the Western and Eastern hemispheres, Baldwin talked of the dangers of isolation and nationalism. He warned his countrymen against the systemic dangers of the nation's dependence on expensive superstructures. "'The white man's Heaven,' sings a Black Muslim minister, 'is the black man's Hell'" and "it has been true for as long as the white men have ruled the world" (Baldwin 1985a, 351). America's twenty-first-century claims to the resources and administering bodies of the Middle East took Christian-Muslim tensions to a new and deadly level. Yet Baldwin saw into the heart of this darkness a generation ago when he stated the following:

> Even leaving out of account the remarkable arrogance that assumes that the ways and morals of others were inferior to those of Christians, and that they therefore had every right, and could use every means, to change them, the collision between cultures—and the schizophrenia in the mind of Christendom—had rendered the domain of morals as chartless as the sea once was and as treacherous as the sea still is. (Baldwin 1985a, 352)

The American public's fear and distrust of the Muslim world are "historical and public attitudes," though they feel natural and justified in the face of what is called terrorism. "Neither civilized reason nor Christian love would cause any of those people to treat you as they presumably wanted to be treated; only the

26. James Baldwin on the Golden Horn, 1960s. Photograph by Sedat Pakay.

fear of your power to retaliate would cause them to do that, or to seem to do it, which was (and is) good enough" (Baldwin 1985a, 340). The "you" is the disenfranchised, regardless of time or place: the idea was as disturbing and dangerous in the 1960s as the 2010s. And the failure of a most fundamental Christian and Muslim dictum is painfully relevant to a twenty-first-century crusade. Baldwin's conclusions are as logical as they are sensitive to the tautological fallacies that fuel human vengeance. Self-serving global power inevitably becomes a target for those who see through the transparent rhetoric that glorifies the globalization of Western "democracy," when such a word is sorely abused. They know very well that their independent well-being does not factor into the reciprocal processes and promises of the global marketplace.

8

Mary Lee Settle's *Turkish Reflections*

Past and Present Recognitions

MARY LEE SETTLE'S BOOK *Turkish Reflections: A Biography of a Place* avoids the requisite march through the chronicles of history that load Turkey down with the weight of recycled facts. Instead, Settle attempts to enliven and expand the present by infusing it with fluid layers of the past. Because time travel constitutes the structural logic of the book we are asked to hold the past and present simultaneously in our minds as we discover not so much the relationships between historical causes and phenomenological effects but rather the past at play in the present, the present playing out dramas rooted in the temporal past.

> Today, the road is wide, the trucks, huge and powerful and showing it at every blind hill, every turn, cruise along it, owning it. Modern conquerors from the Mercedes factory snort and whinny like the warhorses, except when some local farmer and his family, going at five miles an hour in a cart pulled by the family tractor, which has replaced the camel, simply refuses to get out of the way, or even to look behind him as he goes slowly, slowly across Anatolia as he always has, ready to be killed but not to be bullied, changed, speeded up, or suppressed. He is the maddening, surviving strength of Anatolia, and he always has been, with Alexander fuming behind him, Tamerlane cursing, Genghis Khan sighing. (Settle 1991, 166)

Here we have a modern rural highway scene that dramatizes a predicament faced by those who will impose from without a sense of order on a local culture. Alexander the Great from the North, Tamerlane from the East, foreign conquerors who would subjugate Anatolia are contrasted to Genghis Khan who lays equal claim to Turkish heritage. Settle, with her penchant for disturbing a Western reader's sense of order, inverts an Occidental reading of heroes and villains. Genghis Khan, the consummate villain of the West, is an empathetic player in this vignette.

Like modern scholars of Turkish history, Settle in *Turkish Reflections* attempts to rewrite European narratives of "the terrible Turk" by reinterpreting Turkish history beyond the confines of Eurocentric stories of Huns and hordes. She does this by bringing the reader up to speed via modern manifestations of ancient cultural dilemmas. Descendants of those other Huns, German vehicle manufacturers are likewise implicated in this allegorical sketch. Geographically positioned between markets to the West and East, Anatolia adapts the technology of its neighbors to its own particular idiosyncrasies. So it is, so it has always been, as Settle repeatedly reminds us in her leitmotif of a synchronized past and present.

Much is typical of the book as a whole in the discussion of Amasya. Searching for the past in the present in her travels through Turkey, Settle does not seek out monuments for their own sake; her quest is not limited to beautiful testaments to dead ideas, a démodé conception of the aesthetic. Rather, she is in search of lived-in history. It is this sense of the continual past that leads her to Muslim, Turkic, and Seljuk shrines rather than the Christian ruins that tend to occupy most travel books about Turkey published in the West. Because Christianity is one primary purveyor of tourism in Turkey, or anywhere many Western tourists go, what does not immediately speak to an Occidental visitor's understanding of his or her historical and cultural heritage does not appear in the books that guide them. Following the paths of the Crusaders who fought and traded their way through Anatolia in the Medieval Ages, the Christian tourist has a final goal, whether it be on the itinerary or in the heart: to trace the paths of their own holy warriors and ultimately to re(dis)cover their own holy land. And in the process, as Roland Barthes argues in his essay, "The Blue Guide," "Human life disappears into the exclusive benefit of its monuments" (Barthes 1973, 75).

While Settle makes a concerted effort not to reduce geography "to the description of an uninhabited world of monuments," she nevertheless does not always avoid what the *Guide Bleu* sells: an expression of mythologies which are, ultimately, "obsolete" (Barthes 1973, 76). The "hospitable pride" she finds everywhere and associates with what she conceives of as the people's "natural" sense of themselves as keepers of the world's memory, of Christian as well as Muslim shrines, is an assessment fraught with problems that the good intentions of the writer cannot resolve. While Settle provides us with a historicized version of the present and the Anatolians who live in it, the historical past ultimately never informs an authentic vision of the present in spite of her efforts to include real people in the "biographical" narrative of the place. There is an ideological rift in *Turkish Reflections.* Settle's laudable New Historical method, whether a self-conscious approach or not, does not lend itself to a true marriage of the experiential and hypothetical. Much is lost in the translation of the anecdotal to the theoretical. This is mostly due to the Romanticism that muddies the present as well as to the nostalgia that taints the past.

NOSTALGIA AND ROMANTICISM are the bane of good travel writing. Both attest to unfulfilled longing: one for a place that was, one for a place that never was. And both hinder the rendering of time and place that is unsentimental, and thus open to the complex, often contradictory realties of any story told about human beings and their history. Sentimentality is a handicap that Settle struggles with, often quite consciously, in the course of the book. Bodrum, the ancient city of Halicarnassus, the alleged birthplace of Homer, is the site that holds the peripatetic narrative together like bookends. Settle tells us that she first went to Bodrum in 1972 and stayed for three years. She had originally stumbled on the small, dozing fishing village, in flight from what she describes as the rather inhospitable island of Kos. Greek boys, bullies, prove less well behaved, because, she seems to suggest, they lack the hospitable pride that is the cultural inheritance of the better behaved boys six miles away on the Turkish coast. According to Jan Morris in the preface, Settle returns sixteen years later to Bodrum to "search for origins of the happiness she found" in the 1970s, and the book is testament to

> a widening of her interest and intimacy from the first foothold long ago to the whole of the country and its history: to Istanbul, Trabzon, Ankara, and the Troglodyte cities of Cappadocia; to the lost kingdom of Urartu; to the territories of the Seljuks and their illustrious Aladdin-Keykubad. A country, as she quotes from the poet Nazim Hikmet in the epigraph, "coming full gallop from far-off Asia." (Settle 1991, x)

The book is a happy one. Descriptions of the people and the landscape in the 1970s are intimate and richly textured:

> Turkey is more than ruins, or armies, or even the fawn-colored spaces of central Turkey, the mountains, the wild shades of green in the northeast. It is a cared-for plant in a window, a geranium as tall as a small tree and covered with red bloom against a white wall, the controlled tumble of grapevine, the economics of food and shade together on a trellis above a table in a hidden courtyard, the pot of basil in the captain's cabin of a fishing boat. These tell me more of Turkey, the place I knew day by day, than all the great buildings and all the history, even though these things, too, are hints of habits that seem to change without ever being rejected. (Settle 1991, xvi-xvii)

The mythological and historical backgrounds, which inevitably follow, are equally evocative:

> The movement of a tide, of a rock, of the slowly trembling earth of this part of the world calls forth legends. Even the word *meander* comes from the winding Maeander, the river that flowed to Miletus, Priene, Magnesia, and was fed in turn by the Marsyas River, named for the satyr Marsyas, who was flayed of his shaggy goat hide by the Amazon priestesses of Apollo for daring to compete against him in music. (Settle 1991, xvii-xviii)

Even when she "gazes" on poverty, she locates an aesthetic that is not decontextualized: she directs us to see a past richness that lingers in the poverty of the present: "The villagers, with that ever-present sense of style that Turkish people have, make neat symmetrical towers of dung as high as the houses, for their winter fuel, their sides piled carefully in geometric patterns" (Settle 1991, 80).

When Settle does discuss Christian history in Turkey, her explicit aim is not only revisionist, that is, retelling the story of Anatolia from a non-European point of view. She goes a step further than this: she posits Anatolia directly at the center of some of the most enduring narratives that Western culture holds onto in its drive for a unified historical and thus cultural identity. Her discussion of the medieval period and its crusaders is a case in point. In her initial descriptions of Bodrum, the medieval crusader castle that still stands is given equal but not more space than her descriptions of ruined temples to Aphrodite and Hermes, or the Friday open market:

> To the right, all the medieval legends, the knights-in-armor, the Crusades, the castles of childhood rose on a small mountain against the sky. It was the castle

> of Saint Peter, begun in 1402 by the Knights of Saint John, sometimes called the Knights Hospitalers. They came to Bodrum when they were defeated by Tamerlane and lost their castle at Smyrna. It is a stone memory dominating the sky above the town as it has for nearly six hundred years. It was only when, later in that first day, I climbed up to it, that I saw much of it, too, was ruined and snaggled. (Settle 1991, 14)

While any guide book of the area would not fail to mention this attraction, Settle offers us a way to look at it that is not always offered in contemporary travel texts. First, there is her refusal to allow the Christian monument to dominate the page and thus the geography. The imposing castle (the illuminated focus of most tourist posters for Bodrum or the southern Aegean) is one of many things to spend your day with. Settle, herself, spends more time at the market. Second, she does not merely place the Knights of St. John, or Hospitallers, in Bodrum as if by divine intervention as many will: she does not allow crusaders to simply appear or circulate on the Muslim map as if they were in complete control of their movements and destiny. Rather she offers their existence as the effect of a cause not customarily embellished on because it does not reinforce a heroic reading of Westerners as invincible religious warriors. The Hospitallers are chased to Bodrum by Tamerlane, the antihero that we love to hate despite Byron's attempts to seduce us in his play by that name. Eastern forces play an incisive role in the unfolding of Western histories, so much so that the use of binary categories East and West in our narratives of cultural identity appears self-delusional at best.

Settle does not stop at historical relativity. She moves on to other forms of provocation, which aim to further disturb classic heroic representations of the Crusades.

> On that fatal day, Friday, 19 August 1071, known ever after as "that dreadful day" by the Byzantines, Turkish tribes deserted and joined their own, and the Franks refused to fight. In one day, the Byzantine army was destroyed. For the first time a Roman emperor fell into the hands of an enemy. The Seljuks called the new kingdom that began to grow that day the kingdom of Rum because they considered that they had conquered Rome, and they had.
>
> The repercussions of that battle, when the floodgate broke open to the settlement of the whole of Anatolia by Turkish tribes, are still felt today. The traditional Eurocentric attitude toward the Turks began then, when the Pope

> called for the First Crusade to protect the Christian Byzantine Empire when it was already too late. It was then that the name Turk became a pejorative term meaning infidel, savage. (Settle 1991, 77)

Tradition tells us that Pope Urban II instigated the first Crusade in defense of the universal faith: "On beholding the enormous injury that all, clergy or people, brought upon the Christian Faith . . . at the news that the Rumanian provinces had been taken from the Christians by the Turks, moved with compassion and impelled by the love of God, he crossed the mountains and descended into Gaul (Foucher de Chartres 1969, 321). While more recent accounts speak of geopolitics and power, the reputation of the "terrible Turk" still lingers in Western discourse, as most thousand year old habits of mind often will. Settle challenges this naturalized version of history by tracing its etymology. She also puts into question the ethics of Crusade—and in effect the medieval chivalric code—by confounding their origins as defensive or offensive movements. Although it is customary to count the Crusades as eight in number—one reignited approximately every twenty-five years for a duration of about one hundred and seventy-five years, these overseas religious wars went on from the twelfth century well into the seventeenth century. As long as Christians did not have full control of the passage to Jerusalem, there was war.

The people of Asia Minor have always played Hermes to one of the earth's most argued-over trade routes, and Settle traces this condition to the present. Modern Turkey finds itself forever at odds with one world power or another, because there is no pleasing everybody, even if one were so inclined.

> What had been an ancient commercial route to Europe, east to west, north to south, part of the road that Xenophon took and that was the caravan route to the Mediterranean and the Black Sea, had long been abandoned. Merchants from around the East had to go around both Crusader and Türkmen, and the armies of the Byzantine emperors, to get to Europe . . . Near our own time, the Suez Canal was an attempt to control the route. So was the ever-present longing of Russia to take the Bosphorus and the Dardanelles—to say nothing of Churchill's mistake at Gallipoli. The discovery of America was the result of another commercial attempt to go around the Middle East to get to India. (Settle 1991, 115–16)

This global urge to control modern Turkey in order to control international markets can be applied to the invasion of Iraq by American forces in 2003. As many times before, the Turks refused passage to a foreign army whose ultimate ambitions did not serve the interests of Turkey. Against enormous pressures from Washington, and over the urging of the Turkish prime minister himself, the Turkish parliament voted against allowing the American military to invade Iraq via a northern passage through Turkey, a move that jeopardized the economic future of the country and led to celebrating in the streets.

Settle creates a working model for such contemporary observations as the above. But while teaching us to historicize, showing us that we can better grasp the present by studying the past and better see the past by carefully observing the present, her method is not without problems. Speaking fondly of one of her many Turkish contacts that helped guide her, or, rather, helped facilitate her travels through Turkey, Settle calls up another foreign traveler from the past, this time a medieval Moroccan:

> My new, solicitous friend, Ziya, whose name means "luminous," was an elegant, young, English-speaking Istanbul University graduate.
>
> He may never have read Ibn Battuta, the fourteenth-century traveler who was handed from *akhis* to *akhis,* an old Turkish word for the generous organizations of young men who followed the standards of *futawwa* [*sic*]—an ideal of nobility, honesty, loyalty, and courage—but he was following, without considering anything else, the same rules of hospitality. (Settle 1991, 36)

The comparison is rich in historical texture; the roots of the ever-present Turkish hospitality are keenly accounted for. Yet there is a problem in the conclusion that troubles many well-intentioned associations in much of Settle's text: Ziya lacks consciousness. In the passages cited above, Settle's enthusiasm for local color and its cultural, historical contexts creates its own trap. Nostalgia and Romanticism lead to an aestheticizing of place and people that, like ancient Greek mythscapes and their gods, vanish into the recesses of what inevitably proves to be an Orientalist travel text:

> Turn off a main road, wander into a village, go to see an ancient ruin, and you are in another country, the one where people live as they have for so many

> thousands of years. They are not conscious of saving a culture. They are not resisting change. They are digesting it, as they always have. It is so slow that it is more like the erosive carving of rocks. (Settle 1991, xvii)

Though in the paragraph that follows she asserts that the past is not wiped out in the transmission of culture through the generations—"They may have changed the old patterns, but they have not obliterated them"—still we note a tendency to deny cognition or recognition of their historical moment to local people (Settle 1991, xvii). Intuitive beings, they "digest" rather than understand, or, like inert passive nature, they are carved by the elements, the forces of history. Ziya, "without considering anything," is a gentleman. While Settle makes enormous efforts to historicize and, in turn, humanize her subject, she ultimately cannot move beyond a rhetoric that places the Turks, somewhat like noble savages, at the center of a text that, in spite all of its efforts, fails to create a real sense of intersubjectivity between she who is writing and those who are written about.

In her discussion of the travel letters of Lady Mary Wortley Montagu in *Women Travel Writers and the Language of Aesthetics*, the critic Elizabeth Bohls praises the early eighteenth-century wife of the British Consul of Istanbul for her ability to represent a semblance of mutual dialogue between her Turkish subjects and herself: "These letters are perhaps most valuable for their apparent attempt (however partial and intermittent) at actual cultural exchange—a condition of intersubjectivity whose precondition is acceptance of the other as an intelligent, sensitive, acting self (Bohls 2004, 42). While Montagu's efforts may be "partial and intermittent," the letters certainly display a remarkable open-mindedness as well as respect for the people, particularly women, that she speaks for in the letters—a first in the genre. Part of the genius of Montagu's writing is that she shows the subject in action, and acting intelligently. And while she is much concerned with women as spectacles—the result, Bohls argues, of Montagu's own awareness of herself as an equally limited social being in her own culture—she avoids the problems that Settle creates by directing a wry, leveling sense of humor at all subjects, Turk or Infidel. If this is impressive for an early eighteenth-century female travel writer, the contrary inability to imagine and maintain an equal playing field for all human characters is still a problem for any twentieth-century writer schooled in what one hopes are the lessons of our postcolonial condition.

Settle is in love with what she sees as Turkish cool vis-à-vis sights and scenes that juxtapose, almost irreverently, the modern and the ancient, sights and scenes that stop her heart. This is a common New World tourist response to "Old Europe." It is a response born not necessarily out of ignorance but out of a naïve attraction to the exotic. And it is not necessarily a problem of distance and isolation, though it can become that. The veneration of the unknown is tied up with a primal, human desire to forever broaden our personal database, the desire for apotheosis that unites limited beings with the unlimited; it explains the love, and eventual fear, of the iconic. A rural Anatolian viewing skyscrapers from street level in Manhattan for the first, and maybe fourteenth time, will experience a similar sensation of ecstasy or awe. It is merely human. Yet we have to ask, in light of Settle's recurring representation of the ingenuous local, if the Anatolian tourist will assume that New Yorkers have no idea from which forests or ashes the city arose; if he or she will interpret New York cool as a childlike disregard for technologies the natives never think to contemplate. Or, as we may prefer to imagine, the Anatolian might automatically direct his or her sense of awe, and maybe even respect, to the people who seem at ease in their complex environment because they, like their city, are technologically advanced and thus in control of the wonders that surround them. Neither scenario is true, of course. But the logical fallacy is useful. Settle, like many contemporary as well as past travel writers, cannot see beyond her own Western urban prejudices. She overcompensates for the distance her excitement creates by reducing the Anatolians, the New Yorkers, to caricatures of disinterested cool, beings so naturalized in their landscape that they do not seem to have any potential existence beyond it, or even any identifiable distance within it. The naturalized Anatolian, like the ploughman in W. H. Auden's poem "Musée Des Beaux Arts," may

> Have heard a splash, the forsaken cry,
> But for him it was not an important failure; the sun shone
> As it had to on the white legs disappearing into the green
> Water
>
> AUDEN 1991, 179

He may be like "the dogs" that "go on with their doggy life" in spite of "something amazing" (Auden 1991, 179). Or as in William Carlos Williams's poem concerned with the same myth of Icarus, the same aestheticized drama only the artist can experience, the Anatolian may be he who is "ploughing/his field," part and parcel of an equally unconscious nature, a "pageantry . . . concerned with itself" (Williams 2003, 1279–80).

Unlike Auden and Williams, Settle does not maintain a sense of ironic distance from her own recontextualizing of a myth, this one of the "terrible Turk." Both poets offer an anti-Romantic reading of the fate of men as well as of the heroes, antiheroes, and legends we create to sustain ourselves. The poems are often read as modernist exercises in aesthetic distance and nonengagement. But this interpretation works only if we do not allow that both narrators communicate a clear understanding of the limits of their vision as voyeurs or readers or artists: they both rely on Bruegel's painting, Bruegel's eyes, to frame their poems. They self-consciously reveal their sources and in doing so allow for an objective distance that lets them speak about myth and men without folding one into recesses of the other. This is how Bruegel, the "old master," understood it; this is one way, a wonderful way, of considering different facets of human suffering.

Settle's discussion of rural unconsciousness does not offer the same distance or philosophical potential. While she suggests repeatedly that her Turkish characters are noble and stoic under the burden of so much accumulated history, she does not, as Auden and Williams do, reveal her sources. She does not offer, for example, clear economic or political contexts for a people's apparent disinterest. Neither does she apply Turkish fortitude, the need or necessity to carry on in spite of difficult odds, to a general human condition. In her pages life "concerned only with itself" comes to resemble an old travel narrative trope, that of the "inscrutable Oriental." Turkish blind acceptance of, and subsequent resilience to, the "amazing" cultural landscape they inhabit seems to be an isolated condition, one that is the effect of something more than historical circumstances; it seems different somehow from a common human way of getting on with the business of life in spite of dramas that erupt and threaten to change our way of seeing every afternoon. It seems to be in their particular blood, or their DNA, this way of viewing the world through wise and weary eyes. By romanticizing her subjects Settle does them no favors because she essentializes them. Rural Turks, living people, not tableaux, are not allowed an alternative response to their environment (they all seem to feel the same), nor are they assumed to have noticed Icarus falling from the sky or Settle, in the distance and practical shoes, observing them from under her sunhat.

SETTLE IS THE URBAN WESTERN TRAVELER who has the education necessary, she suggests, to see what indigenous people do not see or cannot see. And the difference is important. If they cannot see then there exists in her text the implicit suggestion that local people might negotiate the ruined signs of a collective history, recycle them, live in and on them, but never with them in a holistic way—the way Settle herself would if she were in their shoes. She never, however, explicitly criticizes or judges. She is continually amused by the offhandedness of local innocents; the people in Kayseri who have transformed a *han* (an inn) into workshops and a space for sport are the subject of an enthusiastic paragraph again dedicated to the kind of bliss that only lack of awareness, she seems to say, can afford.

> Boys of what were obviously well-known local teams were playing volleyball in the courtyard below. All the way around the balcony in front of the shops and tiny workshops that were inside the cavelike rooms men stood cheering for their chosen team. They called to each other, or down to the boys in the midst of it all playing volleyball in the courtyard of a *han* that from the arches must have been seventeenth-century Ottoman. There was no sign. Nobody cared. (Settle 1991, 141)

The lack of signs, a lack that could be addressed through funding from local or national government, is read as a lack of interest on the part of the local population. Team sports are a common obsession in poorer nations where one amuses oneself with what one can afford: a few friends, a ball, and the free time that unemployment guarantees.

A dervish kitchen in Seyitgazi near Eskişehir offers a similar example of how a past is only accessible through a privileged gaze:

> It was full of Turkish people who had brought lambs and their food to the kitchens to be sacrificed and cooked, and there was blood on the stones. We were the only Westerners, and probably the only ones who recognized that a baptistery from the Byzantine church had been built into the corner of the courtyard, and the columns were Roman. (Settle 1991, 198)

Again being a Westerner leads to the full recognition of a place, to a holistic understanding of the Ottoman, Byzantine, and Roman scenarios that contribute to a contemporary Turkish scene. It is often argued by Western scholars and some Turkish nationalists that the European Enlightenment never traveled as far as the Ottoman Empire. The responsibility is placed on the shoulders of the caliphs, religious leaders who, it is argued, opted for revelation rather than science. But what these same polemicists often fail to note, and rightly so for it would jeopardize their credibility as post-Enlightenment subjects, is that a jealous Turkish nationalism dating at least from the War of Independence of 1919 and an opportunist Western colonial urge dating from the Middle Ages have made a concerted effort to keep people ignorant of their comprehensive history. It is a common joke with university students, told with a weary laugh, that Turkish history, according to the school books distributed throughout the stressed national education system, begins with Atatürk. Few students have been given access to prerepublic history in its Byzantine or Phrygian manifestations. Turkic, Seljuk, and Ottoman history tend to take the form of legend, an aestheticizing of a past that distances it from the real lives of people. Modern Turks, like modern Americans, lead isolated lives: history begins with their grandparents and ends with them. Everything else, and sometimes even their grandparents' lives, is the stuff of dreams.

It is only relatively recent that Christopher Columbus and Thomas Jefferson have been reduced from myths to men, at least in higher education in the United States. The trickle-down effects of education are slow moving; both characters, in all their two-dimensional splendor, still appear on the back of cereal boxes—a source of information for much of North America's youth. It comes as no great surprise that a young republic like Turkey may still be at work on inventing its national consciousness. It is important for Americans who write about Turkey to be aware of the limitations of self-invention: we of all people should know most about the confidence man. When Settle sees no signs and registers no recognition of this lack, she must remember that some nations are in a position to invest in their national heritage as well as their myths, and some are not. It is a question of power, as always, and the economic freedoms or indulgences that ensue. A related question one might ask oneself as an American is this: why it is that with all our economic advantages we as a general population still tend to know as much about the lives and times of our distant ancestors as the average Anatolian knows about his. Is it because we don't care? Or is it because we are trained not to care?

SETTLE, OF COURSE, CARES and she posits herself as mentor to various young male guides in her travel narrative. A Western female incarnation of the roving dervish, she educates as she wanders, taking pleasure in opening the eyes of smart, uniformed men who repay her efforts with fealty and veneration.

> I kept crashing against the fact that Yusuf was an excited twenty–two year old, finding his country for the first time. He bounded up steep stone steps, over roofs, around towers, up ramps, over piles of stones, and looked back innocently to see if I was following. (Settle 1991, 117)

A lamb, a puppy, a child, Yusuf is all enthusiasm and potentiality. He is the future, the hope of a nation that, were it to gain access to the world's information, the kind of information that Settle has to offer, would no longer need the help of outsiders to penetrate the mysteries of local ruins, to make sense of the fragments that sprinkle their pastures and motorways like fallen sky junk:

> The surprise of the morning was always Yusuf, who began to develop an eye for the hints and fragments, especially Seljuk. The best part of Amasya, and of the other cities we visited, was the discovery, the hints and fragments, the possibilities of conjuring whole buildings from a half-buried cave that had been an *iwan* . . . , from a bit of imperial Roman carving sunk into a wall. It was Yusuf who pointed out a Seljuk *han,* an inn still used for merchants, only now the merchants are the hardware store, where wheelbarrows are piled high against the carved entry, and a builder next door who has left a pile of lumber propped against the wall that reaches to the roof. There are empty oil cans, a *bakkal* [small market], and, in the middle, a pharmacy where they sell the oil of flowers. (Settle 1991, 97–98)

Ignorance may often manifest itself as happy disinterest in her sketches of contemporary Turkish culture. One also notices, however, a suggestion of abuse based on that same ignorance. These "best parts" of Turkey are also its most neglected, she often implies, though never without adding that such neglect creates its own kind of beauty. Something nearing magic is necessary to "conjure" an integrated past, "whole buildings from a half-buried cave." Yet magic, like mythology, relies on the credulity of a people, and Settle's desire is to uncover the empirical data that makes up the biography of a place so that she may pass it on to her reader. Hers is ultimately an educative travel narrative.

It is the abuse, however, that dominates her final chapter about her return to Bodrum after a sixteen-year absence:

> All the way up to the walls of Halicarnassus, the empty hillside meadows were covered with holiday houses, all alike, that looked from a distance like white skulls . . . There were no country people at the *pazar.* The beautiful vegetable market was organized and permanent . . . It was no longer my sweet, kind town. It was, to me, a place that had been changed by invasion, as the cities I had seen in Anatolia had been changed and overlaid centuries ago . . . They were all gone: the carpenter, the fishermen, the sponge divers, the *dolmuses* stuffed with country people . . . The old Halikarnas Hotel on a point at the end of the bay had become a chic and noisy motel-cum-disco that I was told pulsed through the night. In front of it, new Greek temple columns thrust up against the sky—a folly of "ancient" ruins. (Settle 1991, 218)

Settle never fails to identify the "invasion" as one coming this time from the West. Yet the scope of her book does not include a real discussion of the nature of that invasion. Enterprising people in Bodrum, as in the world over, exploit the false magic conjured up by the Romantic longings of the leisured, restless, contemporary Occidental/Oriental traveler: Bodrum has long been the summer destination of upper-middle-class Turks as well as foreign tourists. Such escapism is facilitated by a much larger problem, what Claude Lévi-Strauss in 1955 had already identified in *Tristes Tropiques* as an "exhausted globalism."

> Journeys, those magic caskets full of dreamlike promises, will never again yield up their treasures untarnished. A proliferating and overexcited civilization has broken the silence of the seas once and for all. The perfumes of the tropics and the pristine freshness of human beings have been corrupted by a busyness with dubious implications, which mortifies our desires and dooms us to acquire only contaminated memories. (Settle 1991, 776)

Proliferation, overexcitement, and busyness are the character traits of a global capitalism that must forever create new markets if it is to survive. To romanticize a lost past in the face of ominous economic theory is to underestimate the problems of carpenters, fishermen, sponge divers, and country people in general. Settle chides herself for her bad humor in the face of "progress": "It seemed churlish to mourn. I stopped searching for what was gone and began to enjoy what was there—a new Bodrum, shining white in the sun" (Settle 1991, 219). Her conventional American positivism, the compulsive urge to locate a bright side, is as disingenuous as it is finally doleful. Nostalgia takes over the text. Failing to identify the silent powers, past and present, that work to undermine the integrity of local, diverse communities, Settle gives in to a longing for a place that was, a surrender that puts into question the main thrust of her book—her project to assess the ahistoricized present.

THE NARRATOR in Elizabeth Bishop's poem, "Questions of Travel," expresses a wistfulness about her travels to Brazil similar to that of Settle about her travels to Turkey. Within the space of five lines, however, Bishop contextualizes the global significance of the fatigued country she visits: It would have been "a pity," she insists,

> not to have heard
> the other, less primitive music of the fat brown bird
> who sings above the broken gasoline pump
> in a bamboo church of Jesuit baroque:
> three towers, five silver crosses.
>
> BISHOP 1994

Missionaries and petrol companies, the one paving the way for the other in modern history, are interjected into a pastoral scene with birdsong. Global issues cannot be disconnected from the smallest details of a landscape. The monoculture that Settle finds upon her return to Bodrum, and from which she recoils, is also the result of international market pressures that do not always serve the interests of local people. Nor do they serve the Romantic nostalgia of enlightened writers who come in search of the "origins of a happiness," their "sweet, kind town," now lost among "the shoddy imitations of Western clothes and souvenirs for tourists" (Settle 1991, 218). Settle is aware of the problems of global tourism in *Turkish Reflections* even if she does not make it an explicit topic of discussion. Nevertheless, a central paradox in this educational travel narrative is left for others to uncover. If help starts at home, Settle as a U.S. citizen avoids her own national implications in the contemporary problems of Turkey. Travel writers, if actively engaged in the discovery of a place, do well to remind themselves and the reader just where their authority comes from. Claiming intellectual fixity over others may serve a certain purpose, may bring many forgotten or repressed facts to light, but when all is said, and one is back in New York, life goes on in small towns in Anatolia much as it always has. This is not necessarily something to celebrate. Disinterest may be heroic when you control the narrative. But when you have no voice on the world stage, all you do is endure its direction. Turks know. They too were once its masters.

APPENDIX | WORKS CITED | INDEX

APPENDIX

Historical Timeline

667 BC	Ancient city of Byzantium founded.
330	Constantine, ruler of the Roman Empire, builds his new capital, Constantinople, at Byzantium.
392	Theodosius I reunites the Eastern and Western portions of the Roman Empire.
395	Permanent division of the Empire into Eastern and Western halves after the death of Theodosius I.
532–37	Justinian I builds the Church of Hagia Sophia.
730–87, 813–843	Iconoclasm controversies that result in the loss of many territories in Italy and in the South.
1054	The East-West Schism or Great Schism divides medieval Christendom into Western (Latin) and Eastern (Greek) branches; first official separation between the Church of Rome and the Byzantine Church.
1096	Beginning of the First Crusade; European armies enter Constantinople for the first time.
1202	Beginning of the Fourth Crusade; Europeans attack Constantinople.
1204	Europeans take Constantinople; dismemberment of the Byzantine Empire.
1261	Michael VIII Palaiologos recaptures Constantinople from the Latins.
1326	Ottomans under Sultan Orhan take Bursa and establish their first capital there.
1329	Ottomans under Sultan Orhan take Nicaea. Little of Asia Minor is left in the hands of Byzantines.
1353	Ottomans cross the Hellespont and establish first Turkish foothold in Europe.

1397	First Ottoman siege of Constantinople.
1442	Second Ottoman siege of Constantinople.
1452	Mehmet II, the Conqueror, builds Rumeli Castle.
1453	May 29, Constantinople conquered.
1453–79	Rise of the Ottoman Empire
1520–66	Reign of Süleyman the Magnificent; zenith of Ottoman power.
1699–1792	Decline of the Ottoman Empire.
1839–76	The Tanzimat Period; Mahmut II puts the westernizing Imperial Reform Decree of the Tanzimat into operation.
1853–56	Crimean War; Ottomans side with France and United Kingdom against Imperial Russia.
1856	Paris Treaty; Ottoman Empire to be accepted as a European State.
1876	First Constitution prepared and the first Turkish Parliament established. (Parliament dissolved the next year due, in part, to the Russian-Ottoman war of 1877–18.)
1881	Birth of Mustafa Kemal in Salonika/Thessaloniki.
1908–9	Parliament restored; Abdülhamit deposed; Young Turks take power.
1914	Ottoman Empire enters World War I as an ally of Germany.
1915	Turks repel Allied landings at Gallipoli.
1918	Turks surrender to Allies; Istanbul occupied by Anglo-French army.
1919–22	War of Independence.
1919	Treaty of Sévres; Greek army lands at Izmir (Smyrna). Mustafa Kemal leads Turkish Nationalist movement.
1920	Establishment of the Grand National Assembly of Turkey with Mustafa Kemal (Atatürk) as president.
1922	Ottoman Empire dissolved.
1923	Treaty of Lausanne establishes sovereignty of modern Turkey, defines its borders and arranges for exchange of minorities between Greece and Turkey; Ankara replaces Istanbul as capital.
1925–38	Program of reforms to modernize Turkey, including adoption of the Latin alphabet.
1928	Turkey becomes secular: clause retaining Islam as state religion removed from constitution.

1938	Death of Atatürk; İsmet İnönü becomes Republic's second president.
1939–45	Turkey remains neutral during World War II.
1945	Turkey becomes a charter member of United Nations.
1946–50	Establishment of multiparty democracy.
1950	Republic's first open elections, won by the opposition Democratic Party.
1950	Turkey enters Korean War as a part of United Nations force.
1952	Turkey joins the North Atlantic Treaty Organization.
1960	Military coup against the Democratic Peak Party.
1961	New constitution establishes two-chamber parliament.
1963	Association agreement signed with European Economic Community.
1970s	Period of social violence between members of left-wing and right-wing political organizations.
1971	Military coup by a letter of memorandum against the ruling Justice Party. Prime Minister Demirel resigns. Following the coup, many leftist organizations dissolved and leftist militants arrested.
1974	Turkey's military intervention on the island of Cyprus following a decade of intercommunal violence and the subsequent Athens-inspired coup.
1980	Military coup; constitution suspended and martial law imposed.
1982	New constitution creates seven-year presidency and abolishes the senate, turning back to a unicameral system.
1983	Turkish Republic of Northern Cyprus is established.
1984	Kurdistan Workers' Party (PKK) starts separatist guerrilla war in the southeast region.
1992	Turkish troops enter Kurdish regions in Iraq in anti-PKK operation.
1993	Tansu Çiler becomes Turkey's first woman prime minister.
1995	Major military attack launched against the PKK in northern Iraq; Turkey enters EU customs union.
1996	Welfare Party forms first pro-Islamic government since 1923.
1997	The coalition resigns under pressure by the military (called a "postmodern coup d'état" by some intellectuals); a new coalition led by the center-right Motherland Party is formed.

1999	July, death sentence given to PKK leader Abdullah Öcalan captured in Kenya in February. Later turned into life imprisonment.
1999	August, 17,000 people die in the devastating earthquake with epicenter at Izmit, close to Istanbul.
2002	Islamist-based Justice and Development Party (AKP) wins the general elections with 34 percent of the vote.
2007	AKP wins 46.6 percent of the vote in the elections and is allocated 341 seats.
2007	Turkish Armenian journalist Hrant Dink's assassination by a seventeen-year-old nationalist. At his funeral, one hundred thousand mourners, Turkish and Turkish Armenian, march protesting the assassination.
2009	Investigations into "Deep State" activities.

Works Cited

Adelsen, Charles. 1970. "A Love Affair: James Baldwin and Istanbul." *Ebony,* Mar., 40–46.

Aldridge, John W. 1971. *After the Lost Generation: A Critical Study of the Writers of Two Wars.* New York: Ayer Co.

Algren, Nelson. 1963. *Who Lost an American?* New York: Macmillan.

———. 1965. *Notes from a Sea Diary: Hemingway All the Way.* New York: G. P. Putnam's Sons.

———. 1998. *Nonconformity: Writing on Writing.* New York: Seven Stories Press.

Auden, W. H. 1991. *Collected Poems.* New York: Vintage International.

Bair, Deirdre. 1978. *Simone de Beauvoir: A Biography.* London: Vintage.

Baldwin, James. 1965. "James Baldwin Explains: Interview with Anil Mericelli." *Varlik* 658 (Nov. 15): 10–11.

———. 1968. Introduction to *The Amen Corner.* New York: Dial Press.

———. 1985a. "Down at the Cross: Letter from a Region in My Mind." In *The Price of the Ticket: Collected Nonfiction 1948–1985,* 333–79. New York: St. Martin's Press.

———. 1985b. "White Racism or World Community." In *The Price of the Ticket: Collected Nonfiction 1948–1985,* 435–42. New York: St. Martin's Press.

Baldwin, James, with Richard Avedon. 1985. "Nothing Personal." In *The Price of the Ticket: Collected Nonfiction 1948–1985,* 381–93. New York: St. Martin's Press.

Barthes, Roland. 1973. *Mythologies.* London: Paladin Books.

Beach, Joseph Warren. 1972. *American Fiction 1920–1940.* New York: Antheum, 1942.

Beauvoir, Simone de. 1992. *Force of Circumstance: The Autobiography of Simone de Beauvoir. 2 vols.* New York: Paragon House.

Beauvoir, Sylvie le Bon de. 1997. Preface to *A Transatlantic Love Affair: Letters to Nelson Algren,* by Simone de Beauvoir. New York: New York Press.

Bhabha, Homi. 1994. *The Location of Culture.* London: Routledge.

Bishop, Elizabeth. 1994. *The Complete Poems, 1927–1979.* New York: Farrar Straus Giroux.

Bloom, Harold, ed. 1999. *Herman Melville.* Broomall, Penn.: Chelsea House.

Bohls, Elizabeth. 2004. *Women Travel Writers and the Language of Aesthetics, 1716–1818.* Cambridge: Cambridge Univ. Press.

Bowles, Paul. 1986. *Collected Stories.* Santa Rosa: Black Sparrow Press.

———. 1957. *Their Heads Are Green and Their Hands Are Blue.* New York: Random House.

———. 1949. *The Sheltering Sky.* New York: Ecco Press.

———. 1972. *Without Stopping.* New York: G. P. Putman's Sons.

Byron George. 1986. *The Oxford Authors,* ed. Jerome J. McGann. Oxford: Oxford Univ. Press.

Campbell, James. 1991. *Talking at the Gates: A Life of James Baldwin.* New York: Viking.

Caponi, Gena Dagel. 1998. *Paul Bowles.* New York: Twayne Publishers.

Carr, Virginia Spencer. 1984. *Dos Passos: A Biography.* New York: Doubleday.

Cezzar, Engin. 2004. Personal interview. Mar. 27.

Cirakman, Aslı. 2002. *From the "Terror of the World" to the "Sick Man of Europe."* New York: Peter Lang.

Crane, Stephen. 1964. *The War Dispatches of Stephen Crane.* New York: New York Univ. Press.

Dawood, N. J., ed. and trans. 1954. *Tales from the Thousand and One Nights.* New York: Penguin.

Donohue, H. E. F. 1964. *Conversations with Nelson Algren.* New York: Hill and Wang.

Dos Passos, John. 1962. *Mr. Wilson's War.* New York: Doubleday.

———. 1927. *Orient Express.* New York: Jonathan Cape and Harrison Smith.

Drew, Bettina. 1989. *Nelson Algren: A Life on the Wild Side.* London: Bloomsbury.

Edwards, Justin. 2001. *Exotic Journeys: Exploring the Erotics of US Travel Literature 1840–1930.* Lebanon: Univ. Press of New England.

Emerson, Ralph Waldo. 1981a. "Nature." In *The Portable Emerson.* New York: Penguin.

———. 1981b. "A Yankee Abroad: English Traits." In *The Portable Emerson.* New York: Penguin.

Finkelstein, Dorothee Metlitsky. 1971. *Melville's Orienda.* New York: Octagon Books.

Flaubert, Gustave. 1954. *The Selected Letters of Gustave Flaubert.* London: Hamish Hamilton.

Freely, John. 1996. *Istanbul: The Imperial City.* London: Penguin.

———. 2000. *A History of Robert College,* vol. 1. Istanbul: Yapikredi Yayinlari.

Garwood, Mini. 2004. Personal interview. Mar. 18.

Geismar, Maxwell. 1961. *Writers in Crisis: The American Novel, 1925–1940.* Boston: Houghton Mifflin.

Hamlin, Cyrus. 1878. *Among the Turks.* New York: Robert Carter and Brothers.

Harte, Bret. 1870. *Overland Monthly.* http://etext.lib.virginia.edu/railton/innocent/atlantic.html.

Hemingway, Ernest. 1955. *In Our Time.* New York: Scribner.

———. 1964. *A Moveable Feast.* New York: Scribner.

———. 1979. *Complete Poems.* London: Harcourt Brace Jovanich.

———. 1981. *Selected Letters: 1917–1961,* ed. Carlos Baker. New York: Scribner.

———. 1985. *Dateline: Toronto. The Complete Toronto Star Dispatches, 1920–1924,* ed. William White. New York: Scribner. Page numbers in the text are from the eBook edition, Simon and Schuster, 2002.

———. 1987. *The Complete Stories of Ernest Hemingway.* New York: Simon and Schuster.

Hibbard, Allen. 2003. "Paul Bowles: A Biographical Essay." http://www.PaulBowles.org.

Hicks, Granville. 1974. "The Politics of John Dos Passos." In *Dos Passos: A Collection of Critical Essays,* ed. Andrew Hook, 15–30. Englewood Cliffs, N.J.: Prentice-Hall.

Hirsch, Eric, and Michael O'Hanlon, eds. 1995. Introduction to *The Anthropology of Landscape: Perspectives on Place and Space.* Oxford: Clarendon Press.

Horsford, Howard C. 1955. Introduction to *Journal of a Visit to Europe and the Levant,* by Herman Melville. Princeton: Princeton Univ. Press.

Horvath, Brooke. 2005. *Understanding Nelson Algren.* Columbia: Univ. of South Carolina Press.

Howells, William Dean. 1869. *Atlantic Monthly,* Dec. http://etext.lib.virginia.edu/railton/innocent/atlantic.html.

Kaplan, Caren. 1996. *Questions of Travel: Postmodern Discourses of Displacement.* Durham: Duke Univ. Press.

Kazin, Alfred. 1974. "Dos Passos, Society and the Individual." In *Dos Passos: A Collection of Critical Essays,* ed. Andrew Hook, 101–27. Englewood Cliffs, N.J.: Prentice-Hall.

———. 1997. *God and the American Writer.* New York: Alfred A. Knopf.

Klaw, Barbara. 2000. "Simone de Beauvoir and Nelson Algren: Self-Creation, Self-Contradiction, and the Exotic, Erotic Feminist Other." *Contingent Loves: Simone de Beauvoir and Sexuality,* ed. Melanie C. Hawthorne, 117–52. Charlottesville: Univ. Press of Virginia.

Lecouras, Peter. 2001. "Hemingway in Constantinople." *Midwest Quarterly* 43, no. 1 (Autumn): 29–42.

Lee, Brian. 1987. *American Fiction 1865–1940.* Essex: Longman.

Leeming, David. 1994. *James Baldwin.* New York: Alfred A. Knopf.

Lévi-Strauss, Claude. 1955. *Tristes Tropiques.* New York: Penguin.

Llewellyn Smith, Michael. 1998. *Ionian Vision: Greece in Asia Minor, 1919–1922.* London: Hurst.

Mangan, Timothy, and Irene Herrmann, eds. 2003. Introduction and preface to *Paul Bowles on Music: Articles and Reviews.* Berkeley: Univ. of California Press.

"The Marshall Plan." 2006. Aug. 5. http://london.usembassy.gov/marshall/index.html.

Matthiessen, F. O. 1941. *American Renaissance.* Oxford: Oxford Univ. Press.

Mellow, James. 1992. *Hemingway: A Life Without Consequences.* Boston: Houghton Mifflin.

Melville, Herman. 1851. *Moby Dick.* Reprint, New York: Macmillan, 1964.

———. 1955. *Journal of a Visit to Europe and the Levant,* ed. Howard C. Horsford. Princeton: Princeton Univ. Press.

Michelson, Bruce. 1987. "Mark Twain the Tourist: The Form of The Innocents Abroad." *On Mark Twain: The Best from American Literature,* ed. Louis J. Budd and Edwin H. Cady, 171–84. Durham: Duke Univ. Press.

Moi, Toril. 1992. Introduction to *Force of Circumstance: The Autobiography of Simone de Beauvoir,* vol. 1, by Simone de Beauvoir. New York: Paragon House.

Montagu, Lady Mary Wortley. 1994. *The Turkish Embassy Letters.* London: Virago Press.

Mullins, Greg. 2002. *Colonial Affairs: Bowles, Burroughs and Chester Write Tangier.* Madison: Univ. of Wisconsin Press.

New York Times. 1922. "The New Turkish Peril." Sept. 15. Proquest Historical Newspapers. *New York Times* (1851–2006).

O'Brien, Fitz-James. 1857. "Our Authors and Authorship, Melville and Curtis." *Putman's Monthly Magazine,* Apr., 9: 384–93. Reprinted in *Melville: The Critical Heritage,* ed. Watson G. Branch. Boston: Routledge and Kegan Paul, 1974.

Papayanis, Marilyn Adler. 2005. *Writing in the Margins: The Ethics of Expatriation from Lawrence to Ondantje.* Nashville: Vanderbilt Univ. Press.

Ralegh, Sir Walter. 1956. "The Conclusion of *The History.*" In *Renaissance England,* ed. Roy Lamson and Hallett Smith. New York: Norton.

Richards, Laura Elizabeth Howe, Maud Howe Elliott, and Florence Howe Hall. 1915. *Julia Ward Howe, 1819–1910.* 2 vols. Boston: Houghton Mifflin. http://digital.library.upenn.edu/women/richards/howe/howe-I.html.

Rosen, Robert C. 1981. *John Dos Passos: Politics and the Writer.* Lincoln: Univ. of Nebraska Press.

Said, Edward. 2000. "Orientalism." In *The Edward Said Reader.* New York: Vintage Books.

Sartre, Jean-Paul. 1955. "John Dos Passos and 1919." In *Literary and Philosophical Essays,* 88–96. London: Rider.

———. 1971. "Why Write?" In *Critical Theory Since Plato,* ed. Hazard Adams. New York: Harcourt Brace Jovanovich.

Saturday Review [British; unsigned] Oct. 8, 1870. http://etext.virginia.edu/railton/innocent/satrev.html.

Settle, Mary Lee. 1991. *Turkish Reflections: A Biography of a Place.* New York: Touchstone.

Simon, Daniel. 1998. Afterword to *Nonconformity: Writing on Writing,* by Nelson Algren. New York: Seven Stories Press.

Spurr, David. 1993. *The Rhetoric of Empire: Colonial Discourse in Journalism, Travel Writing, and Imperial Administration.* Durham: Duke Univ. Press.

Steele, Shelby. 2002. "The Age of White Guilt and the Disappearance of the Black Individual." *Harper's Magazine,* Nov., 33–42.

Stephens, Robert O. 1968. *Hemingway's Nonfiction: The Public Voice.* Chapel Hill: Univ. of North Carolina Press.

Stewart, Lawrence D. 1973. *Paul Bowles: The Illumination of North Africa.* Carbondale: Southern Illinois Univ. Press.

Stewart, Matthew. 2003. "It Was All a Pleasant Business: The Historical Context of 'On the Quai at Smyrna.'" *Hemingway Review* 23, no. 1 (Nov.). http://muse.jhu.edu/journals/hemingway_review/v023/23.1stewart.pdf.

Townsend, Ludington. 1996. "John Dos Passos, Modernist Recorder of the American Scene." *Virginia New Quarterly Review,* Autumn. http://www.vqronline.org/articles/1996/autumn/ludington-john-dos-passos/.

Twain, Mark. 1911. *The Innocents Abroad, or The New Pilgrims' Progress; Being Some Account of the Steamship Quaker City's Pleasure Excursion to Europe and the Holy Land.* New York: Harper and Brothers.

———. 1975. *Notebooks and Journals. Volume I (1855–1873),* ed. Frederick Anderson, Michael B. Frank, and Kenneth M. Sanderson. Berkeley: Univ. of California Press.

———. 1976. *Tales, Sketches, Speeches and Essays 1891–1910.* New York: Library of America.

Vidal, Gore. 1986. Introduction to *Collected Stories: Paul Bowles.* Santa Rosa: Black Sparrow Press.

Walcott, Charles Child. 1956. *American Literary Naturalism: A Divided Stream.* Minneapolis: Univ. of Minnesota Press.

White, Hayden. 1978. *Tropics of Discourse: Essays in Cultural Criticism.* Baltimore: John Hopkins Univ. Press.

Williams, William Carlos. 2003. "Landscape with the Fall of Icarus." *The Norton Anthology of American Literature,* ed. Nina Baym, 1279–80. 6th ed. New York: Norton.

Wilson, Edmund. 1952. "Dos Passos and the Social Revolution." In *The Shores of Light*, 429–35. New York: Farrar, Straus and Young.

Wonham, Henry B. 2003. "Joyous Heresy: Traveling with the Innocents Abroad." *Mark Twain*, ed. Harold Bloom, 111–30. Philadelphia: Chelsea House.

Yeats, William Butler. 1979. "Sailing to Byzantium." *The Norton Anthology of English Literature*. New York: Norton.

Zughoul, Muhammad Raji. 2000. "The Emperor and the Sultan in Mark Twain: How Innocent Were the 'Innocents'?" *Journal of American Studies of Turkey* 11: 83–92. http://www.bilkent.edu.tr/~jast/Number11/Zughoul.htm.

Zwick, Jim. 2002. "Mark Twain and Imperialism." In *A Historical Guide to Mark Twain*, ed. Shelly Fisher Fiskin. Oxford: Oxford Univ. Press.

Index

Page number in *italic* denotes illustration.